AF553184

MEDIA VIOLENCE AND CRIME

MEDIA VIOLENCE AND CRIME

2008

SBS Publishers & Distributors Pvt. Ltd.
New Delhi

ISBN 10 : 81-89741-62-4
ISBN 13 : 978-81-89741-62-4

Indian Price - INR 895.00
Foreign Price - USD 45.00

First Published in India in 2008

Published by:
SBS PUBLISHERS & DISTRIBUTORS PVT. LTD.
2/9, Ground Floor, Ansari Road, Darya Ganj,
New Delhi - 110002, INDIA
Tel: 23289119, 41563911
Email: mail@sbspublishers.com
www.sbspublishers.com

Printed in India by SALASAR IMAGING SYSTEMS.

PREFACE

The risks of viewing the most common depiction of television violence includes learning to behave violently, becoming more desensitised to the harmful consequences of violence and becoming more fearful of being attacked. Television, when viewed selectively, along with parents can provide immense scope for learning.

- The onset of violence peaks between ages 14-16
- Prevalence of violence is highest between ages 15-19
- Involvement with violence is usually short-lived, lasting from 1-3 years
- For some individuals violence continues, although this is influenced by whether successful transitions are complete, for example, entry into the work force.

"Risk factors" take on a different meaning—they are barriers to successful development. For example, violence in the family may be a barrier to the development of secure parent-chiid attachments, a nurturing family system, and healthy child management and parenting skills, all of which are necessary for healthy development in infancy. Social contexts are interrelated and overlapping (e.g., individuals are members of families living in neighbourhoods within communities). Moreover, they are nested in that individuals are born into primary groups which are linked to increasingly larger and more distant social settings.

Behaviour is influenced by social contexts and the individual attributes—from the inherent to the acquired—brought to those settings. That answers some of the questions—Why do 1 see what I see? Why do 1 notice a small detail in a film which others don't even see? Why am I moved to tears by an episode that causes others to laugh or to show no reaction at all? Why do I like a film that bores others? Why am I enraged by a scene in which others find nothing special?

Watching TV is no mere passive consumption but rather it has a lot to do with the Viewer. There is a constant exchange between the images seen and the experiences made. The viewer suffers desires and condemns, gets carried away. All this happens because the viewer is involved in television with all his personal experiences and emotions.

Violence harms, hurts body, mind and spirit. Direct violence, visible, destructive is the form most feared. Cultural violence is invisible, but with clear intent to harm—even kills, indirectly, through words and images.

Man today has the measure of the two-sided mirror of his universe of excessive information—the marvelous illusion and the loneliness of being. We are hurt by information, because being informed allegedly changes life. According to the poet Darwich: "The written word hurts without spilling blood. So does the spoken word but remember TV is reality without soul!"

ANJU KHOSLA

CONTENTS

1

THE MEDIA

The media of mass communication, usually called "mass media" or "media," include newspapers, magazines, books, film, radio, television, recorded music, and the Internet. Mass communication usually involves the production of content—such as information, entertainment, or art—by an institution—such as a radio station or a publishing enterprise; this content is transmitted to large, scattered, and heterogeneous "mass" audiences who potentially may be interested in receiving it. Unlike much interpersonal communication, which is face-to-face and unfiltered, this type of communication is mediated by complex technologies of recording—for example, film or television cameras—transmitting—radio transmitters, satellites, computers—and receiving—radio sets, satellite dishes. In this way, the contemporary media are complex, technology-based economic, political, cultural, social, and ideological institutions.

Colonialism and Modernisation

Asia began its modern media under conditions of European colonisation, when missionaries, administrators, and business interests launched commercial printing presses. The first newspapers, in European and Asian languages, appeared in the latter part of the eighteenth century and visibly expanded throughout the nineteenth. The print media, especially periodicals, soon turned into sites of rhetorical struggle between, among others, colonial powers and local independence movements, modernity and tradition, socialism and nationalism, and patriarchal power and women's movements.

Twentieth century products of the West's Industrial Revolution, the post-print media, i.e., recorded music—gramophones—motion pictures, and radio, all arrived in Asia during the colonial times. The state and the private institutions adopted these media quickly, though unevenly. India emerged as one of the world's most productive centers of filmmaking, while many Asian nations did not produce any movies until the 1960s. Unlike recorded music and film, radio was monopolised by the state, under colonial rule and in the nascent independent states, for nation building and external broadcasting purposes.

Asia's media environment is, more than on any other continent, distinguished by uneven and conflicting trends of development and extreme diversity. Asia has two-thirds of the planet's population—at about 3 billion, the world's largest potential audience. It has the largest number of daily newspapers —3,536 out of the world figure of 8,896 in 1994; radio receivers—696 out of 2,183 million in 1996; and television receivers—652 out of 1,361 million in 1996. In terms of the diffusion of media, however, Asia is below the world average and markedly lags behind other continents, excepting Africa. For instance, the circulation of daily papers per thousand inhabitants in 1994 was 63—lower than 96 for the world, and much lower than 135 for America, 278 for Europe, and 214 for Oceania; however, the circulation is higher than 17 for Africa. In broadcast media, the number of television receivers per thousand inhabitants in 1996 was 187, which is considerably lower than 236 for the world, 431 for America, 442 for Europe, 421 for Oceania, but, again, higher than 50 for Africa.

The discrepancy between Asia's potential audience—the largest in the world—and its actual audience—proportionately the smallest after Africa—can be explained by the persistence of poverty, illiteracy, and state control of the media. The percentage of illiterate adults (fifteen years and over) was 74.3 in Pakistan (1981), 70.8 in Bangladesh (1981), 59.2 in India (1981), 22.2 in China (1990), and 18.5 in Indonesia (1990). In India, advanced computer and space industries coexist with high illiteracy rates and the continuing phenomena of serfdom and even slavery. By contrast, Japan has one of the world's most developed media and communication technology markets, cent per cent literacy, and extensive press freedoms, and Hong Kong is known as the "advertising capital" of Asia.

New Media

At the beginning of the twenty-first century, the unceasing revolution in communication technologies and the globalisation of media markets is reshaping Asian societies. The Internet is blurring the borders that divided the rather distinct media of the past, creating media convergence—a "hypermedia," "multimedia," or "post-mass media" era. This involves the production, transmission, and reception of diverse media content—film, radio, television, newspapers, magazines, and books—through the single medium of Internet and the rise of multi-channel satellite and cable television. Equally important is the increasing privatisation of the media or "cultural industry" markets and open-door policies encouraged by the West, the World Trade Organisation, the World Bank, and the International Monetary Fund.

The Birth of Television

The invention of television has exerted a profound and wide-reaching effect on the nature and quality of modern everyday life. More vivid than radio, more intimate than film, television became one of the central and most significant technologies of the twentieth century. Television took a long time to reach maturity, as it required the technology to broadcast as well as receive images, along with the cooperation of government and commercial interests to coordinate the supply of programming. But once television broadcasting became a reality and television sets were for sale to average home, it quickly became the primary source for entertainment and information, first in the United States and England, and eventually throughout the world.

Background

Television—a term first used in 1900—lived in the imaginations of inventors and writers long before it became a technological reality. The desire to transmit images was piqued by the ability to carry sound on the telephone, invented in 1876. Advances in photography, cinematography, and facsimile transmission also stimulated interest in television. The earliest patented design for a "television" system came in 1884 from a German engineer named Paul Nipkow—1860-1940. Nipkow's system consisted of a disk with 24 holes through it in the shape of a spiral. Spinning the disk in a light source produced a pattern of images on a photosensitive cell, which would then produce a varying electrical current. Reception would be achieved by reassembling the dissected image using another rotating disk and a magneto-optical light modulator. Nipkow never actually constructed the system he proposed, but mechanical systems based on the Nipkow disk became the first reliable televisions. Mechanical television systems were, however, challenged nearly from the beginning by an alternative strategy using cathode-ray tubes. For several decades, mechanical and electronic television struggled alongside one another as inventors and engineers tried to make real the dream of transmitting images.

The chief proponents of mechanical television were John Logie Baird—1888-1946—a Scotsman, and an American—Charles

Francis Jenkins—1867-1934. Baird began his television experiments in 1923. His invention was introduced to the public in 1925, during a publicity affair at London's Selfridge's department store. This early apparatus, based directly on the principle of the Nipkow disk, was extremely crude and could transmit only rough patterns of light and dark to represent images. By 1929, Baird had advanced his system of "low-definition" television significantly, and undertook broadcasting experiments with British Broadcasting Corporation —BBC— radio transmitters. Jenkins also began his investigations into television using a Nipkow disk system in 1923. He was issued the first American television broadcasting license by the Federal Radio Commission in 1928, for experimental transmissions from a station in the suburbs of Washington, D.C. The first commercial receivers for the Jenkins system went on sale in 1930, with a viewing screen of 2 × 1.5 inches (5.08 × 3.81 cm)! These early television signals had no more than 48 lines per screen; in comparison, televisions at the end of the twentieth century typically used 525 or 625 lines, giving much finer definition of images suitable for larger screens. Most images produced were black and white or "monochrome", although experiments using colour filters began as early as 1929.

But lone inventors like Baird and Jenkins did not have television research to themselves for long. During the mid-1920s, large companies including General Electric —GE—, America Telephone & Telegraph —AT&T—, and Radio Corporation of American —RCA— joined in the efforts to produce a commercially viable mechanical television. Between 1928 and 1932 both the United States and England had some limited amount of television broadcasting —entertainment programs of various kinds as well as occasional news shows— available to the public. Television broadcasting had begun in Germany as well. American and British efforts focused primarily on bringing television signals into homes. In Germany television was treated as an alternative to cinema and was usually viewed in large theaters.

While broadcasting began with mechanical television systems, a technological competitor was emerging that would leave mechanical television stillborn. The idea of using a cathode ray tube as the foundation for "distant electric vision," as it was called by A. A. Campbell Swinton—1863-1930—in his own proposal in 1908, was first raised by Russian engineer Boris Rosing in 1907. An assistant to Rosing, Vladimir Zworykin—1889-1982—became the driving force behind electronic television. Zworykin emigrated to the United States and joined the Westinghouse company in 1919. While at Westinghouse, and later at RCA, Zworykin designed the "iconoscope," a transmitting tube where an image could be projected onto a photosensitive array. These photosensitive elements would then be scanned by a beam of electrons, which in turn released charged elements to form a picture signal that could be received and displayed by a modified cathode-ray tube. In 1932 in-house field tests of television using the iconoscope began at RCA.

Zworykin and his mighty corporate backers did have strong competition. Philo Farnsworth (1906-1971), an independent inventor, demonstrated publicly the first complete electronic television system in 1934, following more than eight years of development. His system was based upon an invention of his own called the image-dissector tube. In this electronic version of the Nipkow disk, a moving electronic image moved passed a stationary aperture through which passed electrons that in turn stimulated an electrode to collect and reassemble picture elements. While Farnsworth is largely given credit for the invention of electronic television, his system failed to achieve the commercial success of the system backed by RCA.

Of course, for television to fulfill the dreams of its creators required a system for broadcasting. In England and Germany television-broadcasting was run by companies closely affiliated with the government. British broadcasting switched from Baird's mechanical system to an all-electronic system in 1936, but stopped broadcasting entirely in 1939 after the outbreak of World War II. For a time during the war, the German government made use of television for propaganda purposes, including television broadcasts of the 1936 Olympics from Berlin. In the United States, television was promoted by commercial interests—companies including RCA and Columbia Broadcasting System—CBS— that had been enormously successful in the radio industry. Although experimental broadcasts continued, the public was hesitant to invest in receivers for their homes out of fear that they would become rapidly obsolete as several companies competed to dominate the television market. The Federal Communications Commission —FCC—finally endorsed a set of standards in 1941 that would insure compatibility of all receivers with all broadcasts, but the United States entered World War II just a few months later, effectively bringing about a hiatus in the development of television.

Beginning in 1946, the television industry started to grow again. Wartime research produced improved equipment, and the number of stations exploded so rapidly that in 1948 the FCC was forced to place a four-year freeze on the assignment of new stations while problems of interference could be worked out. Another area of contention was colour broadcasting, where rival companies CBS and RCA championed two completely different and incompatible systems. While CBS's "field sequential system," which utilised coloured disks rotating in the signal in the transmitter and receivers, was developed more quickly, RCA's "dot sequential" system, which sent three separate signals carrying different colours, ultimately triumphed following four years of FCC hearings beginning in 1949. Thanks to this controversy, color television got off to a slow start—it was not until the mid-1960s that sales finally eclipsed those of monochrome sets, and colour broadcasting became routine.

Impact

In 1947 there were 16,000 television sets in American homes; in 1949 there were four million, and by the end of 1950, 11 million. This number continued to increase until eventually, virtually every home in the United States had at least one television. Initially, most homes used large rooftop antennas to receive signals broadcast through the air like radio, but alternative methods of delivering signals appeared early and have continued to grow in importance. The concept of "cable" television, where signals are brought to each home via coaxial cable from a central antenna, began in remote areas far from broadcasting centers, in the 1940s. In the 1980s, it became a multi-billion dollar industry that competed successfully with broadcast television throughout the country. The distribution of television programs directly from satellites into homes became possible in 1979 and, like cable television, it continued to increase in popularity and influence.

Television programming was initially controlled by a small number of "networks" of stations broadcasting in major cities and affiliated with existing radio stations. Three of these networks—the National Broadcasting Company —NBC—the broadcasting arm of RCA, CBS, and the American Broadcasting Company —ABC—dominated television broadcasting for more than 30 years. While they remained influential, by the 1980s the growth of cable television provided viewers with new alternatives to the broadcast networks. Forms of entertainment programming, including game shows, variety shows, serial dramas, and situation comedies, appeared very early in television history and continued in popularity. Television also became a vital source of news and information, initially following formats established on radio but soon taking great advantage of the visual medium by incorporating images of events like those formerly shown on cinema newsreels.

Television is truly a dream made real. It has influenced nearly every aspect of life, providing images—profound and profane—that people share and even experience simultaneously. While the technology of television continues to improve and spread to even the most remote places in the world, the impact of even the earliest television broadcasts was very powerful. Although television may someday be superseded by newer technologies, those technologies will undoubtedly have been themselves shaped by television.

1920s: TVs and Radio

The begining of this decade marked the shift in American culture to electronic media for entertainment and news. The first radios were sold in the United States for home use in 1920. By mid-decade, a decent radio could be purchased for about $35, with higher quality models being sold for up to $350. By the end of the decade, more than five million of the battery-powered radios were sold.

At first, the broadcasting on radio centered around music, especially the classics and opera. The featured orchestras were often named after sponsors. Listeners could hear the likes of the Ipana (toothpaste) Troubadours, the A&P—grocery chain—Gypsies, the Champion—spark plugs—Sparkers, and the Hoover—vacuum cleaners—Sentinels. Speeches and lectures were also broadcast. Local meetings of civic and professional organizations—the Commercial Law League and the Foreign Policy Association—were broadcast in full. Although the programming was uninspired, people would gather around their radios just for the pure novelty of listening to sound coming out of a box. By the end of the decade, radios had become a true craze across the country. The popularity of radios during the 1920s provided a mere glimpse into what would become a national obsession with electronic media gadgets in the following decades.

Television

About the same time that Guglielmo Marconi was experimenting with radio transmissions in the late 1890s, other scientists were exploring the possibility of transmitting visual images. The first inventor to do so was Abbe Caselli, an Italian-born priest who succeeded in sending very elemental shadow pictures via the French telegraph lines in 1866. Almost twenty years later an Englishman named Shelford Bidwell developed a device that he called an electric distant vision apparatus. This machine used a selenium cell mounted on a box that moved up and down to scan an image.

While still a student, the German scientist Paul Nipkow designed an electric telescope that divided its target into scanned lines. Using this as a base he developed a photomechanical image scanner in 1884 which he called a *Nipkow disk.* The device was comprised of a metal or cardboard disk perforated with a series of square holes in a spiral pattern, so that each hole was slightly closer to the disk's center than the last. As the disk spun, a light was shone through the holes and onto the target; by looking through the holes one could see the target revealed as a series of horizontal lines. Though the Nipkow disk became the basis for later photomechanical televisions, the technology in the mid-1880s was not advanced enough for Nipkow himself to pursue his work further.

It was a Scottish engineer, John Logie Baird, who eventually continued the research Nipkow had begun. In 1923 Baird designed a television system utilising the Nipkow disk. By adding a photoelectric cell, Baird's system was able to read the areas of dim and bright light that made up each scanned line and convert them into an electrical signal. To play back the image a second

Nipkow disk was used, along with a flashing light bulb. By using the incoming signal to make the bulb flash brightly or dimly, and then by synchronising that flashing to the second spinning disk, a crude but recognisable image was formed. Baird's design was used to send bicoastal and transatlantic transmissions during the late 1920s, and it was his device that was first used by the British Broadcasting Company—BBC.

However, it was becoming very clear to the scientists that the photomechanical systems had their limits, and that an all-electrical device would be far more advantageous. This line of thinking was not new: both the American physicist Charles F. Jenkins and the Scottish-born engineer A. A. Campbell-Swinton had suggested designs for an all electrical television by the turn of the twentieth century. Decades ahead of its time, Campbell-Swinton's design was outstanding in that it was the first to suggest the use of an electron scanner to convert the images.

The basic model for modern television was designed simultaneously yet independently by two scientists: American Philo Farnsworth and Russian immigrant Vladimir Zworykin. Farnsworth got the idea for his "image dissector" as a sophomore at Brigham Young University. He showed his design to several investors who gave him enough money to continue his research. In 1927 he demonstrated a working model of his television, which, though not practical for mass-market production, it showed potential. Unfortunately, Farnsworth's investors soon backed out, and at the onset of World War II, the entire project was abandoned.

Zworykin fared much better. After immigrating to the United States in 1919 he found a job with the Westinghouse Electric Corporation. It was there that he developed his iconoscope, an all-electrical television camera. The iconoscope used a vast array of tiny drops of selenium, each acting as an individual photoelectric cell. As the drops were exposed to light, they stored the amount of light they had "seen" as a very small electric pulse. An electron gun was then used to convert the stored pulses into an electric signal that could be transmitted. With the drops' pulses discharged, the process could be started anew and was repeated many times each second. In 1924, just a year after applying for the patent for his iconoscope, Zworykin developed the kinescope, the precursor to the modern television receiver. Zworykin's tremendous advances in the field attracted the attention of the Radio Corporation of America —RCA—, and in 1929 he began to work for them full-time. It was Zworykin's iconoscope/kinescope system that evolved into the television systems of today.

Television operates by a principle known as persistence of vision—that is, the human eye is slower than the brain, so that if a series of similar images are played rapidly, the brain will blur them together, creating the illusion of animation. This is the same principle by which motion pictures work. In a standard American television set each picture contains 525 lines. These lines are scanned the way a book is done, starting at the top left and going from left to right and from top to bottom. In the first pass, the scanner shows the odd-numbered lines (1, 3, 5) and then goes back to scan the even-numbered lines (2, 4, 6); this practice helps to decrease screen flicker. In all it takes just 1/30th of a second to scan all 525 lines. This method was adopted in 1951 by the National Television System Committee — NTSC—in order to standardise all American television broadcasts.

In the early years of television, all broadcasts were in black and white. It was not until the late 1950s that a viable colour system was approved, and not until after a bitter battle between the two largest television companies, RCA and Columbia Broadcasting System—CBS—. CBS was the first to offer a practical colour image based upon the work of Peter Goldmark. Goldmark's field-sequential colour system delivered colour quality unsurpassed even today; however, the mechanical nature of the Goldmark design would have made it necessary for all television owners to exchange their existing sets for new field-sequential sets. RCA offered a colour system designed by Ernst Alexanderson; this design was not as clear as the one developed by CBS, but it was compatible with existing black-and-white sets. The Federal Communications Commission—FCC—eventually chose to make the RCA colour system the industry standard in 1954. The colour and scanning standards adopted in other countries—SECAM in France and PAL in Great Britain, for example—are not necessarily compatible with American television sets, and digital translators are required in order to receive these images.

In the late 1990s, cathode ray technology continued to develop. The trend in televisions moved towards thinner and flatter—the opposite of the bulk inherent in one big cathode ray tube television, Philips Research Laboratories have devised cathode-ray tube panels (CRP), which are thinner and flatter. Researchers have produced early prototypes that are one centimeter—0.4 in—thick. Japan's Matsushita Television Research Laboratory reduced cathode ray bulk with Flat Vision which has 10,000 tiny tubes, managing the image with an electron beam sweep. The resulting television is merely 25 inches thick, and might become commercially available in the United States by the year 2000. Another television technology in development is 3-D television, being developed in the Computer Laboratory at Cambridge University in England. Called the Cambridge Autostereo Display, the 3-D is created by eight or sixteen scene views being displayed then updated in rapid succession, about thirty times per second. The viewers' eyes see the projected images in 3-D. However, this technology will take years to come to fruition and be available on the consumer market.

What has hit the consumer market in 1998 after 17 years of promise, is high-definition television, also known as HDTV.

The HDTV system offers a much sharper image, comparable to that seen at a movie theater. This is accomplished by transmitting each picture in at least 720 lines and up to 1080 lines—twice as many as in a standard television. Because HDTV can require the transmission of so much information, cable television and direct broadcasting satellite are the preferred HDTV broadcast mediums, though transmission via standard broadcast is possible because of digital multicasting.

DirecTV began broadcasting two channels of HDTV programming in 1998. Available to consumers in 1994, DirecTV is a digital television programming broadcast medium that relies on satellites circling the Earth at 22,300 miles (236,380 km) above the earth. The signals sent by the satellites are picked up by small dishes owned or rented by a consumer that are only 18 inches (45 cm) across. DirecTV, and similar products like Primestar, promoted themselves as an alternative to cable, with up to 150 channels available and sharp, clear pictures. It could reach consumers in rural areas where cable is unavailable. There were several drawbacks to the DirecTV system. Remote controls are unavailable, so channel changing requires going back to one on-screen grid. The dish and television receiver can be costly. As of 1996, there were 1.3 million DirecTV household subscribers. In 1996, DirecTV partnered with Microsoft, to develop multi-media satellite broadcasts with computer links, providing web content related to television. In 1997, the first commercially available link between computer and television was announced: WebTV. A set-top box, WebTV allows viewers to explore the Internet using the television and telephone lines. WebTV Plus, introduced in 1998, allows viewers to watch television while they use the Internet and featured a hard drive to store data and the capabilities for printer hook-up. WebTV and WebTV Plus were priced much less than a computer, as such the future of both television and computers might lie in this kind of convergence.

Television: 1946–Present

Television brought unforgettable sounds and sights of war to the American home front. Geographically isolated from major conflicts, U.S. citizens had become accustomed to reading newspaper and hearing radio reports of distant battlefield action, military and civilian casualties, troop movements, government propaganda, and commentaries about war. Television could do all of these things and more, bringing viewers a new and captivating sense of reality, immediacy, and participation through the combination of moving images and sound. Television narrowed the psychological, emotional, and political distance between the home front and the battlefield: what happened in Korea, Vietnam, Somalia, and Iraq also happened inside American living rooms. Television helped support and form American communication about fighting wars and managing enemies.

Before the Vietnam War, film footage and commentaries about World War I, World War II, and the Korean War were frequently aired on television, but typically in the form of carefully edited documentaries. *Victory at Sea*, for example, was produced in 1952 for the National Broadcasting Company—NBC—by Henry Salomon, Jr. Pieced together from Navy footage taken during actual naval battles, the popular series ran for twenty-six weeks. With a stirring soundtrack, the thirty-minute segments were narrated by a strong male voice. In the 1950s and 1960s, Americans also enjoyed watching war movies and television series with military themes such as *Combat!* The early era of television generally portrayed the excitement, glory, and heroism of war. Television continues to provide Americans with entertaining movies and graphic documentaries about war.

In their pioneering 1951 news program—*See it Now*—the journalists Edward R. Murrow and Fred W. Friendly offered expanded coverage of current events such as the Korean War and the Army-McCarthy hearings. The American Broadcasting

Company's—ABC's—extensive coverage of the hearings encouraged citizens to suspect the motives behind Senator Joseph McCarthy's pursuit of Communist sympathisers inside the military. Documentaries such as Burton Benjamin's *Trial at Nuremberg* (1958) and *From Kaiser to Fuehrer* (1959) conveyed philosophic reasons why Americans must sometimes fight wars. Early television productions about war clearly distinguished between the heroes and the villains, and the power of the military was dramatically connected to national survival.

Television played a significant role in shaping public opinion during the Cold War—1946-1991— portraying the personalities of leaders and describing ideological differences between democracy and Communism. Television linked ideology to world leaders. After Richard Nixon's official visit to Moscow in 1959, Soviet Premier Nikita Khrushchev toured the United States for two weeks, appearing daily on television. In 1960 Khrushchev was filmed walking out of an international diplomatic meeting in Paris, sensationally rebuffing President Eisenhower and other Western leaders. Television viewers observed Khrushchev take off his shoe and bang it on his desk at the United Nations, denouncing those who serve the "imperialist" interests of the United States. In 1962 President Kennedy used television to reach a tense world audience as he demanded the Soviet Union to remove missiles from Cuba. Both the Soviets and Americans telecast their competitive advances in the space race, beginning with the successful orbit of Sputnik I in 1957. Nearly 600 million people worldwide watched two Americans triumphantly walk on the moon in 1969. In 1982 television carried President Ronald Reagan's description of the Soviet Union as a "decaying evil empire". And in 1989, television viewers saw the Berlin Wall fall. Television rendered events as part of the drama and conflict of the Cold War. Viewers could follow developments in the contest between the two superpowers on their TV screens.

In 1962 the experienced war correspondent Walter Cronkite began anchoring *CBS Nightly News*. Within a decade, he became one of the most trusted public figures in America, with over nine million nightly viewers. With a professional reputation for presenting news "the way it was" and without bias, Cronkite's coverage of the Vietnam War eventually included his own criticism of the U.S. government. Along with other journalists, he used television to bring Americans directly to the unedited, uncensored frontline. Television began to show American viewers increasingly dark, violent, chaotic, and controversial aspects of war. Not only were soldiers filmed while fighting, they were filmed getting wounded and killed. The evacuation of the U.S. Embassy in Saigon, accusations of atrocities committed by GIs, pathetic scenes of refugees, mass demonstrations against the war, and the blindly destructive power of modern weapons were all brought home into the living room. In addition to the live news coverage every day, investigative documentaries with a critical orientation also began to appear. Frank Freed, for instance, helped with a view to inform an increasingly fragmented public opinion with his probing NBC documentaries: *The Decision to Drop the Bomb* —1965—, *Cuba: The Missile Crisis*—1964— *And Now the War Is Over: The American Military in the '70's*—1971—, and *Vietnam Hindsight*—1971. Television journalists openly challenged the truthfulness of official government reports during the Vietnam War, focusing public attention on the problem of an alleged credibility gap.

Television continued to inform Americans about military engagements in Panama, the Balkans, Iraq, and Afghanistan. Digital communication between reporters and their networks, satellite phone connections, behind-the-lines broadcasting, and other technical innovations added to television's ability to fascinate viewers. The success of cable television companies, twenty-four-hour programming, and a vast increase in the number of national and international broadcasters also increased television's impact on the home front. Americans can now see their wars from a variety of sources and perspectives.

Both soldiers and civilians relied on the Cable News Network—CNN—for information about the first U.S. air strikes against Baghdad in March 2003. Integrated with fighting units, officially "embedded" journalists provided the first real-time images of American forces in action. Feeling safe at home, Americans could watch their pilots actually aim, shoot, and destroy enemy troops with sophisticated weapons. Between battle scenes, moderators interviewed professionals about the technical aspects of the weapons used, their cost, and their destructive potential. According to Nielsen Media Research, nearly seventy percent of Americans relied on cable networks for information about the war in Iraq, with the audiences of MSNBC, CNN, and Fox increasing almost 300 percent during the first two weeks of the war. Many television networks—as the Public Broadcasting Service (PBS) and MSNBC—supplemented their coverage by hosting Web sites. Networks varied greatly in what they elected to cover the depth of commentary presented, and how much they embraced official U.S. views. Fox, for example, routinely displayed the flag, overtly appealed to patriotic emotions, and generally attracted viewers who supported the government's "War on Terrorism". In contrast, Arab and European networks, widely available to American cable subscribers, related civilian casualties, alternative interpretations of events, and international criticism of the war.

Television functions especially well in bringing fresh, impressive graphics and easily accessible information to viewers. Its coverage of war, however, also leads to controversy. One problem is that networks typically deliver spectacular images without helping viewers interpret what they see. For instance, as television stations transmitted the ongoing terrorist attacks on the United States on September 11, 2001, viewers were left with unexplained horror. Television showed what was happening in New York City, replay after replay. Though the view was perfectly clear, television reporters struggled to comprehend the meaning of the events. Television delivers breaking news in full colour, allowing Americans to see war for themselves, but critics have charged major networks with sensationalism, commercialism, repetition, and superficiality.

Another problem with television during wartime is that the medium becomes entangled in the conflict, employed by the warring parties in their struggle to manipulate public opinion. Embedded journalists, for instance, serve the interests of the military, showing viewers what the government wants them to see. Al Jazeera and other Arabic networks deliver videotaped messages on behalf of terrorists. What networks decide to broadcast may indeed be of strategic importance in war.

Television's evolving coverage of war raises questions about the strategic importance of information access, private ownership of networks, freedom of the press, and the constitutionally protected obligation of the press to report news to citizens. Paradoxically, criticism of television's coverage of war is itself extensively televised, with experts using television to debate the use of television. Television's ability to help Americans observe and make sense of war makes it one of the most important and contested technological innovations.

TELEVISION IN INDIA

In a world of increasing globalisation, the media has much potential. It has the possibility of spreading information to places where in the past it has been difficult to get diverse views. It has the potential to contribute to democratic processes and influences especially on countries and regimes that are not democratic. On the negative side though, it has also the ability to push the ideas and cultures of more dominant interest.

India is one of the world's largest markets for satellite TV, with some 300 million viewers.

The Indian economy opened up in the 1990s after decades of being closed:

- This led to an explosion in global consumer goods.
- There was also an explosion in Indian television.

While globalisation of television has been going on since the 1980s—with the likes of CNN, MTV, Sky, Star TV, etc—in India, demand from urban middle classes came around 1991 for the likes of CNN in view of coverage of international events such as the first Gulf War.

- Star TV —a Hong Kong based company, owned by Rupert Murdoch's News Corp and present in many, more Asian countries—found it easy to penetrate into India. This was because of many reasons, including—
- The existing broadcast was based on an old system.
- The existing broadcast was state-owned, primarily a vehicle for news, education, and social issues, such as how to deal with various health issues, etc. Entertainment was usually films of religious stories.
- While such things were very useful for the rural poor, the growing urban middle class wanted more entertainment, western soaps, etc.
- While televisions used to be rare, they were now becoming widespread.
- Initially Star TV only catered to the small minority of people that spoke English, showing western soaps, serials, Hollywood movies. Hindi's first commercial channel, Zee TV introduced programs in the natural language, Hindi. Zee TV's launch heralded private television. Zee was and is primarily focused on entertainment.

Just 5 years after the launch of Star TV, there are a dozen satellites broadcasting over 50 channels, in English, Hindi, and some 16 regional languages. Furthermore—

- India is the second largest TV market in the world, after the United States.
- These new networks offer many programs. However, India has seen a number of trends including:
- An increase in programming and hours, especially more music, films, talk shows, game shows, soaps, etc.
- But there has also been an increase in the number of repeats, of music channels, etc. The film industry, known as Bollywood, is the largest feature film producer in the world, larger than Hollywood, with some 300 feature films a year.

While there has been a long tradition of cinema movies in India, satellite TV has meant more foreign films being broadcast. Local industries have seen the effects too, for example, by being forced to innovate, to improve effects of their own films, or increase violence, etc. Those television channels that have localised the most are succeeding in the tough competition.

Most parents find television to be a convenient tool to engage their child while they do their work without any interruption. For adults, the television may be a way to relax as they are able, or are supposed to be able to judge the difference between fantasy and reality. Television is primarily considered a medium that reflects the world and which shows viewers what their societies are like. The response to these representations varies from individual to individual and can be assessed in the form of social behaviour.

Movies and television and other forms of popular fiction show us the fallen state of our selves and society, and the creation of the better selves and societies we would like to bring about.

But they don't merely depict these things. They also employ techniques that evoke a state of wholeness and benevolence in viewers, so we temporarily become the same kind of better selves that we are watching on the screen.

Despite their apparent diversity, movies and television express a coherent vision. In essence, they tell stories that depict our deepest desires to lead a full life; see other people treated fairly; and share in a good society. And they show us characters that have to face primordial fears, regressive desires, and landscapes of oppression, as they seek the better selves and societies they know should exist. By understanding the vision they offer, we can get a step closer to creating a world that embodies these same values.

VIOLENCE ON TELEVISION

"Guns don't kill people, picture tubes do. Or at least that seems to be the message behind the clangour of current alarms about television violence."

The Journal of the American Medical Association also stated, "The introduction of television in the 1950's caused a subsequent doubling of the homicide rate, for example., long-term childhood exposure to television is a causal factor behind approximately one half of the homicides committed in the United States, or approximately 10,000 homicides annually...if, hypothetically, television technology had never been developed, there would today be 10,000 fewer homicides each year in the United States, 70,000 fewer rapes, and 700,000 fewer injurious assaults" (June 10, 1992).

Someone once said that a person's perception of reality is a result of their beliefs. In today's age, a lot of those beliefs are in some ways formed via the mainstream media.

The previous century has been characterised by organised group violence on an extraordinary scale; to say that the human race has seen fit to engage in something like 250 significant armed conflicts in the course of this century, during which over 110 million people have been killed, and many times that number wounded, crippled, and mutilated.

The scale of this slaughter is something new in human history. Only 19 million people died in the 211 major conflicts of the Nineteenth Century; 7 million were killed in the Eighteenth, which was marked by mere 55 significant wars. In fact, there have probably been as many casualties from mass violence in the said century as those in the rest of human history combined.

We have become sufficiently used to these numbers and the human sufferings they represent that we forget with how much more social violence we live than did our ancestors, and how much more deadly it has become. Indeed, mass violence on a previously unimaginable scale has become universalised, industrialised, and reutilised. Ours is the age of "ammunition affluence," in the words of John Keegan, the military historian, who noted in the midst of the Lebanese civil war that a typical small building in Beirut carried two or three thousand bullet holes. Large structures might have been hit up to two or three million times. "This is not just the nuclear age," he wrote. "It is also the age that has made ammunition junk, a throwaway commodity, like popcorn or wedding rice."

According to Ted Robert Gurr, who has done the most ambitious data gathering, every form of ethno-political conflict has increased dramatically since the 1950's: violent communal protests and open rebellion are both four times what they were a half century ago. Social violence, in other words, is now more likely to occur than at any other time in human history, and to be devastating in its consequences when it does so.

But why invoke the media in this context? Because it is clear that, taken together, mass media technologies, institutions, professionals, norms and practices constitute one of the fundamental forces now shaping the lives of individuals and the fate of peoples and nations. To be sure, media influence is not evenly distributed in space or time and varies with circumstance. But, overall, media influence is significant, and increasingly so, and as a result the media constitute a major human resource whose potential to help prevent and moderate social violence begs to be discussed, evaluated, and, where appropriate, mobilised.

History of Media Violence

Between 2000 B.C. and A.D. 44, the ancient Egyptians entertained themselves with plays re-enacting the murder of their god Osiris—and the spectacle, history tells us, led to a number of copycat killings. The ancient Romans were given to lethal spectator sports as well, and in 380 B.C. Saint Augustine lamented that his society was addicted to gladiator games and "drunk with the fascination of bloodshed".

Violence has always played a role in entertainment. But there's a growing consensus that, in recent years, something about media violence has changed.

Research indicates that media violence has not just increased in quantity; it has also become much more graphic, much more sexual, and much more sadistic.

Explicit pictures of slow-motion bullets exploding from people's chests, and dead bodies surrounded by pools of blood, are now commonplace fare. Millions of viewers worldwide, many of them children, watch female World Wrestling Entertainment wrestlers try to tear out each other's hair and rip off each other's clothing. And one of the top-selling video games in the world, *Grand Theft Auto*, is programmed so players can beat prostitutes to death with baseball bats after having sex with them.

MEDIA ECONOMICS

Media entertainment is a big business. In 2001, people around the world spent US$14 billion going to the movies. The U.S. domestic box office alone hit US$9 billion—a 75 per cent increase from 1991—and there are huge revenues from home video/DVD sales, rentals and spin-off merchandise. But even these profits are dwarfed by music, the largest global media sector. In 2000, sales reached US$37 billion, with music consumption high among young audiences everywhere. Video games are not far behind: global sales for 2002 were anticipated to be US$31 billion.

American media corporations earn at least half of their profits from foreign sales. And global markets are growing fast as standards of living are rising around the world. Sales of TVs, stereos, VCRs and satellite dishes are increasing, and in the last decade or two, new and expanding markets have emerged in countries that have abandoned state control of media and distribution. Today, U.S. films are shown in more than 150 countries worldwide, and the U.S. film industry provides most of the pre-recorded videos and DVDs sold throughout the world. American television programs are broadcast in over 125 international markets, and MTV can be seen in more foreign households than American ones.

This international success has a tremendous impact not just on the recipient countries, but also on the cultural environment of the U.S. To some extent, the tail is wagging the dog: more and more, the demands and tastes of foreign markets are influencing what popular products get made in the U.S.

In recent years, market forces have driven screen violence to an amazing pitch. As the movies lost much of their audience—especially adults—to television, the studios learned that the way to make their killing, so to speak, was to offer on big screens what the networks would not permit on the small. This meant, among other things, grisly violence—aimed to attract the teenagers who were the demographic category most eager to flee the family room. At the same time, the technologies of special effects steadily advanced to permit more graphic representations. We have witnessed the burgeoning of a genre unknown two decades ago: the "action movie," a euphemism for the debased choreography that budding amateurs throughout the world aspire to imitate. Aiming to recoup losses and better compete with cable, television programmers struck back: the networks lowered their censorship standards and pruned their "standards and practices" staffs; the deregulatory Federal Communications Commission clammed up; and local news fell all over itself cramming snippets of gore between commercials. The financiers, executives, directors, writers, make-up artists, distributors, and others responsible should be covered with shame.

Emulation: In 1982, after the cable television broadcast of The Deer Hunter, several people killed themselves playing Russian roulette, which was featured in the movie. American youths recently were killed and maimed when they lay down on the center strip of a highway, imitating a scene from Disney's movie—The Program. A few months ago, a 17-year-old French youth blew himself up after learning from an episode of MacGyver how to build a bomb in a bicycle handle, at least according to his mother, who is suing the head of the channel for manslaughter. The industry has considerable discretion about what to depict and how to depict it. But from this business truth it does not follow that the captains of entertainment have strong ideological motives.

THE AGONY OF MARKET DEMAND

Nowhere is this influence more evident than in the film industry. In the U.S. and Canada, movies rated "G" (General) and "PG" (Parental Guidance) consistently bring in more revenues than R-rated films. Yet the number of G and PG films has dropped in recent years, and the number of restricted films has risen. Two-thirds of Hollywood films in 2001 were rated "R". Action travels well. Action movies don't require complex plots or characters. They rely on fights, killings, special effects and explosions to hold their audiences. And, unlike comedy or drama—which depends on good stories, sharp humour, and credible characters, all of which are often culture-specific—action films require little in the way of good writing and acting. They are simple, and they are universally understood. To top it off, the largely non-verbal nature of the kind of films that journalist Sharon Waxman refers to as "short-on-dialogue, high-on-testosterone" makes their dubbing or translation relatively inexpensive.

Foreign investors are much less likely to invest in films focusing on serious social themes or women's issues, or ones that feature minority casts. Such films, however brilliant, are not where the big money is. Worldwide appeal determines casting and script decisions—and the overwhelming demand is for white actors and action.

Success breeds success, and the sheer ubiquity of these productions and all their spin-off products and businesses around the world is in turn fueling an ever-growing demand for U.S. popular culture products.

Foreign market pressures are driving the $1.9 billion Canadian film and television industry as well: international sales are essential for a country with such a small domestic market. And so, as the Writers' Guild of Canada points out, "distributors are now the gatekeepers of Canadian television".

Explicit and Violent Music Lyrics Go Mainstream

In the last decade, social analysts have also noted a steady increase in violent and anti-social music lyrics and images. Once relegated to the fringes, "rage" music, filled with profanity and hate, has become a cash cow for the mainstream music industry.

The world's largest music company—Universal Music Group—is putting the might of its international marketing machine behind artists—Eminem, Dr. Dre and Limp Bizkit—all known for their bleak anthems of violence and hatred, often aimed at women, gays and lesbians. This kind of violence reached mainstream status in 2001, when the U.S. Grammy awards nominated Eminem for four awards. He won three, and his 2002 CD, *The Eminem Show* made US$3.63 million in its first month of sales.

Rap music, too, has been co-opted by the major corporations. The Recording Industry Association of America says that rap/hip-hop, which sprang out of the East Coast music scene 25 years ago, replaced pop music in 2001 as the third most popular music genre. Gansta Rap artists are now being accused of destroying the soul of original rap and hip-hop movements with their violent lyrics and lifestyles.

Video Games and Violence

Though there are many challenging non-violent computer and video games, in the last few years video games have become almost synonymous with violence. Their trademark movie-like realism, combined with enormous marketing budgets, has made this entertainment industry the second most-profitable in the world.

In September 2002, the ultra-violent *Grand Theft Auto 3* was the second most popular game in the world (See *Violence in Entertainment Media*, below). The game was initially banned in Australia for its graphic violence and sexual content, but it nevertheless grossed US$300 million by the end of 2002.

The success of *GTA3* (and its successor GTA: *Vice City*) is upping the ante for violence in the next generation of video games. The cost of developing new games is so high that producers need to know that a game is going to be a hit before bankrolling it.

SUPPLY MEETS DEMAND

No one knows better than the communication industries that children and young people represent a huge market, due to their spending power and their influence on family spending decisions. In September 2000, a Federal Trade Commission (FTC) report revealed what many suspected: U.S. media corporations were routinely ignoring their own rating restrictions and actively marketing violent entertainment to children and teens. In fact, the study showed that 80 per cent of R-rated movies, 70 per cent of restricted video games, and 100 per cent of music with "explicit content" warning labels were being marketed to kids under 17.

The report revealed a number of standard (though illicit) practices for marketing adult media products to kids. These included advertising in publications for adolescents, such as *YM*, *Teen* and *Marvel Comics*; screening trailers for restricted movies on TV at times when kids are likely to be watching; and recruiting teens and children (sometimes as young as nine) to evaluate story concepts, commercials, trailers and rough cuts—even for R-rated movies. The study also revealed that the film and videogame industries often target children as young as four with toy tie-ins for adult-rated movies and games.

Follow-up reports from the FTC indicate that the film and gaming industries have improved their practices somewhat. However, ads for R-rated movies continue to appear on television shows popular with kids (TV is considered the most important medium for drawing an audience to a film), and the video game industry still advertises games rated M (Mature) in magazines with young readers. The music industry has done little to clean up its act. All five major record labels continue to advertise albums with explicit or violent content on television programs and in magazines that have substantial followings of kids under the age of seventeen.

COCKTAIL OF SPORTSMANSHIP AND CONFLICT

Sports and sports media appeal to adults and children of all ages. Cheering on a team is an activity that even very young children can enjoy together with parents and friends.

While many sports inspire tremendous physical and emotional accomplishments of strength and stamina, some involve varying degrees of physical violence. Media representations frequently focus on and promote the physical conflicts that are inherent in these sports or, in some cases, have been staged to increase audience appeal.

It is common, for example, for sports reports and play-by-play commentary to contain metaphorical language that glorifies and promotes physical conflict-language that enthusiasts usually enjoy because it's graphic and exciting. Commentators describe plays in terms of "crushing" opponents, throwing a "bomb", and "killing" the clock. Teams are often marketed through aggressive logos depicting ferocious animals that not only identify teams, but tap into or create consumer demand for "spin-off" merchandise. Through graphic visual and sound images, children see and hear about countless real-life examples of extreme competitiveness. Displays of temper and arguments with authority, for example, are not uncommon in televised sports. Such images can be a powerful influence on those who experience them, and may suggest "scripts" to be imitated. It's clear, therefore, that children require images to balance their media experiences of sport. These may be provided through positive modelling of cooperation, skill development and respect in community and school sports programs.

Children also need to learn how and why different media forms, especially television, have the power to increase audience excitement and entertainment by focusing on violent elements in sport; they need to be able to see through the "hype" and staged violence in texts such as televised wrestling events and hockey games. As students develop the concepts and skills required for critically appreciating media representations of sport, they also gain greater awareness of the various strategies that real-life athletes must use to cope with the actual hard work, excitement, frustration and satisfaction of competitive sport.

The Globalisation of Media

Concerns about media violence have grown as television and movies have acquired a global audience. When UNESCO surveyed children in 23 countries around the world in 1998, it discovered that 91 per cent of children had a television in their home—and not just in the U.S., Canada and Europe, but also in the Arab states, Latin America, Asia and Africa. More than half (51 per cent) of boys living in war zones and high-crime areas chose action heroes as role models, ahead of any other images; and a remarkable 88 per cent of the children surveyed could identify the Arnold Schwarzenegger character from the film *Terminator*. UNESCO reported that the *Terminator* "seems to represent the characteristics that children think are necessary to cope with difficult situations".

In a global media world, extravagant terror spectacles have been orchestrated in part to gain worldwide attention, dramatise the issues of the groups involved, and achieve specific political objectives.

The live television broadcasting brought a "you are there" drama to the September 11 spectacle. The images of the planes striking the World Trade Center, the buildings bursting into flames, individuals jumping out of the window in a desperate attempt to survive the inferno, and the collapse of the Towers and subsequent chaos provided unforgettable images that viewers would not soon forget. The drama continued throughout the day with survivors being pulled from the rubble, and the poignant search for individuals still alive and attempts to deal with the attack produced resonant iconic images seared deeply into spectators' memories. Many people who witnessed the event suffered nightmares and psychological trauma. For those who viewed it intensely, the spectacle provided a powerful set of images that would continue to resonate for years to come, much as the footage of the Kennedy assassination, iconic photographs of Vietnam, the 1986 explosion of the space shuttle Challenger, or the death of Princess Diana in the 1990s provided unforgettable imagery. There followed a media spectacle of the highest order. For several days, US television suspended broadcasting of advertising and TV entertainment and focused solely on the momentous events of September 11.

What is the Cost of an Average Crime?

Britain spends more on law and order per person than any other country in the western world. But is it money well spent?

Every five minutes, someone, somewhere has their mobile phone stolen. And the cost of this? You'd be surprised.

CRIME IS AN EXPENSIVE BUSINESS

For an average theft, £878 is the estimated cost of catching the criminal and processing the case.

If it goes to court, probably before a magistrate, we're looking at another £704.

And if our thief is convicted and sent to prison—maybe for not more than a month—we can add, roughly, another £1,000.

But what about the hidden cost of a crime? The emotional impact of crime is quantified by government number crunchers and these figures are greater than you might expect.

The Home Office suggests that £1,000 is a suitable estimate for any time taken off work or school.

The average bill for illness or trips to the doctor which may arise from the crime is given as £483.

And there's even a calculation for how much an individual crime will affect your life in the long term. The sum they give for the emotional and physical impact of a robbery is £3,048.

So from one individual action, the theft of an item worth around £100, it is possible to calculate the total cost of the crime. And it is a staggering £7,200.

In this case that is 72 times more than the value of the item stolen.

Crime is clearly an expensive business.

Lethal violence is a distinctively American problem too. The rate of criminal homicide in the U.S. is four to fourteen times higher than in other Western industrialised nations. That is what Americans fear, but the common belief is that the high rate of killings is the natural consequence of a large number of criminals and a high crime rate.

Crimes such as burglary and theft are part of modern urban life worldwide. Only when it comes to lethal violence does the U.S. outpace other Western nations, with homicide rates many times greater. Most killings in America do not have their origins in criminal activity—most stem from arguments. One study compares the death rate to victims of different types of crime in the U.S. for the first time. Except for assault, robbery is by far the most dangerous American crime, with a death rate per thousand crimes 2 1/2 times greater than rape and 50 times as deadly as burglary.

Why are the streets of American cities so much more lethal than those of other countries with just as much crime and just as many criminals as the U.S.?

AGE AND LEARNING

Kids today live in a media culture where they are constantly exposed to violence in movies and television, video games and music. Violence has always played a role in entertainment, but in recent years dramatic changes have taken place. Research shows that media violence has increased in quantity and has also become much more graphic, sexual and sadistic.

Children, especially till the age of seven or eight are at a stage of development that does not equip them to distinguish reality from fantasy. Moreover, with the advent of 24-hour satellite channels, there is a constant stream of images of violence or sexual behaviour that may have an undesirable impact on young children.

It has been found that there is a tendency among children to imitate the stunts performed by models in the advertisements. Increasingly, research on the subject seems to be pointing out that children who watch programmes replete with violence-based content are more prone to thinking of aggression as a way of life and problem solving, to get what they want.

Violent behaviour is learned, and often it is learned early in life. But just as children can learn to be violent, they also can learn to be kind-hearted. They can learn constructive ways to solve problems, deal with disagreements, and handle anger. Children who learn these skills early in life actually are learning violence prevention; something that will be valuable for the rest of their lives. With these skills, children are far less likely to grow up to be violent, or to be victims of violence.

First and foremost, a child needs to feel safe at home. There is no surer way to start children on the right path in life than to provide consistent, reliable, loving care. How you relate to the children inside your home is perhaps the most powerful tool for protecting them from violence outside the home.

Children learn how to behave by watching people around them. Your child learns by watching characters on television, in videos, and in movies. And, above all, your child learns by watching you. Think for a moment about how you react to difficult situations. How do you act towards your spouse?—Your friends?—Your neighbors?—Other family members?—You are teaching your child, by example, how to get along in the world. When you and others come together to solve your problems peacefully, your child learns how to deal with people in a positive way. But when you or someone close to your child is aggressive and destructive, the child learns to act the same way.

When children, even very young children, see a violent act, they are deeply affected by it. This is especially true if the violence involves a family member or someone they know in the neighborhood. What can you do to help? First, allow the children plenty of time to talk about violence they have seen at school, in the neighborhood, or on TV. Encourage them to express their feelings about it. Second, make sure your children get to see many more examples of people dealing with each other in a spirit of friendly cooperation rather than by threatening violence or hurting each other. The children will gradually realise that there are many ways to deal with people and resolve conflicts peacefully, and that violence is not the best way to get what they want.

Sadly, children themselves are sometimes the victims of violence. A child who is being abused lives with constant fear and pain. And while the physical wounds may heal, the emotional scars can last a lifetime. If you know of a child who is being abused, or if you suspect that someone may be abusing a child in your care, seek help immediately. Otherwise, that child may grow up to become a violent adult or may fall into a pattern of repeatedly being victimised.

A few years ago, a child's daily routine included an hour's play at the local park. But nowadays this trend has diminished. Thanks to the television, children prefer staying indoors to the idea of feeling the wind rush past their cheeks in outdoor play. The result: lack of exercise.

Moreover, parents allow children to have their meals while watching programmes. The dinner table is the only place where the entire family can hope to be together for a while. But with television breaking into that time, inter-personal communication is hampered to a considerable extent.

Television Statistics

According to the A.C. Nielsen Co., the average American watches more than 4 hours of TV each day (or 28 hours/week, or 2 months of nonstop TV-watching per year). In a 65-year life, that person will have spent 9 years glued to the tube.

I. FAMILY LIFE

Percentage of households that possess at least one television: 99

Number of TV sets in the average U.S. household: 2.24

Percentage of U.S. homes with three or more TV sets: 66

Number of hours per day that TV is on in an average U.S. home: 6 hours plus 47 minutes

Percentage of Americans that regularly watch television while eating dinner: 66

Number of hours of TV watched annually by Americans: 250 billion

Value of that time assuming an average wage of S5/hour: S1.25 trillion

Percentage of Americans who pay for cable TV: 56

Number of videos rented daily in the U.S.: 6 million

Number of public library items checked out daily: 3 million

Percentage of Americans who say they watch too much TV: 49

II. CHILDREN

Approximate number of studies examining TV's effects on children: 4,000

Number of minutes per week that parents spend in meaningful conversation with their children: 3.5

Number of minutes per week that the average child watches television: 1,680

Percentage of day care centers that use TV during a typical day: 70

Percentage of parents who would like to limit their children's TV watching: 73

Percentage of 4-6 year-olds who, when asked to choose between watching TV and spending time with their fathers, preferred television: 54

Hours per year the average American youth spends in school: 900 hours

Hours per year the average American youth watches television: 1500

III. VIOLENCE

Number of murders seen on TV by the time an average child finishes elementary school: 8,000

Number of violent acts seen on TV by age 18: 200,000

Percentage of Americans who believe TV violence helps precipitate real life mayhem: 79

IV. COMMERCIALISM

Number of 30-second TV commercials seen in a year by an average child: 20,000

Number of TV commercials seen by the average person by age 65: 2 million

Percentage of survey participants (1993) who said that TV commercials aimed at children make them too materialistic: 92

Rank of food products/fast-food restaurants among TV advertisements to kids: 1

Total spending by 100 leading TV advertisers in 1993: $15 billion

V. GENERAL

Percentage of local TV news broadcast time devoted to advertising: 30

Percentage devoted to stories about crime, disaster and war: 53.8

Percentage devoted to public service announcements: 0.7

Films and Violence

Gerbner warns that the search for a link between media violence and real life aggression is in itself a symptom of the problem itself. For Gerbner, media violence demonstrates power: "It shows one's place in the 'pecking order' that runs society."

For example, Gerbner's decades-long study of television violence indicates that villains are typically portrayed as poor, young, male members of visible minorities, while the victims are overwhelmingly female. He argues that by making the world look like a dangerous place, especially for white people, the majority will be more willing to give the authorities greater power to enforce the *status quo*.

Violence is the foundation of many films, TV movies, and action series. In fact, violence is often synonymous with "action". Without violence, there would be no story. A crime, a murder, a fist-fight are used to launch TV and movie plots. Violence is often the very pretext for the action that follows.

TV and film plots begin with violence, and impending conflict continues to drive the story. The hero is never safe. Danger is always just around the corner. As the story unfolds, outbreaks of violence against people and property make sure that viewers stay in their seats. TV violence doesn't bleed. There are lots of shootouts and fist fights, but amazingly no one gets seriously hurt. TV rarely shows the consequences of violence. Occasionally, unlucky characters (but never the hero!) end up in a nice clean hospital bed. In general, films depict bleeding, the immediate consequence of violence, more often than TV. In fact, horror movies celebrate gooey, graphic, glory scenes. But even in these films, the real world consequences of violence—the physical handicaps, financial expense, and emotional cost—are never a part of the plot. Perhaps the most chilling aspect of the media's portrayal of violence is that when people are killed, they simply disappear. No one mourns their death. Their lives are unimportant.

Media violence takes place in a world of good and bad. In most TV programs and movies, viewers' emotions have to be enlisted very quickly. Starkly contrasting good and bad characters help accomplish this. Deeper, more realistic, more ambiguous characterisations make it hard for viewers to know whom to root for. It also requires more screen time that takes away from on-screen action.

As a result, TV and film criminals are reduced to caricatures. They are 100% bad. No one could care about them. They have no families. Many of them don't even have full names, only nick names. They deserve no sympathy and they get what they deserve.

Bad guys have to be really bad otherwise good guys wouldn't be justified in clobbering them. Good guys are peaceable. They are driven to violence only as a last resort in their struggle against these bad—bad people. Good guy violence is justified. To see how this self justifying formula works, ask a child why a particular character is getting beat up. Their answer is simple: "He's a bad guy."

CHILDREN see model behaviour in the media. If kids don't see the consequences of violence, it teaches them that violence doesn't cause serious harm. When heroes use violence, it sends a message that violence is an appropriate way to respond to problems. Early childhood is the important period for observational learning; the social-cognitive observational learning model suggests that normative beliefs about aggression, hostile biases about the world, and aggressive social scripts are all learned from observing violence.

Identification with same-sex aggressive TV characters and the perception that violent TV shows tell about life "like it is" predicted adult aggression for both genders, these factors exacerbated the effect of TV-violence viewing only for male participants. Boys who viewed TV violence *and* identified with male aggressive TV characters or perceived TV violence as true to life were most at risk for adult aggression.

Media violence may have short-term effects on adults, but the real long-term effects seem to occur only with children. We need to be aware that media violence can affect any child from any family. The psychological laws of observational learning, habituation/desensitisation, priming, and excitation transfer are immutable and universal.

True, media violence is not going to turn an otherwise fine child into a violent criminal. But just as every cigarette one smokes increases a little bit the likelihood of a lung tumor some day, every violent TV-show increases a little bit the likelihood of a child growing up to behave more aggressively in some situation.

The violent films and TV programs that probably have the most deleterious effects on children are not always the ones that adults and critics believe are the most violent. What type of violent scene is the child most likely to use as a model for violent behavior? It is one in which the child identifies with the perpetrator of the violence, the child perceives the scene as telling about life like it is, and the perpetrator is rewarded for the violence.

ADULTS see much more violence in the media than actually exists in real life. That's because producers believe that they have to include extraordinary violence in order to keep viewers interested. As a result, heavy TV viewers think that the world is more dangerous and violent than it actually is. This phenomenon is often called the "mean world" syndrome. How high is your mean world quotient? Do the shows you watch make you feel more fearful?

A longitudinal research men who were high TV-violence viewers as children were significantly more likely to have pushed, grabbed, or shoved their spouses, to have responded to an insult by shoving a person, to have been convicted of a crime (according to state records), and to have committed a moving traffic violation (according to state records). For example, men who were high TV violence viewers in childhood were convicted of crimes at over three times the rate of other men. Women who were high TV violence viewers as children were more likely to have thrown something at their spouses, to have responded to someone who made them mad by shoving, punching, beating, or choking the person, to have committed some type of criminal act, and to have committed a moving traffic violation. For example, women who were high TV-violence viewers as children reported having aggression for both men and women but with indirect aggression punched, beaten, or choked another adult at over four times the rate of other women.

We must recognise the economic realities of media violence. Violence sells. Both children and adults are attracted to violent scenes by the action and intense emotions. Many of the most popular shows and popular films for children have contained violence. Violent TV shows appear to be a little cheaper to produce on the average. Hamilton (1998) reported that from 1991 to 1993, the average production fee per hour for network prime time TV programming was about $1,094,000 for nonviolent shows and $998,000 for violent shows—in other words, about 10% cheaper.

Each additional violent act seems to reduce the cost by about $1,500. Of course, these are only averages for production costs. What really counts is the ability of a TV show to attract enough sponsors to cover its cost or to attract enough syndicated buyers and the ability of a video game to attract enough buyers to cover its cost.

Foreign markets become very important in these calculations, and generally violent shows and games are easier to sell in foreign markets than are other kinds of games or shows. More specifically, the probability of a TV show being exported successfully increases about 16% if it is violent (Hamilton, 1998).

CRIME AND MEDIA

Media reports of crime clearly influence general perception; a more serious problem is the way in which the media covers specific crimes and specific individuals who are suspected of committing those crimes. At times public is not provided with any opposing evidence indicating the suspect's possible innocence. There is a strong tendency to form a negative impression based on the primacy effect. Moreover people tend to believe assertions made in the media.

Those crimes that make news are often terrible ones, and the public is eager to identify and punish the individual responsible for the evil deed. People tend to leap to assumptions of guilt long before the evidence with respect to guilt or innocence is presented in court.

The most serious problem is that the members of the jury are also drawn from the same public whose opinions have been influenced by the media. As a result pre-trial publicity tends to help the prosecution and harm the defense.

Some people connected with television industry claim that watching violence on TV is beneficial—viewers discharge some of their own aggressive impulses through viewing, thus reducing the likelihood that they will perform aggressive acts. Freud would probably have agreed with this claim; an instinct or drive theory of aggression assumes that aggression builds up until it is discharged by some form of aggression act, either actual or vicarious. Girls tend to imitate aggression behaviour much less than boys unless they are specifically reinforced for doing so. Most of the aggression roles on TV are male, the female is less likely to find aggressive models to imitate. There is a 'critical period' in a boy's development when he is maximally susceptible to the influence of violent TV, and regular viewing of such programs during this periods leads to the development of a more aggressive life style. The boy's preference for violent TV at age eight influences both his current aggressiveness and his aggressiveness ten years later. By the time he is nineteen, however his TV preferences are not related to his aggressiveness.

Aggressive behaviour has many causes and the influence of TV models on behaviour depends on whether the models of behaviour imitated prove effective in daily interactions. The child who is punished for imitating acts observed on TV, either by parents or peers, is apt to show no change in behaviour or even a decrease in aggressiveness—although behaviour that is prohibited in one setting may be displayed in another where there is less fear of punishment.

Many factors are involved in the instigation of aggression; condition of poverty, overcrowding the actions of authorities such as policemen, the values of one's sub-group within the society.

Playing violent video games can cause increases in aggression and violence (Anderson Ph.D. 2000). Here are a few of the facts that were highlighted concerning TV and movie violence by Professor Rowell Huesmann of the University of Michigan:

1. Exposure to violent TV and movies causes increase in aggression and violence.
2. These effects are of two kinds: short term and long term. The short-term effect is that aggression increases immediately after viewing a violent TV show or movie, and lasts for at least 20 minutes. The long-term effect is that repeated exposure to violent TV and movies increases the violence prone of the person watching such shows.
3. Both the long term and the short-term effects occur to both boys and girls.
4. The effects of TV and movie violence on aggression are not small (Anderson 2000).

• • •

2

MEDIA VIOLENCE AS FREE SPEECH

The Root Cause of Problem

The notion of violence as a means of problem-solving is reinforced by entertainment in which both villains and heroes resort to violence on a continual basis. The Center for Media and Public Affairs (CMPA), which has studied violence in television, movies and music videos for a decade, reports that nearly half of all violence is committed by the "good guys". Less than 10 per cent of the TV shows, movies and music videos that were analysed, contextualised the violence or explored its human consequences. The violence was simply presented as justifiable, natural and inevitable—the most obvious way to solve the problem.

Many pundits argue that media violence is at least partly to blame for the school shootings in Littleton, Colorado, Taber, Alberta and Erfurt, Germany. Ex-army psychologist Dave Grossman, a leading American activist, points the finger squarely at movies and video games. He argues that Hollywood films have desensitised the kids to consequences of violence, and video games have taught them how to handle a gun. But others, like psychiatrist Serge Tisseron, maintain, "Just because a film has a murder scene doesn't mean people are going to commit the act.... That overstates the power of the image and under-estimates the role of parents."

Comic-book creator Gerard Jones contends that violent video games, movies, music and comic books enable people to pull themselves out of emotional traps, "integrating the scariest, most fervently denied fragments of their psyches into fuller sense of selfhood through fantasies of superhuman combat and destruction". Pullitzer-Prize-winning author Richard Rhodes says that video game violence enables young people to safely challenge their feelings of powerlessness.

Psychologist Melanie Moore concludes:

> "Fear, greed, power-hunger, rage: these are the aspects of our selves that we try not to experience in our lives but often want, even need, to experience vicariously through stories of others. Children need violent entertainment in order to explore the inescapable feelings that they have been taught to deny, and to reintegrate those feelings into a more whole, more complex, more resilient selfhood."

Video Games

Violence in general and sexual violence in particular, is also a staple of the video game industry. The current trend is for players to be the bad guys, acting out criminal fantasies and earning points for attacking and killing innocent bystanders. Although these games are rated M, for mature audiences, it's common knowledge that they are popular among pre-teens and teenaged boys.

Web Sites

Virtual violence is also readily available on the World Wide Web. Children and young people can download violent lyrics (including lyrics that have been censored from retail versions of songs), and visit Web sites that feature violent images and video clips. Much of the violence is also sexual in nature.

Many kids view sites as the online equivalent of harmless horror movies. But their pervasive combination of violence and sexual imagery is disturbing.

The presence of violence, degradation and cruelty in a range of media means that children are exposed to a continuum of violence.

Television is also so pervasive that it's hard to locate people who have lived without it.

HISTORY

In the 19th and 20th centuries, at the start of the industrial revolution, communications were generally bad, and so information was most easily produced and consumed in the towns where there was a market for it. In the countryside few people could read and write. It was only really with the development of the telegraph and the railways in the 19th century that a national press and publishing industry could develop in the main industrial countries. But still, it was the publishing houses and newspapers in the national capitals which could most easily sell their products throughout the country as a whole. They had the benefit of (a) higher circulation and more readers, (b) greater income because of this, (c) more revenue from advertising, (d) larger machines to reduce production costs, (e) a better road and rail network for distributing their books, papers and magazines, and (f) a better network of writers and reporters in different parts of the world. Gradually over time newspaper and publishing firms have tended to become bigger and bigger as the larger companies have bought up more and more papers, sometimes in more than one country.

Two other developments in the press were noticeable around the beginning of the 20th century. The first was the development of "news agencies", specialised firms that produced and sold news to the newspaper companies but which did not publish their own newspapers. Not all newspapers had enough money to keep their own reporters in cities and countries in other parts of the world, so it was convenient for them to simply buy news from these agencies. The best known of these are Reuters and Associated Press, which are international, but many countries have their own official news agencies, such as TASS in Russia and the former Soviet Union. The other development was that of the popular or "tabloid" press-papers like the sports papers in Japan which cover mainly sports, sex and scandal. The newspaper industry is thus divided between the quality—news—and the popular—entertainment— papers, with different places in the market. In many cases, as with the News International newspapers in the US, Australia and the UK, the same company owns both.

The owner of News International is a man called Rupert Murdoch who has media interests in Australia, the UK and the US, and who is now becoming involved with satellite TV both in the UK and in Asia. He actually controls most of the satellite broadcasting in both the UK and China. He started as the owner of a tabloid paper in Australia, which he took over when his father died. He increased the number of readers of his newspapers by including more and more sex and scandal, and started to buy up other newspapers both in Australia and the US. He moved into the UK newspaper industry by buying a British paper—The Sun—in the late 1960s. The Sun had been started as a politically left-wing newspaper, but Murdoch turned it into a sex-and-tabloid. (The paper is very famous for the "page three girls"—photographs of nude models which appear on page three every day.) The Sun soon became the most popular paper in the UK, with a circulation of about 4-5 million (out of a population of 55 million). Politically it was very important, because it supported the Conservative Thatcher government, and there is evidence that the Conservatives won the 1992 British election because the Sun decided to support them. After the success of this paper, Murdoch bought The Times, the most famous of all the UK papers, which remains a quality newspaper. Murdoch is also important because he forced the press labour unions to accept new technology. He did this by closing down the old printing factories when the workers went on strike, and opening new ones with new technology and new workers who did not belong to the old unions.

The cinema developed very quickly in the early 20th century, once the technology had been invented to make copies of films and transport them around the country cheaply. Sound recording and film technology were eventually brought together in the talking film. The existence of these other technologies meant also that: (a) Prints of the same films could, therefore, be carried easily around the country and shown in different places at the same time. (b) The cinema also added moving pictures to the news in the form of the weekly newsreel, the main source of visual news for most people before the arrival of the television. This was very important during the Second World War. (c) The cinema also changed the social lives of many people, with a visit to the cinema on either Friday night or Saturday (rarely Sunday) being a weekly event for a large number of people. Cinema audiences were at their highest from the 1930s, with the invention of the talking film, to the early 1950s, when more and more people started to watch television.

Once more, competition led to a situation in which the larger companies tended to get bigger, and the smaller ones tended to disappear. The bigger companies had more money. The bigger film Companies could pay the most popular stars to work for them, and they could pay for the best sets, the best costumes, and the best film technology. "Gone with the Wind" (1936) was a particularly important film because it was long and in colour, which made it very expensive. It was also based on a best-selling novel. The bringing together of literature and film in this way was another important development for the future of the media industry later on. Not all expensive films have been so successful: Hollywood has a long tradition of films that have left producers and whole film studios bankrupt because they were expensive but nobody wanted to see them.

Radio had a slightly different role. Film was nearly always commercial, being an extension of the theatre industry in the 19th century. The early cinemas looked like theatres, and often could be used for plays and music as well as films. But radio often existed both in a commercial form, and in a state controlled form. Like the film newsreel, it was particularly important during the Second World War, as a source of information, instruction and propaganda, in addition to entertainment. It also gave a mass audience to recorded music, including the soundtracks, songs and theme music from films.

Different collaborations between these various media were possible. In the case of a successful film, it would often also produce theme music which could be sold on record, and as sheet music, involving the publishing industry as well. So a successful film could also earn money from the recording and publishing industries. In more recent years, the links between these different industries have become much closer, so that the same company often has links with all of them.

The period when these different industries started to come together was with the increased popularity of television in the 1950s. The cinema audiences began to disappear as people began to spend more time at home watching the television. Radio audiences also fell. (At first the films could provide colour which television could not, but colour television had also appeared in many countries by the end of the 1970s.) But while the cinema industry started to get smaller, the film industry only grew bigger, as it began to produce films for the television market.

For the film companies making television films, especially series of "soap operas", was important because it guaranteed a steady stream of work for technicians and actors. (They were called "soap operas" because they were shown mostly in the daytime, their audiences were housewives, and many of them were sponsored by the soap and shampoo companies!) Successful television shows could carry on with weekly episodes for many years. The size of the American market compared with the other industrialised countries was also important. Many more people had televisions in the US than elsewhere in the 1950s and 1960s, so that American production companies could sell their films to more television stations more cheaply. This meant that it was much cheaper for television stations elsewhere to show American material, either with the voices changed to the local language, or with subtitles. American television shows and films established a dominance in the world market which they still have, and the companies which produced them grew extremely wealthy and large.

More links between publishing and television also started to develop. The largest example is the Time-Warner company, which was set up when the owner of the Warner Brothers film studios, Ted Ross, took over Time-Life Inc., which publishes Time and other popular magazines. The present boss is Gerry Levine, and it is now one of the world's largest media companies. In addition to publishing magazines and making films, it makes CD's, organises concerts, and manages artists such as Madonna and Michael Jackson. It has close links with another company, CNN, which was started by Ted Turner (the husband of Jane Fonda). This specialises in selling news coverage to other companies, rather like the press agencies, Reuters etc, do in the newspaper business. CNN was lucky to be in the right place to cover two big stories: the Chinese Tiananmen incident in 1989, and the Gulf War with Iraq in 1992. Soon press companies began to have an interest in television and vice versa. The Rupert

Murdoch newspaper company—News International—also owns the British Sky satellite broadcasting system, with all-day films and coverage of news and sporting events. When he started the company, cable and satellite TV was not very popular in the UK, and so Murdoch used his money to buy the rights to major sporting events, especially soccer and cricket, which could only be seen on his television channel. The number of people using satellite TV grew rapidly! Through his links with Hong Kong, he has also started a satellite TV company in China, which will be a huge market in the future as the economy grows. He has also bought up one of the largest American film studios, 20th Century Fox, and so their films can be seen on Murdoch Star Satellite TV. Japanese companies have also been active, with Sony also involved in making and marketing CDs and buying film studios in California.

The reason why the big firms like News International, Sony, Disney, or Time Warner are successful, therefore is not that they are better or more efficient: it is because they also have control of the marketing system. The big companies are able to make sure that their best-selling paperback books, CDs and software are to be found on the book and record stands of the stations, airports and supermarkets throughout the world. Of all the Japanese computer companies, Sony may be able to make most use of the internet because of the information resources (movies, music) that it controls, in addition to the hardware. With the new computer technology, you should soon be able to access download Sony films (Columbia Studios) and Sony Music (CBS Records) from the internet and play them either on your Sony Play-station or your Sony Vaio computer or your Sony minidisk recorder.

Smaller companies lack this distribution network, and so sell less copies. The next ten years promise to be very interesting ones for the media, with small producers able to become increasingly active in areas which the big companies concerned only with mass entertainment and publishing do not wish to exploit. It remains to be seen whether, in the end, the new technology will be a force giving people more power over their own lives, or a force which simply strengthens the position of the major international corporations over what people see, listen to and read. With people like Bill Gates increasingly controlling information technology and the internet, it is very likely that the large corporations will remain in control of the economy and, through their money, the political system.

Representation of Crime Issues

The most comprehensive research on this has been conducted by Robert Reiner, Sonia Livingstone and Jessica Allen. The advantages of their research are that it covers a significant historical sweep: 1945 to 1991. It also covers the representation of crime issues in a range of different media: newspapers, film and television.

What did Reiner and colleagues find? In general, the media does cover crime more than in the past, and this coverage has shifted towards more serious and violent crimes. Alongside this, they argue that news and editorial values tend to represent crime as ever-present and common; an everyday threat rather than a one-off disturbance, as they more commonly did in the past.

Does media representation of crime have an impact on its audiences? One way it could have an impact is by making it more likely someone will go out and commit a crime. There was much speculation at the time of the trial of the two boys who killed Jamie Bulger about whether their video viewing habits may have led them to do some kind of copycat killing. But the research on the impact of watching, say, violent videos, is at best inconclusive.

The annual British Crime Survey examines, among other things, public fear and anxiety about crime in relation to the types of newspapers they read. Asked if they were very worried about being attacked by a stranger, six per cent of broadsheet readers said that they were, compared with 17% of tabloid readers. Similar differences were found in the case of burglary, mugging and rape.

Tabloid readers might have other reasons to be more fearful of victimisation of course. Compared with the broadsheets, tabloids have their core readership among the working class, and the British Crime Survey also tells us that the poorer you are, the greater your risk of victimisation. So tabloid readers might have just cause to be more fearful than their better off broadsheet-reading peers. Nonetheless, these figures are suggestive. The British Crime Survey also found that tabloid readers were far more likely to believe that the national crime rate has risen (nearly a half of them thought so) than were broadsheet readers (only a quarter thought so).

The American Booksellers Foundation for Free Expression lists a number of reasons to protect media violence as a form of free expression:

- censorship won't solve the root causes of violence in society;
- deciding what is "acceptable" content is necessarily a subjective exercise;
- many of the plays, books and films banned in the past are considered classics today;
- it's up to individuals and not governments to decide what's appropriate for themselves and their children;

Heath and Gilbert (1996) find that the relationship between media presentations and crime is dependent on characteristics of the message and the audience.

Presentation of large amounts of local crime news engenders increased fear among the larger public (Brillon, 1987; Sheley and Ashkins, 1981), while the presentation of large amounts of non-local crime news has the opposite effect by making the local viewers feel safe in comparison to other areas (Liska and Baccaglini, 1990).

WHAT THE LAW OF JUSTICE SAYS

The burden of proof: a provable link

Perhaps the most direct challenge that has come to program producers has been the charge that they are responsible for imitative actions on the part of viewers. Suppose a 16-year-old boy watches a wrestling match on a cable channel and then while trying to imitate the feigned violence breaks his buddy's neck. Can the parents of the victim sue the cable channel and the wrestling producer for inducing the damage? To date, the courts have ruled against such torts.

In fact, no court has granted monetary compensation for harm allegedly caused by a television program or music recording, because the courts doubt the existence of a provable link between television and violence. In *Zamora v. Columbia Broadcasting System, Olivia N. v. NBC, Walt Disney Prod. v. Shannon, DeFilippo v. NBC,* and *Waller v. Osbourne,* the plaintiffs were denied damages when they alleged that they were victims of violence incited by television programming or, in the last case, an Ozzy Osbourne recording. Instead, the courts sided with the defendants' claim to a First Amendment right to freedom of expression. Based on Brandenburg v. Ohio (1969), the scope of the advocacy of "imminent lawless action" doctrine has been limited; the Supreme Court has specifically ruled that televised violence does not fall into that category, especially if it is entertainment. The same is true of the "clear and present danger" standard articulated in Schenck v. United States (1919). That test was strengthened in Whitney v. California (1927), where Justice Louis Brandeis in a concurring opinion joined by Justice Oliver Wendell Holmes wrote: "Fear of serious injury cannot alone justify suppression of free speech.... Men feared witches and burnt women. It is the function of speech to free men from the bondage of irrational fears. To justify suppression of free speech there must be reasonable ground to fear that serious evil will result if free speech is practised."

Media violence and social violence

Some have argued that violence in the media contributes to violence in society as a whole; thus government has a compelling interest to reduce and/or censor violence in programming. A host of national policymakers has brought pressure on producers and broadcasters of violent programming to curtail "gratuitous violence." In 1994, for example, Rep. Edward Markey, D-Mass., told the television networks to figure out a way to label violence in programming or the Congress would do it for them. In 1995, good to his word, he attached legislation to a communications bill that required the installation of a so-called V-chip in all new television sets. The legislation was signed into law, and then further amended when the ratings were found to be too vague by some in Congress.

Reed Hundt, the then chairman of the Federal Communications Commission, warned that networks might be legally responsible for the effects of their programs and that the FCC had the power to regulate the content of programs. Speaking before the executive committee of the National Association of Broadcasters in February 1994, Hundt called for "new family programming" to "educate and instruct" children. Appearing before Markey's committee later that year, Surgeon General Joycelyn Elders attacked the networks for not doing enough to reduce violence on television. With the resignation of Elders, Attorney General Janet Reno emerged as the point person on this issue. She told Congress that regulating the content of programming did not violate the rights of broadcasters because they are second-class citizens under the First Amendment.

In February 1995, Sen. Kent Conrad, D-N.D., introduced a bill to ban "gratuitous violence" from television between 8 a.m. and 10 p.m. Sen. Bob Graham, D-Fla., coerced the Defense Department, the Postal Service and Amtrak to agree not to place advertisements in "excessively violent" programming on television. Sen. Fritz Hollings, D-S.C., introduced legislation to ban violent television programs when children are "reasonably likely" to compose a "substantial part of the audience". Since that time Sens. Joseph Lieberman, D-Conn., and John McCain, R-Ariz., have held hearings and warned producers that regulation is just a bill away. The resulting changes in the V-chip rating system with its confusing list of letters to characterise violence, violent language, sexual material and the like have not been challenged in the courts, perhaps because producers would rather play along with the letter game than offend Congress and risk greater controls.

Predictably, politicians have been unable to resist the urge to blame television for society's many ills. In 1954, for example, Sen. Estes Kefauver, D-Tenn., investigated the relationship between juvenile delinquency and television programs. Sen. Thomas Dodd, D-Conn., revived this issue in the early 1960s; he eventually persuaded President Lyndon Johnson to establish the Eisenhower Commission on the Causes and Prevention of Violence in 1968. Since its conclusions were not in accord with his impressions, Sen. John Pastore, D-R.I., requested that the surgeon general issue another report on the problem. Three years later under the watchful eye of the Congress, a report was published that hinted at a weak correlation between the viewing of violence and violent activity: "The effect is small compared with many other possible causes, such as parental attitudes or knowledge of and experience with the real violence in society. The evidence does not warrant the conclusion that televised violence has a uniformly adverse effect ... [or] an adverse effect on the majority of children." Nonetheless, the surgeon general appeared before Pastore's committee and claimed that a causal link had been documented though "carefully phrased and qualified in language acceptable to social scientists".

By the fall of 1974, FCC chairman Richard Wiley was urging the three commercial networks to curtail "sex and violence" on television. Unfortunately, his call intertwined indecency with violence. In reaction, the networks and the National Association of Broadcasters Television Review Board adopted the "family viewing" policy, which moved violent and sexual programming into the 9–11 p.m. time slot. Nonetheless, the FCC made clear that "industry self-regulation" was preferable to governmental regulation, that such standards were highly subjective and raised "serious constitutional questions" (*Broadcast of Violent, Indecent, and Obscene Material,* 1975). Sure enough, in November 1976, the courts found the "family viewing" hour unenforceable and unconstitutional in *Writers Guild of America W. Inc. v. FCC.* More recently, the courts have ruled that the FCC can put in place a restriction on "indecent" material limiting it to broadcast to between 10 p.m. and 6 a.m., but they have not included "violent" material in their rulings.

The vagueness of the term "violence" is one of the most persistent problems for those who seek to regulate it because it encourages arbitrary regulation that collides with free and creative expression. The Supreme Court has consistently ruled that inhibiting speech is unconstitutional, especially when the inhibition is caused by the application of an "arbitrary and capricious" standard. Television programs from reruns of "The Three Stooges" to "Will & Grace" achieve comic effects using what some have called violent activity. Because conflict makes drama, it is hard to find a serious fiction, whether it is *Macbeth* or "The West Wing", that is not violent in some way. Furthermore, philosophically, it is not difficult to demonstrate that violence can be used to reinforce into the mind of audience members what is moral and what is immoral. In *The Case for Television Violence,* Jib Fowles demonstrates that violence in programming is cathartic and might actually prevent further violence on the part of viewers.

Social-science Studies

Thus, the use of social scientific studies in the courts is a troubling question. President Bill Clinton's last surgeon general, David Satcher, issued a report in 2000 linking violence with the media. It came under immediate attack by numerous scholars. For example, Karen Sternheimer, a sociologist at the University of Southern California and a researcher at the Center for Media Literacy, wrote: "One of the studies the surgeon general cites equates programs as diverse as cartoon and police dramas with video games and action movies." This procedure, claims Sternheimer, negates "the importance of context and meaning". The surgeon general's comparisons are misleading and dangerous because they ignore the more likely causes of violence such as "alcohol abuse, the deterioration of public education and the lack of economic opportunity in impoverished areas". Thus, the issue of causation is a problem for social scientists because they can never eliminate all possible causes and must rely instead on a substantial "correlation" of activities to make their case.

Indianapolis Case

The most recent case in this regard concerns an ordinance written by the city of Indianapolis attempting to limit access to violent video games by minors in arcades. The ordinance defined "graphic violence" in two ways. First, it bracketed "graphic violence" with obscenity, arguing that it caters to a "morbid interest" and is "patently offensive to prevailing standards in the adult community as a whole ... and lacks serious literary, artistic, political or scientific value". Secondly, the ordinance defined "graphic violence" as "amputation, decapitation, dismemberment, bloodshed, mutilation, maiming, or disfigurement". The trial court approved the implementation of the ordinance on the grounds that psychological studies of other games provided enough data to convince the court that such games induced minors to aggressive acts of violence. The case was appealed to the 7th U.S. Circuit Court of Appeals in 2001. Judge Richard Posner wrote for the court in *American Amusement Machine Association v. Kendrick.* Citing *Winters,* which makes clear that "depiction of torture and deformation are not inherently sexual". Posner refused to equate violence with obscenity; he likewise took exception to the use of court-sanctioned obscenity prohibitions as applied to violent depictions. Furthermore, Posner argued that "no showing has been made that games of the sort found in the record of this case" induce violence. "The grounds" for such an ordinance, he added, "must be compelling" not merely plausible because "[c]hildren have First Amendment rights" (Erznoznik v. City of Jacksonville, 1975; Tinker v. Des Moines School District, 1969). Posner compared the video games to literature containing graphic violence and concluded that video games, despite their interactive nature, were still stories that taught various lessons.

As in the case of video games above, there has been much research on the effect of broadcast violence on its audience. However, much of it is subject to criticism because of methodological flaws.

Edward Donnerstein is one of the leading experts on violence in the media. He recently gave a lecture in which he argued that "viewing violence *per se* does not cause people to become violent". Donnerstein pointed out that countries with much more violence on broadcast media than America do not have high levels of violence in society. He cites Japan and Canada as his examples. What America has that Japan and Canada lack—a high level of poverty, excessive gun ownership, drug abuse, broken homes, illegitimacy and gangs. Donnerstein notes that violence in America has declined for every age group except teenagers, where the increase skews the results for the rest of the population.

James Q. Wilson, the Collins Professor of Management and Public Policy at UCLA, reached a similar conclusion in his book—*The Moral Sense.* Wilson points out that in Japan incredible violence pervades the media. And yet Japan has remarkably low rates of crime, especially violent crime.

Conclusion

Given the controversy over social scientific data, the courts have usually found that violence in programming cannot be regulated without creating a chilling effect on its content. Such an effect could only be justified if convincing data existed to establish an actual causal link between violence on the media and violence in society. Despite periodic claims to the contrary, studies to date have yet to establish such a link.

Furthermore, because violence is difficult to define, it presents regulators with the opportunity to censor in an arbitrary and capricious manner, which is also unconstitutional. Thus, until a viable, legally tenable definition of violence can be found, regulating it may prove impossible in the light of the arbitrary and capricious standard. The movement to conflate violence with indecency has also fallen on deaf ears. Other remedies, such as the V-chip, have been imposed only because the media involved have cooperated with regulators. The constitutionality of such government-mandated labels has not been tested.

Thus while members of Congress and others seek way to curtail violence in the media, it is likely to remain a staple of the entertainment industry.

The V-chip technology and accompanying ratings system is meant to give viewers the power to regulate programming in their homes by blocking programs they found unacceptable.

While regulators have been obsessing over flashes of skin and course language, TV violence, or at least the repercussions of that violence, have got more graphic, powered by the success of gritty police procedurals like Law & Order.

Many people think that the context of violence is relevant to whether or not it is justified. Some representations of violence are seen as worthy, educational or artistically justified, whilst others are described as 'gratuitous'. In other words some representations 'explore', whilst others 'exploit'.

It takes resources to isolate the biological, sociological, and psychological factors that are associated with violence, to untangle the ball of wax in which they are found, and to determine what the causes of violence are and what are its effects.

CDC's Youth Risk Behaviour Survey (YRBS), is a school-based survey designed to produce nationally representative sample of risk behaviours among students in grades 9-12.

The 1997 YRBS reported that:

- 18.3% of high school students carried a weapon (e.g., gun, knife, or club) during the 30 days preceding the survey, down from 26.1% in 1991.
- 5.9% of high school students carried a gun during the 30 days preceding the survey.
- 8.5% of high school students carried a weapon on school property during the 30 days preceding the survey.
- 7.4% of high school students were threatened or injured with a weapon on school property during the 12 months preceding the survey.

Other facts from the 1997 YRBS report included:

- Nationwide, 4% of students had missed 1 or more days of school during the 30 days preceding the survey because they had felt unsafe at school or when traveling to or from school.

- The prevalence of weapon carrying on school property on 1 or more of the 30 days preceding the survey was 8.5% nationwide. Overall, male students (12.5%) were significantly more likely than female students (3.7%) to have carried a weapon on school property.
- Nationwide, the prevalence of students who had been threatened or injured with a weapon on school property one or more times during the 12 months preceding the survey was 7.4%. Overall, male students –10.2%– were significantly more likely than female students –4%– to have been threatened or injured with a weapon on school property.
- Nationwide, 14.8% of students had been in a physical fight on school property one or more times during the 12 months preceding the survey. Overall, male students–20%–were significantly more likely than female students –8.6%–to have been in a physical fight on school property. This significant difference was identified for white and Hispanic students and all grade subgroups.
- Approximately one-third–32.9%–of students nationwide had property—car, clothing, or books—stolen or deliberately damaged on school property one or more times during the 12 months preceding the survey.

CDC's School Health Policies and Programs Study (SHPPS) provides information about school health policies, including violence prevention. The 1994 SHPPS showed that among all school districts, 91 percent have a written policy prohibiting student violence and 80.3% have a policy that specifically addresses weapon possession and use among students.

• • •

3

WOMEN AND MEDIA

Many different types of domestic violence—physical, sexual, verbal, emotional, psychological, economic—indicated that there is a wide range of conduct that threatens the safety and well-being of the person subjected to abuse. She indicated that the main reasons for abuse were related to need for power and control.

Violence in children's programmes, even in cartoons, is extremely problematic. Children are influenced by the programmes. The portrayal of women on television is very problematic—they are portrayed, as are sex objects. Violence in our society is institutionally sanctioned and glorified to maintain masculinity.

The disadvantageous social position of women affects the widespread diffusion of certain female images—images possessing the characteristics of a stereotype: a long-standing division of sexual roles due to gender stereotypes.

The Declaration and Platform for Action adopted by the Fourth World Conference on Women (Peking, 1995), where media were invited to promote strongly a less stereotyped image of women, to develop strategies for the application of an equal participation of men and women in TV shows and programmes and to increase women's participation in decision-making roles.

European monitoring team on Media (EuroMediaWatch) constantly monitors gender images in media content throughout Europe. The Model was adopted by analogous structures in Canada (MediaWatch, since 1981) and in the USA (Women, Men & Media, since 1989). Their goal is to start up a discussion among the main media producers and among women's organisations and media female professionals.

Politics and Media

The relationship between politics and television has also many dimensions.

Politics presents itself on television in three ways: as the content of the media (TV discussions about politics), as the subject of the media (politicians entertain and inform), and as a context of the media (TV is situated in an arena that—as in our case—has a strong political component).

From this perspective the relationship between media and politics cannot in any way be reduced to just an informative relationship but something that is much more complex and arbitrated, involving networks of reciprocal constructed relationships.

From a semiotic point of view, the relationship between media, information and politics poses, above all, a narrative problem: how are events constructed by the media? Who, at different times, are the individual protagonists, the interests, methods and strategies attributed to them?

And how do these—strategies and representations—vary according to the sex of the person on screen?

At the same time, each televised speech also is always argument, made up of assumptions, proof, and conclusions. It plays with generalisations and peculiarities that involve judgments; how are these judgments conditioned by the gender identity of the person who is involved? The characteristics of an appearance, for example, are:

Stereotypes and roles this appearance assumes:

- The type of "action" that this appearance involves—a political action, an interpretative action, a defensive action, an entertainment action.
- The methods of interaction—discourse, gestures, proxemics—with the other actor present;
- The "passions" of the appearance, the emotional tone that was mainly assumed.

Identity-and also gender identity-is, above all, the product of social discourse and practice. What needs to be looked at is how political and televised discourse contribute to the dominance of certain stereotypes, subverting some and creating new ones.

Aspects which influence attitudes:

- The choices that every programme makes with regard to possible themes—dominance of political issues, policy issues, campaign issues, personal issues....
- The roles that actors assume—who plays what role in the televised political communication.
- The communicative styles of the actors—starting from a lexical analysis of the discourse produced by each person.
- The management of the interaction between the actors—turns to speak, times, freedom....

The organisation of space and the placement and movement of the actors in the space;

We cannot avoid stereotyped visions about genders, but we must fight in order to prevent them from becoming fixed stereotypes which no one can criticise. We all automatically classify people, using identity principles previously set, thus dividing men and women into two groups and thereby making any other difference within the social body *null and void.*

By referring to "women" as a group with pre-defined common features, we are generalising, such common features being discrimination in political representation and in accessing higher ranks in decision-making hierarchies.

Stereotypes or prejudice, like other generalisations, frequently serve as mental shortcuts and especially are likely to be applied when people are busy or distracted. In one of the typical studies of American culture, it is demonstrated that having had their attention diverted for about 25 second, students remembered more of the stereotype attributes of a person than a sequence of numbers.

Once a stereotype is activated, it can be reactivated by something as simple as a disagreement with someone in the stereotyped group, and if brought to mind frequently enough, can become chronically accessible. Thus, even though media-based stereotypes may seem harmless when considered individually, their cumulative effect over time can be substantial. Once stereotypes are learned—whether from the media, family members, direct experience, or elsewhere—they sometimes take on a life of their own and become "self-perpetuating stereotypes".

Test for bias

One of the most popular techniques for probing implicit biases is the Implicit Association Test, or IAT. The Implicit Association Test has been used to measure a variety of hidden associations, such as implicit racial and gender stereotypes, attitudes toward elderly people, and preferences for particular political candidates. The IAT is a computer-based test that measures how rapidly people are able to categorise various words and images, and it capitalises on the fact that most of us identify words and images more rapidly when they come from closely related categories than when they come from unrelated ones. For example, the two words femininity and irrationality are linked in common-place thinking, and instantly associated with typically stereotyped terms like sensitivity, sweetness, and emotiveness, etc. On the other hand, if we come across two terms like masculine and sweetness, we take far longer to find associated terms since the two words are not connected by stereotypes. Thus, by comparing the speed with which people categorise words or images, the IAT indirectly assesses how closely people associate certain elements with each other. When stereotypic representations of behaviour are activated, relevant behaviour also becomes activated. In addition to the effects of priming, people who are stereotyped face a second burden: the threat that their behaviour will confirm a negative stereotype. This burden, known as "**stereotype threat**," can create anxiety and hamper performance on a variety of tasks (Steele, C., 1997).

How and why do we create stereotypes?

The creation of stereotypes is a concomitant of the process by which all human beings become individuals. Its beginnings lie in the earliest stages of our development.

The vulnerability of children to stereotype threat implies that stereotypes are learned early in life. Several studies have observed in-group biases by age 3 or 4 and the development of racial and gender stereotyping soon after. The infant's movement from a state of being in which everything is perceived as an extension of the self to a growing sense of a separate identity takes place between the ages of a few weeks and about five months. As the child comes to distinguish more and more between the world and self, anxiety arises from a perceived loss of control over the world. Stereotypes reflect certain basic perceptual categories, which are in turn projections of internalised, often repressed models of the self and the other. The resulting basic categories of difference reflect our preoccupation with the self and the control that the self must have over the world. The definition of the reality and of the other must incorporate the basic categories by which we define ourselves.

Stereotypes arise when self-integration is threatened. They are, therefore, part of our way of dealing with the instabilities of our perception of the world. We can and must take the distinction between pathological stereotyping and the stereotyping all of us need to do to preserve our illusion of control over the self and the world. Our perception of the world as "good" and "bad" is triggered by a recurrence of the type of insecurity that induced our initial division of the world into "good" and "bad". Everyone creates stereotypes. We cannot function in the world without them. They buffer us against our most urgent fears by extending them, making it possible for us to act as though their source were beyond our control.

Stereotypes can and often do exist parallel to the ability to create sophisticated rational categories that transcend the crude line of difference present in the stereotype. We retain our ability to distinguish the "individual" from the stereotyped class into which the object might automatically be placed. While the deep structure of the stereotype seems simple, its realisation is much more complex. The complexity of the stereotype results from the social context in which it is to be found. The deep structure of the stereotype can reappear in the adult as a response to anxiety, an anxiety having its roots in the potential disintegration of the mental representations the individual has created and internalised.

The models for control are linked to structures in society, which provide status and meaning for the individual. Self-esteem is linked to the image of the self and of the meaningful objects in the social world. Our self-image not only reflects our mental representation of the external world, but, by influencing our perception of objects and their integration into that mental representation, shapes it as well. The objects exist, we interact with them, they respond to (or ignore) our demands upon them. But when we relate to them, we relate to them through the filter of our internalised representation of the world.

Infants are often able to discriminate between female and male faces by the age of 9 months, and sometimes as early as 5 months exceptionally strong moulding and emphasis of in-group/out-group aspects and stereotypes can be seen as a natural process during certain periods of the identity development.

Young people can become strikingly intolerant and cruel in their rejection of those who are "different". Such intolerance can, for a period of time, be a necessary defensive measure to guard oneself against loss of identity, which can occur because of all the adjustments that adolescence entails. Young people help each other to cope with these troubles by forming coteries and creating stereotypes of themselves and their enemies.

Gender Identity

Gender identity forms in the first three years of life and has powerful psychological determinants that constitute male and female, but this may be independent of biological sex.

Self-recognition as male or female is the first process in becoming men and women.

Theories

Two classes of theories—biological and soco-psychological—have attempted to explain these gender differences in personality traits. The biological theories consider sex-related differences as arising from innate temperamental differences between the sexes, evolved by natural selection. Evolutionary psychology predicts that the sexes will differ in domains in which they have faced different adaptive problems throughout evolutionary history. For example, for biological reasons, including pregnancy, childbirth, and lactation, women have more invested than men in relations with children.

Women who were more agreeable and nurturing may have promoted the survival of their children and gained evolutionary advantage. Other biological theories have been proposed to account for gender differences; for example—in feelings and emotions. These explanations point to hormonal differences and their effects on mood and personality. But some studies considered that the evidence in support of these explanations was inconclusive.

Social psychological theorists argue for more proximal and direct causes of gender differences.

The social role model explains that most gender differences result from the adoption of gender roles, which define appropriate conduct for men and women. Gender roles are shared expectations of men's and women's attributes and social behaviour, and are internalised early in development. The same problems of gender differences affect gender roles: there is considerable controversy over whether they are purely cultural creations or whether they reflect preexisting and natural differences between the sexes in abilities and predispositions.

The social psychological approach called the 'artifact model' explains gender differences on personality scales in terms of method variance. Social desirability bias may lead men and women to endorse gender-relevant traits and some traits—such as fearfulness—may be less undesirable for women than for men. The magnitude of gender differences might also be related to cultural dimension *masculinity*. Male or Female concerns first of all the emotional roles in the home. In some societies, men specialise in ego-boosting, and women in ego-effacing, roles. In others, the emotional roles are more equally divided, with men also being oriented toward ego-effacing goals.

Masculinity is identified with the prevalent capacity to be assertive, rational and orientated towards material success and reinforcement of the ego, while the femininity of a context defines the degree of diffuse empathy, cooperation and orientation towards quality of life and social goals. In masculine cultures (like Japan and Austria), emphasis is placed on occupational advancement and earnings; in feminine cultures (like Costa Rica and Sweden), cooperation with co-workers and job security are valued. Religion and sexuality are the major areas in which society maintains implicit masculinity and femininity.

Gender Stereotypes

Gender stereotypes concern differences in the "psychological makeup" of women and men. We define them as the constellations of psychological traits that are said to be more characteristic of one sex than the other.

Gender stereotypes are not only a widely shared set of beliefs about the characteristics of individual because of gender, but also a rigid and "nearly" perpetual system of beliefs that have spelt discrimination and segregation for women.

Theories

Over the centuries gender stereotypes have generated a sexist ideology.

A case of the phenomenon is what Max Weber defined as *Herrschaft*, a relationship of dominance and subordination; through this system a most ingenious form of "interior colonisation" is achieved. It is one, which moreover tends to be sturdier than any form of segregation, and more rigorous than class stratification, more uniform, and certainly more enduring. However muted its present appearance may be, sexual dominion obtains nevertheless as perhaps the most pervasive ideology of our culture and provides its most fundamental concept of power.

Psychoanalytic theories of sexism have shown that sexism has many modes: it can involve idealising women, derogating them and emphasizing their "castrated" physical and mental inferiority, envying and fearing their bodies and reproductive capacities, viewing them as "other" than the fathers, excluding them from male peer groups, using them indirectly for homoerotic purposes. These different modes have diverse developmental origins – developmentally, they constitute many layers of sexism, and they command or suffuse diverse kinds of social organisations.

It is recognised that some stereotypes may be false and have no objective behavioural data to support them. Other stereotypes may contain elements of truth but fail to take into account the individual differences in traits occurring within groups or the degree of overlap between groups. Thus, if we speak of men as more aggressive than women, we are ignoring important individual differences in this trait among both men and women. Contrary to the implications of the stereotype, there are wide variations in aggressiveness among persons of both sexes, and there are some women who are more aggressive than some men. The stereotype makes no allowance for this variability and, when we use it uncritically, we act as though all men were more aggressive than all women.

Sex roles are defined in terms of activities of social significance in which the two sexes actually participate with differential frequency—that is, predominantly male activities, such as repairing cars and doing construction work, and predominantly female activities, such as keeping house and nursing.

Sex stereotypes, on the other hand, have to do with general beliefs about men and women, and they may be conceptualised as operating at two different levels: **sex-role stereotypes**, which consist of beliefs concerning the general appropriateness of various roles and activities for men and for women; and **sex-trait stereotypes**, which consist of those psychological characteristics or behavioural traits that are believed to characterise men with much greater (or lesser) frequency than they characterise women. Sex roles (there are more men than women construction workers) are often "explained" by reference to sex-role stereotypes —construction jobs should be performed by men—which in turn are "explained" by reference to sex-trait stereotypes—men are strong, robust, and so on, and are, therefore, more suited for construction jobs. The sex-trait stereotypes underpin both the sex-role stereotypes and the sex roles themselves. Supporting the belief in the appropriateness of the conventional adult sex roles are the male and female sex-trait stereotypes. These stereotypes purport to describe differences in the psychological characteristics of males and females, which, if accepted as true, make reasonable the assignment of men and women to different occupational, homemaking, and leisure roles.

Old and new gender stereotypes

Even when people encounter a stereotyped group member who violates the group stereotype, they often continue to maintain the stereotype by splitting it into subtypes. For example, when encountering a "strong woman, good at mathematics!"—people with gender stereotypes may distinguish that woman from the other "sentimental, fragile and irrational women" by creating a subtype for "smart women". As a result of sub-typing, stereotypes become impervious to disconfirming evidence.

Traditional displays of prejudice have not disappeared, but rather contemporary forms of prejudice are often difficult to detect and may even be unknown to the prejudice-holders.

"Modern sexism," is a form of prejudice analogous to the "modern racism". In contrast to old-fashioned sexism—which portrays women as unintelligent and incompetent—modern sexism can be characterised by a denial that sex discrimination continues to be a problem, antagonism toward women's groups, and a belief that the government and news media show too much concern about the treatment of women. Sexism is marked by an ambivalence and "ambivalent sexism" includes two separate but interrelated components— (1) hostile sexism, which involves negative feelings towards women, and (2) benevolent sexism, a chivalrous ideology that offers protection and affection to women who adopt conventional gender roles. Because benevolent sexism may superficially seem like positive regard rather than prejudice, it can go unnoticed or even be perpetuated by women themselves. As in the case of positive stereotypes, however, benevolent sexism is far from benign. Not only does it restrict women's freedom and encourage dependence upon men, but the presence of benevolent sexism among females means that women often act as prisoner and guard at the same time.

Researchers studying these modern forms of prejudice point to the strong evidence that, for example, behaviours toward women and current structural inequalities are inconsistent with the more liberal attitudes toward women and women's roles that are reported. Again, this is evidence of the existence of modern sexism! The positive stereotype of women as nurturing can be used, for example, as a justification to limit women to careers of education, childcare and nursing. This stereotype is dissonant with the image of women as trained soldiers marching into battle or cutthroat executives managing a hostile takeover.

Such terms as "covert discrimination," "subtle discrimination," and "unintentional discrimination" are beginning to appear with greater frequency in common parlance, newspapers, textbooks, and feminist articles. There has been an increased awareness of the importance of addressing non-overt sex discrimination.

Gender stereotypes and television

Lupton (1998) calls the 'major binary opposition in discourses on emotion...: "'Emotional woman' and the 'unemotional man'..." (p. 105; Parkin 1993). Emotion and emotionality are generally culturally viewed as feminine, while rationality (or lack of emotion) is represented as masculine. 'Ideal' femininity includes such attributes as gentleness, empathy, sensitivity, a caring disposition and heightened awareness to others' feelings. Additionally, women are also viewed as having negative emotions which they find difficult to control, and these might include envy, jealousy, rage, irrationality and aggressiveness.

Men, in binary opposition, on the other hand, are constructed as rational, tough, direct, self-controlled, logical, strong and unemotional.

Femininity has been linked with the private and emotionality, while masculinity has been linked with the public and rationality (Lupton, 1998; Parkin, 1993; Putman and Mumby, 1993). Women are given the 'expressive' role within the private sphere, which is apolitical, sexual and emotional. Men are given the 'instrumental' role and can thus dominate women's lives '...through the gender divisions of labour, management, power, authority and leadership in organisations'.

Socialisation

Socialisation is the way people learn about their culture and acquire its values, beliefs, perspectives, and social norms. It is an ongoing social process; we are socialised and re-socialised throughout the life cycle. Traditionally, parents, peers, teachers, and the clergy have had the major responsibility for socialisation. Numerous studies have found, however, that, in today's society, the mass media play a very important role in the socialisation process.

Social or observational learning theory examines the role of modeling in a child's social development. It posits that viewers, especially children, imitate the behaviour of television characters in much the same way that they learn social and cognitive skills by imitating their parents, siblings, and peers.

The actual processes of media socialisation, however, are different from those used by more traditional agents of socialisation. Media socialisation does not permit face to face social interaction and may lack some of the seductive or coercive powers of traditional agents who have the tools of interpersonal communication at their disposal. Nevertheless, the media have their own brand of seductiveness, and much of the socialisation through the media may involve observational and/or social learning.

Television provides not only specific responses but the strategies and rules viewers may apply to copy what they observe. As we already know, stereotypes are conventional representations or standardised images or conceptions. Stereotypes, in particular, play an important part in television's role as an agent of socialisation. Stereotypes typically lack originality, they fall back on commonly known and often one-dimensional elements of portrayal. Television stereotypes provide simplistic models of behaviours, strategies, and rules that appear regularly in many different genres of programs, which means that the more time viewers spend on television, the more likely their conceptions about the world and its people will reflect what they see there. TV gender stereotypes appeal to people's emotions rather than their intellect and their creative fantasies. Television programs with limited time to devote to character development often resort to stereotypes. Research on the impact of such images with regard to conceptions about sex roles points to the existence of a relationship between television viewing and having more stereotypic conceptions about gender roles. These relationships exist in all stages of the life cycle. In essence, television may be contributing to the maintenance of notions of more limited roles for women in society because the images seen on television typically foster the maintenance of the *status quo vis-à-vis* men's and women's roles in society. The concern is that viewers, especially children, who are continually exposed to television's stereotyped roles, may develop conceptions and perceptions about people that reflect the stereotypical images they see in the media.

Television has scant interest in faithfully reflecting reality, offering above all fictions, shows and entertainment. What it does set out to do, however, is to construct a reality of its own that is endowed with a truth value equal to that of the real world. In order to do so it must draw upon the widest possible consensus, and so exploit, for example, the most widely shared representations of women—the traditional, stereotype brand. It is after all clearly by starting off from observations most definitely shared by the majority of the population that it can organise the new values in such a way that, combined with the traditional values, they become authoritative sources of truth.

Thus it makes ample recourse to generalisation and categorisation, creating models that facilitate understanding of the new elements but using old materials.

• • •

4

UNDERSTANDING THE BASIC TERMS

Deviance

"All crime is, by definition, deviant behaviour, but not all forms of deviance are criminal."

"Societies create deviants by making the rules that lead to their infraction."

Crime is the breaking of written rules and deviance is the breaking of social rules.

"Deviance" is a wide-ranging term used by sociologists to refer to behaviour that varies, in some way, from a social norm. In this respect, it is evident that the concept of deviance refers to some form of "rule-breaking" behaviour.

In relation to deviance, therefore, the concept relates to all forms of rule-breaking—whether this involves such things as murder, theft or arson—the breaking of formal social rules—or such things as wearing inappropriate clothing for a given social situation, failing to produce homework at school or being cheeky to a parent, teacher and so forth—more-or-less the breaking of relatively informal social rules.

As should be apparent, criminal behaviour is a form of deviance—one that is defined as the breaking of legal rules—and, whilst we will be concentrating upon this area of deviance, it needs to be remembered that it is only one aspect—*albeit* a very significant one—in relation to the concept of deviant behaviour in any society.

Deviance involves acts of non-conformity that violates significant norms and is negatively viewed by society. Deviant behaviour refers to actions that transgress commonly held norms. What is regarded as deviant can shift from time to time and place to place; "normal" behaviour in one cultural setting may be labeled "deviant" in another.

Sanctions, formal or informal, are applied by society to reinforce social norms. *Crimes* are acts that are not permitted by those laws.

Deviance is learnt in one's neighbourhood, on the job or among friends and will occur when individuals find that they are rewarded more for criminality than for conformity.

The concept of anomie states that criminal behaviour is more visible where the norms of society are no longer clear or applicable.

Crimes are deviant acts that are subject to criminal or civil penalties. In violating criminal or civil codes crimes can be classified as violating significant norms and thus constitutes deviant behaviour.

Crimes involving the use of force or threat of force are called crimes of violence.

Murder—non-negligent manslaughter or willful killing or aggravated assault is the most violent and rarest of major violent crimes.

Forceful rape also comes under this category.

Robbery involves personal confrontation and the threat or use of force.

Assault or an attack for the purpose of inflicting severe bodily injury constitutes violent crime.

For maintenance of peace and order in society the government of the land makes certain laws and punishes the persons who go against the same. State laws may differ not only from one country to another but also from time to time in the same country.

The law may be written or unwritten. When the law is not written then crime is generally recognised as transgressing against the traditions or mores of the community. Crime, therefore, may be regarded as behaviour of individuals which the group strongly disapproves.

Criminal behaviour may be defined as anti-social conduct that violates established laws and entails some penalty. What constitutes a crime varies with time to time. Since societies do not have uniform standards of right and wrong and since standards change in a society from time to time, criminal behaviour is relative and absolute.

Elliot and Merrill state "crime may be defined as anti-social behaviour which the group rejects and to which it attaches penalties". In this way all those activities for which society lays down punishments are crimes. Those activities to which no punishments attach may be sinful but they would not be criminal. But some thinkers have deemed it fit to call all anti-social activities criminal, and have defined it comprehensively. According to Karl Mannheim, "Crime is an anti-social behaviour." This constitutes a definition of crime from the social viewpoint. From the legal viewpoint violation of law constitutes crime. In the words of Gillin and Gillin,"From the legal point of view, crime is an offence against the law of the land." This definition does not include those anti-social activities which are not prohibited by law. Actually criminality should attach both to anti-social activities and to activities forbidden by law. According to Krout, "A crime is an act opposed to the established attitudes of a group as defined by law at a given time or place." This definition of crime is more appropriate.

Treason, murder, incest, and theft are universal crimes. The surest single generalisation that may be made is that society regards as criminal all acts that endanger or interferes with the welfare and preservation of society or transgress established customs and individual rights.

Biological and psychological theories have been developed claiming that crime and other forms of deviance are genetically determined, but these have been largely discredited. Sociologists argue that conformity and deviance intertwine in different social contexts. The divergence of wealth and power in society strongly influence opportunities open to different groups of individuals and determine what kinds of activities are regarded as criminal. Criminal activities are learned in much the same way as are law-abiding ones and in general are directed toward the same needs and values.

Deviant socialisation means the idea that we learn to be deviant–through the family, mass media and so forth. In this respect, the deviant is seen as a victim of forces beyond his/her control and the motor of abnormality, here, is individual experience rather than individual genes.

Various psychologists, from Freud onwards, have identified childhood experiences as bring the key to our understanding of deviant behaviour. Usually, it is the mother who takes the blame for producing maladjusted offspring.

When is an act deviant?

Some sociologists believe that deviance is socially defined. For an act to be seen as deviant or not depends on its social setting, this means that the time and place an act takes place and who sees it is as important as the act itself. Many sociologists would argue that these circumstances—how people react, define and label what they see and hear—results in an act being labeled deviant. Deviance is, therefore, defined by the social setting of the act.

Types of Deviance

It tends to be assumed that "deviant behaviour" is somehow always behaviour that is generally frowned upon by people in a society—the very name seems to imply that such behaviour is, at best, "not very nice" and, at worst, downright criminal. That this is not necessarily the case can be shown by looking briefly at the way in which we can categorise various basic forms of rule-breaking behaviour in terms of three basic ideas:

1. **Admired behaviour:** An example of deviance that might be considered as "good" or "admirable" behaviour—whilst also breaking social norms—might be something like heroism—the saving of the life of another person whilst putting your own life in great danger—for example.

2. **Odd behaviour:** Many forms of behaviour—whilst not being criminal—are frequently considered to be somehow "odd" or "different" to normal behaviour. These forms of deviance range from such things as outlandish modes of dress, through mildly eccentric forms of behaviour—the person who shares their house with 50 cats, for example—to outright madness.

3. **Bad behaviour:** Deviant behaviour in this category tends to be restricted to law-breaking or criminal behaviour—behaviour that in some way is seen as being something more than simply outlandish or eccentric. Depending upon the time

and place, forms of behaviour in this category might include crimes of violence, crimes against property and so forth.

Culpable and Non-Culpable Deviance

A further distinction we can have between different types of deviant behaviour, is one that recognises the idea that there is a qualitative difference between people who commit deviant acts consciously—and with a full understanding of the fact that they are behaving deviantly—and those whose deviant behaviour may, for example, be accidental or no fault of their own.

Culpable deviance refers to acts for which the individual perpetrator can be held personally accountable. They are, in short, acts of deviance committed by people in the knowledge that such acts are deviant. Examples here might include crimes such as murder, theft or violence, as well as a wide variety of non-criminal deviance.

Non-culpable deviance, on the other hand, refers to acts for which the individual perpetrator is not held personally accountable. Examples of this type of non-culpable deviant behaviour might include deviant acts committed by:

1. People classified as "mentally ill". This, in effect, means that the mentally ill refers to:

2. Children—the age of criminal responsibility varies for different forms of crime. It is, however, a general rule that children of under-age cannot be held responsible for any criminal acts they commit.

In terms of deviant behaviour, on the other hand, there are acts for which even very young children can be held responsible—for example, hitting another child.

Another category of non-culpable deviance might be people who fall into various categories of "behaviour" that are considered deviant because they do not conform to the norm in society. In this respect, the disabled are frequently treated as "deviant" even though, through no fault of their own, they are unable to participate fully in the social life and activities enjoyed by the able-bodied. Similarly, those with long-term illnesses or who have been "disfigured" in some way are often also included within this type of non-culpable categorisation.

Major Deviance

Homosexuality

Suicide

Drinking alcohol

Being married to more than one person at the same time

Women wearing trousers

Killing someone

Hagan suggests that there are three main ways to measure the seriousness of deviant behaviour.

1. *The degree of agreement about the wrongfulness of the act:*

In this respect, there might exist a range of possible levels of agreement which go from almost total disagreement to high levels of agreement.

2. *The societal evaluation of the harm inflicted by the act:*

In this respect, what is significant is a general social assessment of both personal and, most importantly, wider social, harm caused by the act of deviance.

3. *The degree of severity of the social response to the act:*

In all cases of possible deviance, the "social reaction" to behaviour is going to be significant and, as you might expect, the range of responses goes from fairly minor, highly-localised, responses—telling someone to go away—through such "personal" responses as physical violence to more society-wide responses such as imprisonment and even Capital Punishment.

Hagan makes a distinction between both "crime" and "deviance" and the varieties of likely social response to each are described below:

1. Crime:

a). Consensus—for example, murder, theft, etc.

Crimes about whose seriousness there is a general agreement. For Hagan, crimes in this category are seen as being most serious precisely because there is some form of general agreement about their seriousness.

b). Conflict —for example, public demonstrations, drug offences, illegal abortion etc: Crimes over which "public opinion" is divided. For Hagan, crimes in this category are seen to be treated less seriously, precisely because arguments and conflicts surround them. For example, "drug abuse" may be defined as a "medical problem" and therefore one where the drug user is in need of help rather than punishment—these kinds of crimes are sometimes referred to as "crimes without victims"—since no person other than the drug abuser is directly "injured" by the behaviour—other forms of such crime might be things like tax evasion, illegal parking, *etc*.

2. Deviance—non-criminal deviance:

a). *Social deviations—for example, insanity, betrayal of trust, juvenile pranks etc.*

These types of behaviour will be viewed as deviant because they will, in some way, break social norms; but they are not viewed as criminal because, for example, they are:

Highly localised, a betrayal of trust may only involve a couple of people.

Something the individual has no control over and therefore no responsibility for—insanity.

Not particularly serious in relation to the social harm they do.

b). Social diversions—for example, styles of dress, mannerisms etc.

Behaviour in this category tends to be used more as an indication of likely forms of potential deviance, although, in many cases they may be mildly deviant forms of behaviour, than anything else.

For example, dressing as a "hippy" may indicate to people that here is someone who is likely to be involved in some form of drug abuse—which, if you're interested, represents a form of stereotyping.

In general, we can note that behaviour that falls into the criminal category is behaviour that is regulated by some form of formal social process of attempted regulation—police, legal system and so forth—whilst behaviour that falls into deviance category is likely to be regulated by informal control agencies—parents, peer groups and so forth.

Delinquents

Sheldon and Eleanor Glueck claimed to have discovered an apparent relationship between physical build and delinquent behaviour in males. They argued that stocky, rounded, individuals—known as mesomorphs—tended to be more active and aggressive than people with other types of physical build.

The characteristics of delinquents

1. *Some of these traits appear to be fundamental personality factors*:

- Hyperactivity
- Tendency to alcoholism
- Psychosis
- Low measured intelligence

- Small stature and poor health
- Male rather than female

2. *Some characteristic modes of social interaction—bad temper*:

- Unpopular with peers
- Disruptive behaviour in school
- Parents found him a difficult child
- Likely to be violent
- Poor work and bad results at school

3. *Some background traits*:

- Environmental
- Living in a slum area—living in an area of high delinquency—social class—father unskilled labourer
- Family dynamics
- Poor surveillance—irregular discipline—lack of affection—family interaction, characterised by antisocial behaviour—family breakdown—poverty

These young people are recognised as being difficult by parents, other children and teachers. The onset of these problems is very often early in the child's life, and the first steps into delinquency is often taken as early as 9 or 10 years old

Juvenile delinquency is the term used for crime committed by children and adolescents under statutory age are referred to as delinquencies. The maximum age limit varies but in most states offenders under sixteen or eighteen are classified as juvenile delinquents.

Classification of crime

Crime

1. Weapon violence
2. Physical abuse
3. Rape/date rape

With respect to their relative seriousness crimes are divided into treason, felonies, and misdemeanors.

Treason—the most severe and infrequent type of crime—consists in levying war against one's country or in giving aid and comfort to the enemy.

Felonies are serious crimes such as murder, manslaughter, forgery, aggravated assault, fraud, robbery, burglary, and rape, punishable by death, imprisonment, or heavy fines.

Misdemeanors are minor offenses. Some examples are larceny, drunkenness, disorderly conduct, and vagrancy.

ORGANISED CRIME

In this type of crime a group of persons pre-plan their strategies and the same or other set of persons are given training to carry out the plan. Persons who indulge in organised crimes are self-centered, impulsive, and epicurean in temperament. Cheating and exploiting others is part of their nature.

FACTORS IN CRIME

HEREDITY: No person is inevitably destined to become a criminal because of his heredity. In some cases, however, the inheritance of unfavourable physiological and mental traits may increase the probability that a person will encourage criminality. The significance of heredity is most marked in cases of persistent criminality and in those cases where criminal tendencies are associated with personality defects.

It is suggested by some psychologists that the criminals may possess 'XYY' combination of genes. Normally in males there is a combination of 'XY' genes, when in its own it becomes 'XYY' the change in behaviour is seen in violent aggressive behaviour.

Early sexual maturity, mental defects and nervous instability etc. are abnormalities which an individual inherits which may lead a person towards criminal behaviour.

Critics are quite right, there are no genes "for" crime, and no biosocial scientist claims that there are. There are genes, however, that lead via various neurohormonal routes to traits—e.g., low levels of empathy, IQ, self-control, conscientiousness, and fear, and high levels of sensation-seeking, egoism, negative emotionality, and aggression—that increase the probability of criminal behaviour.

Chronic criminals remain young children. As they grew older, they retained their childhood priorities for instant self-gratification without having developed the emotional inner voice necessary to generate a sense of discipline, responsibility, and the recognition of the rights of others.

SOCIAL DISORGANIZATION—In both primitive and contemporary society, it has been observed that the stability of the social order is an important controlling factor in the incidence of crime. No society, however stable, is totally free of criminals, but fewer violators appear in stable, isolated and homogenous communities than in disorganised, migratory, and heterogeneous population groups. The pathogenic life situation of criminals includes:

FAMILY DISRUPTION—The family life of delinquents and criminals is characterised by disorganisation, discord, and general instability. It has been found that delinquents are more often reared in home broken through desertion, divorce, separation, or the death of one or both parents. More important than the absence of one or both parents is the presence of unfavorable intra-familial tensions and conflicts that produce psychologically broken homes.

DEFECTIVE SOCIAL INSTITUTIONS—The dowry system, wrong system of mate choice, consumption of alcohol, caste system have also been responsible for increasing criminal activity. There are a large number of crimes committed under the influence of alcoholic stimulants.

CHANGE IN SOCIAL VALUE—There has been a tremendous change in social values in India. New notions like materialism, individualism, rationalism, the respect for wealth, absence of sex restrictions etc., are becoming very popular in the country. This has led to a disregard of ancient social values. There is no common agreement or opinion on any of these values. This disorderly state inspires crime because any individual can put forth an argument to justify his/her acts.

ECONOMIC ASPECTS—The majority of criminals and delinquents come from poor homes and are either unemployed or engaged in unskilled and low-income occupations. Many take to robbery, stealing when they are frustrated by continued unemployed. Among the main economic reasons is poverty, unemployment, industrialisation, and urbanisation.

BAD COMPANY

SOCIAL CHANGE—In modern times there is rapid social change which can bewilder youths who cannot decide their course of action. Rapid social change gives rise to new standard of conduct. These standards are at times misinterpreted by youths and they become inclined towards antisocial activities.

In industrial cities, there is congestion which breeds crimes. In cities the society fails to exercise social control.

ABSENCE OF SOCIAL CONTROL—Earlier the caste, panchayats in villages, kept control over the behaviour and conduct of the members of the caste. It was extremely difficult to conceal crime in the village and any crime was revealed the caste panchayats meted out very stern punishments, going to the extent of exterminating the guilty person from the caste. This tended to control and check crime effectively. With better facilities of transport being available the criminal can commit the crime and abscond from the village to town or to the village from the town.

In urban areas no one seriously considers caste bindings. In big cities one is lost in a crowd. There are more of impersonal relations. One can commit a crime and can conceal his identity. The disappearance of the control of caste organisation is the cause of crime in India.

RACE—A race is a large division of human beings distinguished from others by relatively obvious physical characteristics presumed to be thoroughly inherited and remaining relatively constant through numerous generations.

No race is inherently more criminal than any other. Cultural traditions and restrictions, together with environmental influences may, however, increase or decrease the frequency of law violations and determine the nature of offenses committed by a particular racial group.

Elliott Currie (1985) suggests that America's high crime rate reflects its cultural emphasis on individual's economic success frequently at the expense of family and community cohesion.

EDUCATION—Ethical education has no place in modern education. Thus the importance of character building is not considered important. Thus the future generation believes in selfishness, disorderliness and impertinence.

CINEMA—Cinema has helped in the increase of crime in India. The cinema arouses criminal tendencies in man by teaching crime techniques, by exhibiting many kinds of crimes, by stimulating the desire for wealth and comforts by showing ways and means of appropriating them illegally, by arousing profound sexual urges, by stimulating day dreams of criminal activities.

GEOGRAPHICAL LOCATION—Lombroso has stated that crimes of rape are more common in plains than in the mountains or plateaus. According to some criminologists in hot countries there are more crimes against the person while in cold countries more crimes are committed against property.

POLITICAL REASONS—Many political causes also encourage crime including inflicting injury or defaming opponents. Criminals are encouraged by inefficiency, immorality and corruption.

PSYCHOLOGICAL AND PSYCHIATRIC FACTORS

INTELLIGENCE—The intelligence of apprehended criminals and delinquents is slightly lower than that for the general population. Moreover, they are impulsive, aggressive, and immature in their way of living. It may be due to the fact that the dull offenders are easily apprehended and the bright ones are more apt to escape detection.

NEUROSES—Personality inventories and clinical observations indicate that delinquents and criminals are somewhat more neurotic than the general population, but the differences are not very marked.

PSYCHOSES—Psychotic individuals who commit criminal offenses are classified as criminally insane. Although there is no infallible test, insanity is determined in modern courts mainly by having qualified psychiatrists to examine offenders suspected of being mentally deranged. Criminals adjudged insane are not held responsible for their offenses.

PSYCHOPATHIC PERSONALITY—Individuals possessing average or superior intelligence who are neither neurotic nor psychotic but at the same time are social misfits and borderline mental cases are labeled psychopathic personalities or constitutional psychopathic inferiors. This is a general psychiatric category that includes pathological liars, sexual perverts, tramps, amoral individuals, misanthropes, eccentrics and certain types of emotionally unstable individuals. It is generally assumed that constitutional factors consisting of hereditary defects and disturbed parent-child relationships in early childhood play important roles.

NEUROPHYSIOLOGICAL FACTORS—In some criminals there is more excitability in the neuro-physiological waves and the central nervous system while in others certain marks of inhibition of impulses which gives rise to criminal behaviour.

PHYSICAL TRAITS—One study co-related criminal tendencies to physical traits. It found that hardened criminals had bigger and wider ears, flat nose, narrow temples, and longer arms, well-built. The whole body looked quite strong and well structured.

PROFFSSIONAL CRIMINALS

WHITE-COLLAR CRIMINALS—It is crime committed by people of respectability and high social status in the course of their profession. It includes embezzlement, bribery, marketing of unsafe products, false advertising etc.

This category of people are found in big towns, in big government and semi-government offices and established great business centers where certain officials and other persons accept bribes from those in need. They are called white-collar criminals as they are not taken as criminals in their official attire.

A new survey says that white collar crime cost Irish business more than two billion pound last year, and that 34% of companies surveyed had taken disciplinary action against their own staff.

The survey looked at fraud, embezzlement and internet crime as well as cheque and credit card fraud.

Some of the country's largest companies, with total sales of eight billion pound, were surveyed.

The survey found almost half of companies believe the problem will worsen. Four-fifths of firms say if it emerged they were the victims of these crimes it would damage their reputations.

One new area of concern is the internet, where fraudsters frequently masquerade as internet banks and send customers messages seeking their account details.

PSYCHOPATHIC CRIMINALS—The super-ego of the people in this category curses him for some sin or crime committed in the past and in order to get off the self-guilt the person commits another crime with the sole aim to get punished. Once punished for the criminal act the person feels relieved and encouraged to indulge in other crimes. Thus the cycle goes on.

BRAIN ACTIVITY OF PSYCHOPATHS

Kent Kiehl, Robert Hare, and colleagues studied eight male criminal psychopaths, all inmates of a maximum-security prison in Canada, comparing them to eight non-criminal, non-psychopathic controls. The researchers controlled for a wide range of factors including age, parental socioeconomic status, education level, and IQ.

The subjects participated in a test in which they viewed concrete words—such as "table"—abstract words—such as "justice"—and pseudo-words. All words were selected to be emotionally neutral to eliminate emotional response as a factor. Subjects viewed word groups containing either concrete words and similar-looking pseudo-words, or abstract words and similar-looking pseudo-words. They were instructed to raise one hand each time a real word appeared, and to raise the other hand if a pseudo-word appeared. During the tests, the researchers investigated brain changes in the participants using functional magnetic resonance imaging (fMRI).

Psychopathic subjects, Kiehl *et al.* say, "Performed more poorly, manifested as slower reaction times, than control participants, when processing abstract word stimuli." This is consistent, they say, with studies showing that psychopaths have trouble processing abstract words, performing abstract categorisation tasks, understanding metaphors, and processing emotionally weighted words and speech.

In particular, the psychopaths showed clear deficits in activating one brain area, the right anterior superior temporal gyrus, when processing abstract stimuli. This region failed to differentiate normally between abstract and concrete stimuli. The researchers say, "These data support the hypothesis that there is an abnormality in the function of the right anterior superior temporal gyrus in psychopathy."

"Perhaps," the researchers say, "psychopathic individuals have difficulty engaging in cognitive functions that involve material that has no concrete realisation in the external world. We might speculate that complex social emotions such as love, empathy, guilt and remorse may be a form of more abstract functioning. Thus, difficulties in processing and integrating these conceptually abstract representations to regulate or modulate behaviour would be [seen] in these individuals."

THEORIES OF CRIME

1. *Theological school:* According to this school, crimes increase when the religious tendency diminishes. But it is not inevitable that a religious person will do no criminal act while

an atheist will do it. Sometimes even religious people are seen committing the most heinous crimes.

2. *Hedonistic:* According to this school, an individual indulges in criminal activity when he thereby stands to gain more pleasure than pain. However, he may commit crimes by force of habit through compulsion proceeding from the circumstances in which they are placed.

3. *Ecological school:* Economic and geographical conditions of different areas are the causes of crimes. This view does not explain the personal causes of crime.

4. *Geographical school:* Geographical conditions such as heat, cold, climate, weather, etc. are causes of crime.

5. *Typological school:* Criminal is of a unique type. He is born a criminal and, therefore, commits crime. The view does not take into consideration the social, individual, and other causes of crime.

6. *Economic school:* Crimes take place due to economic causes. It also does not take into account the social, personal, and other causes of crime.

7. *Sociological school:* They look upon social condition as the cause of crime. This view is also prejudiced.

8. *Multiple cause school:* There are many causes of crime. Neither one cause can be regarded as the origin of all crimes and nor can crime be considered as originating in any one cause. Actually the causes of crime are of many kinds such as social, economic, geographical, ecological, etc. and the reason for a person's having committed a crime can be discovered only after seeing his circumstances of life. There can be no universal formula for it. In connection with the cause of crime this view is the most appropriate and most modern criminologists agree with it.

Society and Crime: Sociological Theories

Functionalist theories see crime and deviance as produced by structural tensions and a lack of moral regulation within society. Durkheim introduced the term *anomie* to refer to a feeling of anxiety and disorientation that comes with the breakdown of traditional life in modern society. Robert Merton extended the concept to include the strain felt by individuals whenever norms conflict with social reality. Subcultural explanations draw attention to groups, such as gangs, that reject mainstream values and replace them with norms celebrating defiance, delinquency, or nonconformity.

Interactionist theories focus on deviance as a socially constructed phenomenon. Sutherland linked crime to *differential association*, the concept that individuals become delinquent through associating with people who are carriers of criminal norms. *Labeling theory* is a strain of interactionist theory that assumes that labeling someone as deviant will reinforce their deviant behaviour. It is important because it starts from the assumption that no act is intrinsically criminal (or normal). Labeling theorists are interested in how some behaviours come to be defined as deviant and why certain groups, but not others, are labeled as deviant.

Conflict theories analyse crime and deviance in terms of the structure of society, competing interests between social groups, and the preservation of power among elites. Deviance is viewed as deliberately chosen and often political in nature.

Control theories posit that crime occurs when there are inadequate social or physical controls to deter it from happening. The growth of crime is linked to the growing number of opportunities and targets for crime in modern societies. The theory of broken windows suggests that there is a direct connection between the appearance of disorder and actual crime.

Victims and Perpetrators of Crime

Rates of criminality are much lower for women than for men, probably because of general socialisation differences between men and women, and the greater involvement of men in non-domestic spheres. Unemployment and the "crisis of masculinity" have been linked to male crime rates. In some types of crimes, women are overwhelmingly the victims. Rape is almost certainly much more common than the official statistics reveal. There is a sense in which all women are victims of rape, since they have to take special precautions for their protection and live in fear of rape.

Popular fear about crime often focuses on streec crimes—such as theft, burglary, and assault—that are largely the domain of young, working-class males. Official statistics reveal high rates of offense among young people, yet we should be wary of moral panics about youth crime. Much deviant behaviour among youth, such as antisocial behaviour and nonconformity, is not in fact criminal.

White-collar crime and corporate crime refer to crimes carried out by those in the more affluent sectors of society. The consequences of such crime can be more farther reaching than the petty crimes of the poor, but there is less attention paid to them by law enforcement.

Organised crime refers to institutionalised forms of criminal activity, in which many of the characteristics of orthodox organisations appear but the activities engaged in are systematically illegal.

Cyber-crime describes criminal activity that is carried out with the help of information technology, such as electronic money laundering and Internet fraud. Although cyber-crime is a relatively new type of crime, there are indicators that it is already on the rise.

Introduction to Sociology

TOWARDS AN INTEGRATED THEORY OF CRIME
(mainly robbery, burglary and homicide)

CHARACTERISTICS OF INDIVIDUALS	CHARACTERISTICS OF SOCIAL INTERACTION	STRUCTURAL FACTORS	PROCESS FACTORS
- Age and Sex	- Differential Association offending families deviant friends	-Structural Strain Merton: disjunction between goals and access to means	Labeling -crimes -offenders -stigma contests -secondary deviance
- Intelligence		-Class Structure -Racial stratification -Opportunity structure	
- Personality: weak self-control			
- Mental Illness	- Subcultures (subcultural deviance)	- Social control (stake in conformity): attachments investments involvements beliefs	All interact to produce → CRIME
- Testosterone		-Anomie (lack of social and moral Integration	
- Drug Use			

Storytellers and Crime

Storytellers also find crime lends itself to an ideal literary device: the trial. A crucial part of the criminal process, the trial is custom-made for literature. The adversary legal system has conflict and resolution. Consider John Mortimer's stories about the veteran English criminal lawyer Rumpole of the Bailey. A criminal trial builds suspense and uncertainty, especially while the verdict is up in the air. Erle Stanley Gardner's Perry Mason books always have a criminal trial for a climax. "The Witness for the Prosecution," a story of a criminal trial by Agatha Christie, ends with a famous surprise. In *A Passage to India* by E. M. Forster, a man is acquitted of rape but we never know if the rape actually occurred. And we have to wait until the end of *Anatomy of a Murder* by Robert Travers to find out if the defendant wins because he could not help but yield to an "irresistible impulse".

Crime easily lends itself to literary calls for reform. Many gifted writers of fiction have seared the consciences of their readers by describing how poverty, parental abuse, bad living conditions, prejudice, and other societal factors lead to crime. Think of Charles Dickens's moving portraits in several of his novels, particularly *Oliver Twist*, or Jean Valjean, the hero of Victor Hugo's *Les Misérables*, driven by poverty to steal a loaf of bread for his family and for which he is sentenced to the gallows. E. L. Doctorow's *Billy Bathgate* tells the story of a boy's growing up amid Bronx gangsters in the 1930s.

Literature also shows how the legal system can err by convicting the innocent while following the forms of justice. Medieval justice, wrote Hugo in *The Hunchback of Notre Dame*, "had little concern for clarity and accuracy in criminal proceedings. The main thing was to see that the accused went to the gallows"—Victor Hugo, *The Hunchback of Notre Dame*, 179–180, Lowell Bair, trans. Bantam Books, 1981. A memorable example of this flaw is George Bernard Shaw's trial scene in *St. Joan*. No less memorable is the unjust conviction of Edmond Dantes in *The Count of Monte Cristo* by Alexandre Dumas. In the twentieth century, Franz Kafka wedged his way into our consciousness with *The Trial*, in which the hero, Joseph K., is convicted and imprisoned for unknown crimes.

Whatever the reason, literature relies heavily on crime, but not always in the same way. Fiction writers use crime in their work in two different ways. In one type, represented by Fyodor Dostoyevsky's *Crime and Punishment* and Theodore Dreiser's *An American Tragedy*, crime and its consequences are the primary focus. In the other, crime is a subordinate though often crucial theme of the literary work. Examples of both kinds of crime literature abound and go far back in time.

In the mid-nineteenth century, a new form of crime literature arose—the detective or mystery novel. Invented by Edgar Allan Poe in America, this genre usually has a crime or mystery to be solved and a highly intelligent hero who, through logic or patient investigation or preternatural understanding of the criminal mind, finds the solution. Poe's stories "The Purloined Letter" and "The Gold Bug" and his clever detective Dupin started a popular literary trend that shows no sign of abating.

The mystery novel next flourished in England with *The Moonstone* and *The Woman in White*, both by Wilkie Collins. Arthur Conan Doyle's Sherlock Holmes tales are classics of the form, as are the works of Dorothy Sayers, Agatha Christie, and P. D. James. In the United States in the twentieth century, Raymond Chandler, Dashiell Hammett, Mickey Spillane, and Rex Stout made, with their tough, lean prose, enormous contributions to the modern crime novel.

AGGRESSION

Aggression is often due to a conflict between the interests of two or more individuals. Conflicts arise over limited resources such as territories, food and mates.

Types of aggression

Moyer (1968) distinguished between:

- predatory
- inter-male
- fear-induced
- irritable
- territorial
- maternal
- instrumental

Brain (1981), divided aggression into:

- predatory attack
- self-defensive behaviours
- parental-defensive behaviours
- social conflict

Aggression in psychology defined by the World Book Encyclopedia is hostile behaviour that may hurt or upset other people. Such behaviour may take the form of physical attack against people or their possessions, or verbal abuse (Larsen, 2000).

Aggression may be an automatic response to such experiences as pain or danger. In other cases, it is a deliberate action with a definite purpose (Larsen, 2000). Some people act out of hostility to gain money, pleasure, power or prestige. Other aggressive behaviour is intended to cause physical or psychological injury (Larsen, 2000). An aggressive behaviour can be negative or positive, accidental or intended and physical or mental. There is no justification for violent aggression such as spouse, child, or sibling abuse, criminal assault, rape, bullying, or any other physical harm or psychological insult to another person.

To be called assertive is a compliment. To be told that you are aggressive is viewed as a criticism, and to be considered violent is to be condemned (Hirsch 1981). What is the difference between the three? The Webster's Dictionary defines assertive as "positive; aggressive; and dogmatic." Aggression is defined as "an unprovoked offensive attack, invasion, or the like" and violence as "rough or injurious physical force, action, or treatment; an unjust or unwarranted exertion of force or power...(1993). These dictionary definitions are obviously different from that of psychologists, social workers and psychiatrists. Aggression involves complete lack of concern for the other person and major emphasis on the "gimme" syndrome without consideration for the others involved (Hirsch 1981). Assertiveness, on the other hand, does not involve attack. It focuses on meeting one's needs. Self-respect is an example of assertive behaviour. It has been found that women who are assertive are often labeled as aggressive. Influencing this attitude is the concept that women are innately less aggressive than men, and therefore, any demonstration of definite behaviour is perceived negatively, since it is unexpected (Hirsch 1981).

The definition of aggression portrays two distinct types of aggression, hostile and instrumental. Hostile aggression is aggression driven by anger and performed as an end in itself.

Instrumental aggression is aggression that is a means to some other end (Myers 1999). Distinguishing between the two can be difficult at times. Three main ideas thus includes: (1)There is an inborn aggressive drive, (2)Aggression is a natural response to frustration and (3)Aggressive behaviour is learned (Myers 1999).

Every night on the news there are reports about murders, wars, and rapes. But the news isn't the only place where people encounter violent or aggressive behaviour. Driving home from work, people get cut off and cussed at on a daily basis. At school, children fight over who will be the first in the lunch line. On the street, people get pushed out of the way if they are not walking fast enough. The list could go on and on and on. The point is that humans exhibit aggressive behaviour on a regular basis. However, does anyone know why people display these behaviours? Why do certain people seem more aggressive? Is there just one thing that controls when and how aggressive someone becomes? These are all questions that researchers have been addressing for many years.

TYPES OF AGGRESSION

	Physical	**Verbal**
Active	Hitting	Name-Calling
Passive	Don't shake hands	Don't say Hello

Aggression is an action. It is intended to harm someone. It can be a verbal attack—insults, threats, sarcasm, or attributing nasty motives to them—or a physical punishment or restriction. Aggression also seems to be a way of maintaining social order among many species. Animals compete with each other over food, mates, and dwelling spaces, often showing aggression and occurring among virtually all vertebrate species, including humans. However, if aggression is an effective way of maintaining social order, reckless violence appears to be a poor survival mechanism. Nevertheless, this trait has not been wiped out. Since it hasn't disappeared, it is logical that researchers have tried to understand the nature of this behaviour. In doing this, there has been an ongoing argument of what its source is.

The nature vs. nurture topic has been a continuing debate for many aspects of human behaviour, including aggression. There have been many studies indicating that chemical relationships between serotonin, testosterone, and frontal lobe brain chemistry may play a key role in determining aggressive behaviour, while other studies have explored environmental and societal factors that have been said to control patterns in human aggression.

The argument for nature surrounds the possible biological reasons for why human aggression is exhibited. The reasons for why there is aggressive behaviour in humans include a range of hypotheses. Aggression may have a chemical, hormonal, or genetic basis. Research has shown that stimulation of certain parts of animals' brains leads to aggression. Stimulation of other parts stops aggression. Some researches believe that it stems from low levels of serotonin.

The Frustration-Aggression Hypothesis model states simply that: "Aggression is always a consequence of frustration." and "The existence of frustration always leads to some form of aggression," where Frustration is blocking a path towards the goal and Aggression is a series of actions whose goal response is injury to another organism or its substitute.

Frustration-aggression theorists define frustration as the thwarting of an action that would have produced reward or gratification.

The Social Learning Theory denies that humans are innately aggressive and that frustration automatically leads to aggression.

Instead Bandura (1973) argues that aggression is learned in two basic ways: (1) from observing aggressive models and (2) from receiving and/or expecting payoffs following aggression. The payoffs may be in the form of (a) stopping aggression by others, (b) getting praise or status or some other goal by being aggressive, (c) getting self-reinforcement and private praise, and (d) reducing tension.

There are different reasons why a person may act aggressively towards other human beings. The person may act this way because of his culture or the way he was brought up in society. The person does not, however, act this way based on instinct alone. Aggression is a moulded, learned behaviour. A human being must have both environmental and instinctual factors in order to display aggression. Some of a person's natural instincts are to desire food, reject certain things, escape from danger, fight when challenged, sex desire, care for the young, dominate, and to accept inferior status. The combination of instincts and environment determines a person's behaviour. This is based on the theory that everything human beings do would have to be learned from other human beings. Aggression must be learned; it is not simply there from birth. Rather than being an uncontrollable instinct, a person's behaviour is something that is taught to him.

In order for an individual to display aggression, it must be driven by an instinct interacting with that person's surroundings. McDougall defines the word instinct as "an inherited or innate psycho-physical disposition which determines its possessor to perceive, and to pay attention to, objects of a certain class, to experience an emotional excitement of a particular quality upon perceiving such an object, and to act in regard to its particular manner, or, at least, to experience an impulse to such action". This definition basically explains that people have different reactions for different stimuli. Therefore, an individual is prone to act in a certain way when he is stimulated to do so from his surrounding environment. For example, the Eskimo does not have an innate instinct that allows him to survive in his climate. He is taught to work with his people in order to survive when he is very young.

When people are brought up in a society, they learn certain customs and traditions. These customs are usually taught to them because it's part of their society's way of life, even though some of the customs may seem cruel and repulsive to others. For example, cannibalism is abhorrent to us, but in some primitive cultures, to eat an enemy is to gain his or her strength. This aggressive behaviour was taught to the people of this culture and is the reason for its existence. People need to have exposure to aggressiveness in society in order to act aggressive. For example, there was a tribe in New Guinea, the Fentou, who were fierce warriors that were always fighting and killing. The children of these people learned this hostility from their parents and then acted in the same way. A parent's method of child rearing lays the foundation for aggression. The child rearing practices themselves are the overall design of a particular culture.

Theories of Aggression

Negative Affect Theory: Proposed by Leonard Berkowitz, it states that negative feelings and experiences are the main cause of anger and angry aggression. Sources of anger include: pain, frustration, loud noise, foul odours, crowding, sadness, and depression.

The likelihood that an angry person will act aggressively depends on his or her interpretation of the motives of the people involved.

Offensive and defensive aggression was distinguished on the basis of associated events. Behaviour delivering noxious stimuli was defined as defensive when it is a response to a threatening situation and as offensive when it was an unprovoked act.

Biologists' viewpoints will suggest that humans share certain "genetically determined tendencies" toward aggressive behaviour. The behaviourist argument suggests that aggression is acquired through experience, and learning.

Lorenz argued that aggression in animals and humans is an inherited, spontaneous tendency much the same as the motivation to eat, drink and make love.

Action specific energy accumulates in a reservoir until released by the appropriate external stimulus, represented by weights on a scale pan, or until the pressure on the valve causes an action pattern to occur spontaneously—vacuum activity. The consummatory response or fixed action pattern(s) released vary depending upon how much action specific energy is released from the valve.

This theory predicts that:

- Aggression is inevitable—the accumulating energy must find an outlet.
- Humans & animals will actively 'look for fights'.

It is now realised that aggression is not simply due to an accumulation of internal action specific energy.

We now appreciate that aggression is influenced by a variety of internal and external factors.

For example, in North America and Europe the number of assaults peaks during the **hottest** months of the year (Anderson, 1989).

Sex differences in human aggression

Over 80% of homicides are committed by men. Most of the victims are also men. The most common cause of homicide is due to the escalation of a relatively trivial disagreement over status that starts with words and escalates into lethal violence.

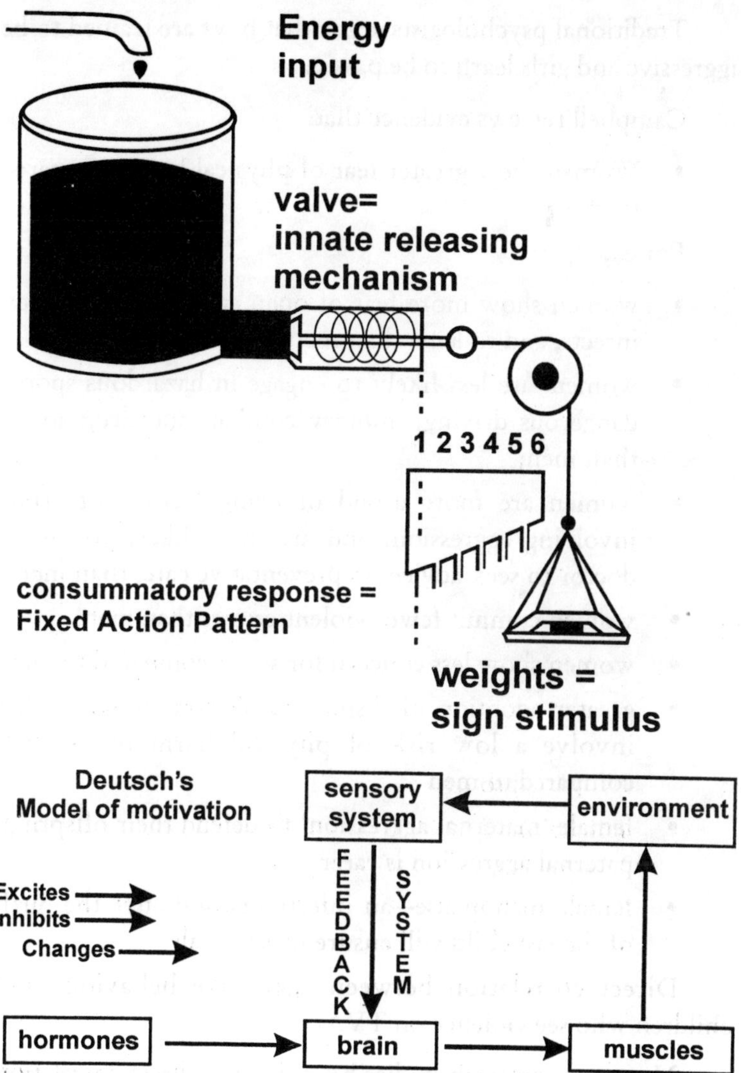

It seems that men resort to violence to protect or gain status and honour.

This sex difference is found across all cultures. Criminal violence is most likely between the ages of 14 and 24.

Traditional psychologists argue that boys are trained to be aggressive and girls learn to be passive.

Campbell reviews evidence that:

- Women show greater fear of physical harm compared to men.

For example:

- women show more fear of open spaces, dogs, snakes, insects, and rodents than men;
- women are less likely to engage in hazardous sports, dangerous driving, military combat, and drug abuse, than men;
- women are more afraid of being victims of crime involving aggression, and are more likely to visit a doctor to seek advice on preventative care, than men;
- women commit fewer violent crimes than men;
- women show less concern for status compared to men;
- greater adoption of dispute resolution strategies that involve a low risk of physical harm by women compared to men
- female 'maternal aggression' to defend their offspring; paternal aggression is rarer
- female menopause—an infertile period after the birth of the last child will ensure its survival;

Direct correlation between aggressive behaviour and children who see violence on TV.

Numerous research studies have shown a direct correlation between aggressive behavior and children who see violence on TV or play violent video games. A 2004 study, which looked at violence in video games, showed that teens who play violent video games for extended periods of time demonstrate the following behaviours:

1. Tend to be more aggressive.
2. Are more prone to confrontation with their teachers.
3. May engage in fights with their peers.
4. See a decline in school achievements.—Gentile *et al*, 2004.

Violence

The Concise Oxford Dictionary defines violence as unlawful exercise of physical force; Olweus—1999—also confines violence to the use of physical force. He defines violence/violent behaviour as aggressive behaviour where the actor or perpetrator uses his or her own body as an object —including a weapon—to inflict—relatively serious—injury or discomfort upon an individual. With such a definition there is an overlap between violence and bullying, where bullying is carried out by physical aggression.

There is a tendency, at present, towards viewing aggression, bullying and violence as being synonymous. While few will disagree that bullying and violence are sub-sets of aggressive behaviour, disagreements are encountered, especially in respect of what constitutes bullying and violence.

However, violence has been defined in a broader sense to include behaviour by people or against people liable to cause physical or psychological harm —Gulbenkian Foundation, 1995.

Novas Res, defines violence as follows:

"Violence is aggressive behaviour that may be physically, sexually or emotionally abusive. The aggressive behaviour is conducted by an individual or group against another, or others. The aggressive behaviour can involve pushing, shoving, shaking, punching, kicking, squeezing, burning or any other form of physical assault on a person(s) or on property. Emotionally abusive behaviour, is where there is verbal attacks, threats, taunts, slugging, mocking, yelling, exclusion, and malicious rumours. Sexually abusive behaviour is where there is sexual assault or rape."

Olweus (1999) confines violence to the use of physical force. He defines violence/violent behaviour as aggressive behaviour where the actor or perpetrator uses his or her own body as an object —including a weapon—to inflict—relatively serious—injury or discomfort upon an individual. With such a definition there is an overlap between violence and bullying, where bullying is carried out by physical aggression.

Aggression is defined as "any form of behaviour directed toward the goal of harming or injuring another living being who is motivated to avoid such treatment".

However, violence has been defined in a broader sense to include behaviour by people or against people liable to cause physical or psychological harm —Gulbenkian Foundation, 1995.

Another definition of violence defines violence as occurring "where persons are verbally abused, threatened or assaulted in circumstances related to their work."

According to one source, the FCC picks up its definition of violence from Morality in Media, a group best known for its anti-indecency crusading.

MIM's definition, found in its 2004 comments on the FCC inquiry: "Intense, rough or injurious use of physical force or treatment either recklessly or with an apparent intent to harm."

A broad definition of violence as a forced crossing of boundaries—be they boundaries of the body, the mind, or society. Traditional Western culture is under pressure from subordinate masculinities (gay, nonwhite, non-Western) and women to blur dichotomous gender boundaries. In response to this crisis, violence becomes the means by which white men who have a "failing sense of masculinity" try to preserve the traditional masculine control of society. Any being or group that does not subscribe to the traditional Western gender roles is perceived as "other". Thus "others" are already in boundary violation and therefore violent. This perceived potential violence is then averted by violence on the part of the "masculinities".

A "monster hybrid" male, in sports, military, media, entertainment, and law—the areas—in which the traditional gender dichotomy is not only perpetuated but under attack.

CAUSES OF VIOLENT BEHAVIOUR

BIOLOGICAL CAUSES

Hormones like testosterone, transmitters in the brain like serotonin, and blood abnormalities like hypoglycemia are only a few causes.

Biological factors do not have to be hereditary. They could be caused by a head injury, poor nutrition, or environmental events, such as exposure to lead paint.

Fortunately, the National Academy of Sciences just reviewed hundreds of studies on the relationship between biology and violence, and it came to one clear bottom-line conclusion: "No patterns precise enough to be considered reliable biological markers for violent behaviour have yet been identified." (1) The National Academy of Sciences found many promising leads that should be vigorously pursued by researchers, but so far, it could point to nothing as a proven, or even close to proven, biological risk factor for future violence.

SOCIOLOGICAL CAUSES

We know the most about social factors and violence, because social factors, such as demography, are relatively easy to measure and because people have been measuring them for a long time.

America is a country with crime surplus. Compared with Japan, a nation of roughly comparable industrialisation, with cities much more crowded than the US, homicide rate is over 5 times higher, the rape rate is 22 times higher, and the armed robbery rate is an astounding 114 times higher.

Within America, violence is subject to great regional variation. The murder rate, for example, is almost twice as high in the South as it is in the Northeast, but the robbery rate is almost twice as high in the Northeast as it is in the South. Communities within all regions of America differ drastically among themselves in how violent they are. People who commit violence on the street are disproportionately poor and unemployed. Majority—close to 90 percent—of the people arrested for crimes of violence are men and that despite enormous changes in gender roles in recent decades, this figure has not budged for as long as criminal records have been kept.

Violence is primarily the work of the young. People in their late teens and twenties are much more likely to be arrested for violence than younger or older people. The arrest rate and the victimisation rate for violent crime for African-Americans is now about six times higher than for the Whites. Official violent crime rates, as high as they are, drastically underestimate the actual rate of violence in America, particularly violence within the family. Poverty and race, for example, are related not just to violence but also to each other. It is also possible that, at least for some people—like an "impulsive" temperament—causes them both to be violent and to be unlikely to keep a steady job.

PSYCHOLOGICAL CAUSES

The developmental processes that most of us go through, successfully, but some of us face great difficulty; the family—the filter through which most of the sociological factors, such as a parent's being unemployed, and many of the biological factors, like poor nutrition, seem to have their effect on a child growing up. All types of families share something in common. Whether they are married or cohabitating, biological or adoptive or foster, single or dual, gay or straight, and whatever their ethnicity, virtually all parents try to raise their children to be neither the victims nor the perpetrators of violence.

While many aggressive children go on to be law-abiding adults, aggression at age 8 significantly predicts violent convictions well into the thirties, in every culture in which it has been studied. Most children who have been physically abused by their parents go on to be perfectly normal adults. Yet, physical abuse doubles the risk that a boy will have convictions for violent crime as an adult. Failure of a child in school is one of the most enduring correlates of later violence. Four out of five violent offenders in prison never finished high school. Stability matters; the more changes of placement a foster child experiences while growing up, the more likely that child will later be arrested for a violent crime. Lack of parental supervision has been consistently related to delinquency, including violent delinquency. A study found that for children growing up in very disadvantaged and violent neighborhoods, who look like they have everything going against them, the one factor that seems to protect that child from growing up to be violent is having a parent—overwhelmingly, a mother—who supervises her child very strictly and who nips misbehaviour at the bud, rather than waiting for the principal to call or the police officer to knock on the door.

We know much about the relationship between illegal drugs and violence. But it is important to remember that the connection between one legal drug—alcohol—and violence is beyond dispute. About one-third of all violent offenders are alcoholic, and the earlier an adolescent starts to drink, the more likely that teen will be violent as an adult.

Root Causes of Violence Today:

- Increases in Oppressive Social Problems, Such as:
  —Economic Distress
  —Family Dysfunction
  —Racial Tensions
  —Teenage Pregnancy
  —Alcohol & Drug Abuse
- As a Result, People feel that everything is out of control.

They Turn to Violence to get what they want

- Money
- Power
- Self-esteem
- "Respect"

Top 10 Causes of Violence in the Order that Children Cited Them

1. 1. The Media
   2. Substance Abuse
   3. Gangs
   4. Unemployment
   5. Weapons
   6. Poverty
   7. Peer Pressure
   8. Broken Homes
   9. Poor Family Environment/Bad Neighbourhoods
   10. Intolerance/Ignorance

Real violence, fictional violence

One must first of all distinguish clearly between what is real violence—with all the necessary reservations concerning a real which has been captured by a cameraman, edited, given sound and commentary by a journalist, and thus has become a constructed real and what defines fictional violence.

Aside from reality and news programming, most violence on television is acted; it is not real. When viewers see a motion picture, they know that it is not real. So how does one measure the impact of violence that is not real, but imagined? Sometimes violence is described as aggressive behaviour; sometimes it is described as verbal abuse and teasing.

U.S. television networks are free to sprinkle their programs with shootings, slashings, torture and other gore because the government has no regulatory authority over violent programming. Violence could be treated similarly to broadcast indecency, with its airing prohibited during times when children might be watching. In USA TV violence had reached epidemic proportions, increasing 75% in six years.

Violence in television is at the core of a wide debate. After the initial indictment of fiction, all the other programmes were called to the witness stand: cartoons, talk-shows, reality-TV shows, Commercials. News programmes were not spared. The daily news, investigative reporting, and other programmes were the alleged victims of the downward levelling of standards induced by the necessity to integrate the requirements of increasingly competitive programming policies.

In Latin, *informare* means to fashion, to formic and, by extension, to give a shape, a structure, a meaning. The mission of these programmes is, therefore, to report on the world, but also to go further and to give it a meaning, to provide the keys to unlock and decrypt our reality, showing its complexity and richness.

Violence is a fact of life. Physical, psychological, economic, social, or environmental violence is an essential part of humanity and its works. Accordingly, it has its place in the news programmes. But it should not be part of a spectacle or just another piece of gossip.

Television news images rarely have significance or meaning in themselves and, no matter what they are concerned with, they need to be replaced within their context and explained. When images or commentaries may prove too explicit for the audience, this marking process is a necessity, the more so as emotion is here an integral part of the viewing experience. This is the reason why the presentation of any kind of footage or statement should not be ambiguous or unclear as to the reason why these items are broadcast at this time and place.

Maybe the criticism stems from the discrepancy between the violent nature of the broadcast information and the lack of a *raison d'être*, a relevance which would justify their presence on the screen. The image and the commentary become obscene when they have no foundation, when the trust between the broadcaster and the audience is broken. The ethical responsibility of the journalist acquires here its full meaning and scope.

The media are a safeguard of democracy, through the information and the tools, which we use to fashion our perceptions and opinions of the world. The popularity of the daily news programmes indicates the importance of their role in our everyday lives.

Modern technology allows information to be relayed so fast that increasingly often the journalist has to make decisions on his own and without the benefit of the larger perspective. It is most important to know and to understand the production process of sequences, which at the end go on the air. Where do the images come from? What conditions do journalists and cameramen work in? What influence does competitive pressure have on them? These are the questions we need to answer to improve our knowledge of their activity. Next, we need to consider the integration of the news reports in the editorial line of the channels and the answers that their managers provide to the issue of violence.

Violence takes many forms and is understood differently in different countries and among different cultures. While there is no universally accepted definition of violence, the World Health Organization has proposed the following as a working definition of violence:

"Violence is the intentional use of physical force or power, threatened or actual, against oneself, another person, or against a group or community that either results in or has a high likelihood of resulting in injury, death, psychological harm, mal-development, or deprivation."

Three main categories of violence can be identified:

Self-inflicted violence refers to intentional and harmful behaviours directed at oneself, for which suicide represents the fatal outcome. Other types include attempts to commit suicide and behaviours where the intent is self destructive, but not lethal—e.g., self mutilation.

Interpersonal violence is violent behaviour between individuals and can best be classified by the victim-offender relationship, either among acquaintances or among persons who are not acquainted. Interpersonal violence may also be specified according to the age or sex of the victim. Violence against women is an important example and is occurring worldwide, often unrecognised. Such violence may occur in the family or within the general community, and may be perpetrated or condoned by the state. Other types of interpersonal violence include child abuse, bullying, harassment and criminally-linked violence such as assault and homicide.

Organised violence is violent behaviour of social or political groups motivated by specific political, economic or social objectives. Armed conflict and war may be considered the most highly organised types of violence. Other examples include racial or religious conflicts occurring among groups and gang or mob violence.

Violence is not one behavioural pattern but several. One approach has been to classify violence according to the underlying motivation of the aggressor. A frequently used distinction is between *hostile* and *instrumental* motivation. In hostile violence, the major goal is to inflict harm or injury. In other words, hurting is an end in itself. In instrumental violence, actions may cause harm but are not motivated by the desire to cause harm *per se*. Rather, they are motivated by goals such as taking resources from others. In both cases, this distinction depends on the individual's intent, not on the act itself.

Certain types of violence such as armed robbery, murder-for-hire, and terrorism generally are well planned, goal-directed, instrumental actions. Offenders are acting to maximise their benefits and minimise their costs. Many prominent models of criminal behaviour emphasise the rational choice component of crime—e.g., Cornish and Clarke. This type of planned behaviour is distinguished from more impulsive and hostile violent actions often characterised by loss of control, irrationality, and rage. Such impulsive violent behaviors are frequently labeled emotional violence and are linked with emotions such as anger and fear. Biological models of violence have identified distinct neural patterns that characterise each type of violence. For example, the "low-arousal" aggressor more likely to commit instrumental violence is under reactive and responds sluggishly to stressors. In contrast, the "high-arousal" aggressor who is more prone to hostile violence tends to be hyper-vigilant and easily frustrated—Niehoff.

Violence can be grouped into categories based on variables such as the agents of violence—e.g., gangs, youth, collective groups—the victims of violence—e.g., women, children, minority groups— the relationship between aggressor and victim—e.g., interpersonal, non-related—perceived causality—e.g., psychopathological, situational, learned, and type of harm—e.g., physical, psychological, sexual—These criteria are frequently combined to examine particular forms of violence, such as psychological abuse of women in intimate relationships, youth sexual violence, instrumental collective violence, and so on.

THEORY LINKS VIOLENCE, LIMBIC "KINDLING"

Harvard psychiatrist Anneliese Pontius believes that some "loners" who commit senseless acts of violence are suffering from a seizure disorder which she has dubbed "limbic psychotic trigger reaction".

Pontius, who has examined hundreds of violent criminals, has documented the cases of 17 individuals she believes suffer from the syndrome. These individuals—13 murderers, three arsonists, and a bank robber—are characterised, she says, by the following pattern:

- None had histories of violent or criminal behaviour.
- All committed motiveless, unplanned, out-of-character crimes, generally against strangers, and appeared "flat" and emotionless while committing the crimes.
- Immediately prior to committing their crimes, each subject experienced a profound sense of puzzlement, followed by hallucinations associated with past events. Some experienced delusions of grandeur.
- While committing their crimes, subjects experienced nausea, vertigo, "ice cold" sensations, profuse sweating, incontinence, or other visceral reactions.
- All subjects were disoriented for several hours following their crimes.

- All confessed openly to their crimes, and were distraught and bewildered by what they had done.

Pontius notes that this pattern is consistent with seizures, which often are preceded by "auras"—frequently cause irrational behaviour and loss of normal bodily functions, and are generally followed by a sense of disorientation. She suggests that her subjects committed crimes while experiencing seizures of the limbic system, a brain region associated with memory and emotion.

Although a number of her subjects had abnormal EEGs suggestive of seizures, and nearly half had experienced significant head injuries—a strong risk factor for seizures—Pontius suggests that another mechanism, known as "kindling," is involved. Kindling, a phenomenon well documented in rats, mice, rabbits, dogs, cats, and primates, occurs when animals are exposed repeatedly and intermittently to mild, harmless stimuli such as low-level electric shock, isolation, or small doses of drugs. Animals at first show no response to the stimuli, but after a short period they begin having small seizures, and eventually they develop generalised convulsions.

Because her subjects were "loners," Pontius believes they may have brooded continually over mild traumas or slights, rather than talking them over with friends or family, and that this brooding eventually "kindled" seizures when subjects were exposed to people or objects that triggered their obsessive memories.

Dominance behaviour

Dominance behaviour is designed to achieve, or maintain, high status—to obtain power, influence, or valued asset—over a co-specific. Humans use threats and violence to dominate, but we also resort to cheating, deceit or negotiation to obtain status and valued resources. In fact a lot of our behaviour involves strategies for existing with each other without causing or risking actual physical damage.

Dopamine abnormalities linked to violence

A new study adds to evidence that abnormalities in the brain's use of the neurotransmitter dopamine play a role in violent behaviour.

•••

5

EMOTIONS

Elations, gaieties, lusts, rancor, miseries, apathies, and despairs of living organisms catch the eyes and hold the attention of passersby. They intrude into the perceptual fields and practical concerns of others. Our emotions reorient others; disturb their trains of thought, seep into the blueprints of their projects, contest them, and afflict them with misgivings and self-doubt. Power among humans is not simply the physical force with which one material body may move another; it is the force to distract, detour, maneuver, and command. Every pleasure we indulge in and every pain we suffer exerts power over others — Lingis 2000, 17–18.

Emotions situate actors in relationships and shape their social interactions. Culture defines both the qualities of individual identity and the constitution of social groups with distinctive values and practices. Emotions, then, are necessarily experienced and acted upon in culturally inflected forms that define not only the conventions of their articulation through individual and collective action.

Emotions are defined as "first and foremost, modes of relating to the environment: states of readiness for engaging, or not engaging, in interaction with that environment"

Aristotle taught us that pity and fear are the deep, tragic emotions. The media moves audience from the comfort of secondary emotions to the primary emotions.

Secondary emotions—pity, fear, contentment: These constitute the defenses that the ego has developed to displace and discharge anxiety. The motives the ego requires for its maintenance—safety and self-esteem—find in secondary emotions the means to resolve conflict in a way that distances and protects the ego from the threat of all disruptive experiences.

Pity: It is the effort to short-circuit anxiety by turning suffering into something one can only experience passively as undeserved misfortune that comes as a result of factors over which one has no control and limited responsibility.

Fear: It is also the effort to externalise anxiety by displacing inner conflict into concern with matters outside the psyche.

Contentment: It is the feeling of well-being that banishes all sources of anxiety through the obsessive-compulsive iteration of the sentiments that tranquilise the subject's relationship to itself.

Primary emotions—anxiety, humiliation, envy, cruelty, melancholia: These, in contrast, burden the subject in which it finds that its being existentially at issue and at risk. Such emotions are defined by the absence of any inner distance between what one feels and who one is. One is assaulted from within by the force of the conflicts that are central to one's being.

Anxiety: It is existence as the awareness of responsibility to reverse the control that the other —parents, social and ideological forces, religious authorities—has over one's psyche.

Envy: It is the need to destroy anything that makes one feels contempt for oneself or that activates the memory of possibilities one has squandered.

Melancholia: It is "wakeful anguish of the soul"; the desire to engage the coreconflicts of one's psyche in active reversal.

Compassion: It is the love as the refusal to succumb to the appeals of pity and the fixations of desire so that one may conduct one's relationship to others on the basis of uncompromising psychological honesty.

Cruelty: It is the the desire to poison what is vital in another's psyche so that one can watch the other bring about his/her own destruction.

Primary emotion shatters the ego and awakens the psyche. The ego is the system of defenses whereby an illusory identity is maintained through vigorous opposition to two things: reality and the inner world. Psyche is joined whenever that system breaks down and the subject is forced to engage the conflicts of its inner world. Secondary emotion is the system of feelings we construct in order to deliver us from that process.

Fineman—1999; 2000—provides an answer to the emotion challenge to rationality, suggesting that this comes in three forms. These are: that emotions interfere with rationality; that emotional processes serve rationality; or that 'emotions and cognitions are inextricably *intertwined*, that rationality is a myth' —Fineman, 1999, p. 293. Rationality can be an 'efficient organising principle'. Many writers point out the dualities that occur when considering rationality and emotion or irrationality, as binary opposites. Other dualities recognised throughout the literature include: rational/emotional; mind/body; objective/subjective, order/disorder, public/private, sexual/asexual, task/process, and male/female—Parkin, 1993; Albrow, 1997—; culture/nature—Tanton, 1994; Albrow, 1997.

The competing divide between these binaries have been further developed by feminists and others who relate mind to the seat of reason, and rationality, objectivity, public and culture to the realm of masculinity. The remainders less valued characteristics are relegated to femininity. A gender lens is then adopted, with Gherardi (1995) suggesting that:

Rationality and emotionality clearly belong to that continuum of symbolic values which delineates gender: the male, the rational, the public, activity, separation, thought, the mind, hardness, coldness, the vertical; as opposed to the female, the emotional, the private, receptivity, connection, sentiment, the *body, softness, warmth, the horizontal* —Gherardi, 1995, p. 34.

Rationality is revered because it involves objectivity, order and cognition, a feature of masculinity, while emotionality or irrationality is likened to subjectivity, chaos and bodily drives, all of which depict a 'negative, feminine world view'— Gherardi, 1995, p. 40.

The interpretations and definitions of emotion range from a set of biological, Neuro-physiological grievance to a social constructionist perspective, and other viewpoints in-between, demonstrating the evolutionary development of this concept. Other approaches to the inquiry into emotion and emotionality, include the psychoanalytic, postmodernist, social constructionist, phenomenological, post-structuralist and feminist, for example—Lupton, 1998. These competing discourses have enriched the debate, and opened the way for ongoing discussion and analysis. The view that emotions 'are inter-subjective, a product of the way systems of meaning are created and negotiated between people'—Fineman, 2000, p. 2— has considerable acceptability among theorists who no longer question that emotions and emotionality are an integral part of the workplace; that, in fact, emotions create the meaning of work.

This view is reinforced by Gherardi—1995—who suggests that the meaning of an emotion 'lies primarily within the socio-cultural system'; that emotions 'adapt to social contexts and regulate cognition and behaviour', and that they 'constitute social roles, [which are] institutionalised ways of interpreting and responding to particular kinds of situations'—p.154. Lupton—1998—asserts that: 'socio-cultural processes and the influence of the unconscious in emotional experience'—p.38—also need to be incorporated for greater understanding of emotions.

The view remains that emotions are unruly, undesirable and need to be contained or managed to reduce unpredictability, and ensure rationality and order—Fulop and Linstead, 1999.

Emotional Labour

Emotional labour is the term used to 'typify the way roles and tasks exert overt and covert control over emotional displays' —Putman and Mumby 1993, p. 37. Emotional labour is so defined because it requires 'effort, planning, anticipation and adjustment to situational factors in order to display emotions' —Putman and Mumby, 1993, p. 258—emotions that one must exhibit, but may not feel privately.

The major object of emotional labour is to provide predictability and maintain harmony. The concept of emotional labour is derived from the work of Hochschild—1983—who demonstrated that physiological and psychological stress may occur because 'emotional deadening and distancing ...is caused by repeatedly suppressing felt emotions while expressing contradictory, unfelt feelings'—Martin and Meyerson, 1998, p. 332. This has been described as 'emotional dissonance'. This dissonance occurs 'when one's display emotions differs from one's actual emotions'—Ashforth and Tomiuk, 2000, p. 185—and hence is positively associated with work alienation and job dissatisfaction. Organisations should not, therefore, treat employees' feelings as a commodity.

One of the by-products of emotional labour can be ambivalence. This occurs because one is required to suppress positive feelings—such as physical attraction to another—which may then provoke a negative emotion—such as frustration or guilt.

Emotional labour work can be emotionally and physically demanding, but requires skill and competencies that are not acknowledged—Myerson, 2000; Nicolson, 1996.

Emotional labour itself can be highly stressful, particularly when the expected appropriate behaviour, including constant courtesy and smiling, must be maintained in difficult circumstances for long periods of time when there is no access to 'back regions' in which to 'be oneself'. Emotional exhaustion results in cynicism and disconnection from others. Morris and Feldman—1997—also note that emotional dissonance negatively impacts on psychological well-being.

Toxic handlers

Another form of stress related to emotions has been identified as fallout from 'toxic handling'—Frost and Robinson, 1999. These authors point out that toxic handlers are not new to organisations, since organisations have always generated stress and chronic emotional pain. Toxic handlers are those within organisations who '...voluntarily shoulder[s] the sadness, frustration, bitterness, and anger that are endemic in organisational life'—Frost and Robinson, 1999, p. 97. They carry out a range of roles, include that of empathic listening, solution provision, confidant, working behind the scenes to prevent and alleviate pain, and reframing of difficult messages, making them more palatable to others. This work is often in the context of downsizing or organisational change, although policies and practices can exacerbate the toxicity of the workplace, increasing stress levels of employees. Frost and Robinson recognise the danger to toxic handlers of managing the emotional health of the organisation: psychological and professional burnout.

Counter productive behaviour

Finally, the failure to acknowledge emotions and emotionality in the workplace may result in a range of counter-productive behaviours. On reviewing the literature in this area, Fox, Spector and Miles—2001—note that counter-productive work behaviours are often '...an emotion-based response to stressful organisational conditions'—p. 291. Such behaviours may include theft, bullying, teasing, aggression, sabotage, harassment or vandalism, for example. The emotions driving such behaviours are often linked to injustice —Harlos and Pinder, 2000), frustration and lack of autonomy. It may result in violation of employee trust, particularly in the areas of psychological contract violations. Many ideas to recoup or heal or impact come from media serials.

Ashforth and Humphrey—1995—note the constructive, as well as the destructive effects of emotions. They suggest that positive emotions in the workplace may spread, increasing empathy, solidarity, cohesion, increasing psychological involvement and maintaining a motivated self. The negative effects of emotional contagion may include anxiety, fear, despondency, apathy and withdrawal rapidly spreading in the surroundings, inhibiting problem-solving and creating a potentially abusive climate.

Background emotions

The notion of "background emotions" is derived from Simmel's—1971—conception of the "blase attitude"—a state of mind he thought arose in Western societies to protect us from the bombardment of those intense, disruptive, and disturbing emotions inevitably generated out of the richness and diversity of urban life. In this attitude certain emotions are banished from public life, dismissed to the private internal sphere as a narrow range of individually experienced subjective and personal feelings—love, hate, fear, anger. Such—irrational—feelings, indulged in the public sphere, would divert individuals from the rational pursuit of market interests. Still other emotions "disappeared" through redefinition as attitudes or components of culture. This banishment, though, can never be fully realised because, the instrumental rationality of market competition still depends on subterranean emotions: "commitment to the purposes at hand, loyalty to the employing organisation, joy in success to encourage more success, and dissatisfaction at failure to encourage success, trust in those with whom cooperation is necessary, envy of competitors to spur the pursuit of interests, and greed to encourage aggrandisement"—1998, 59. Under practical rationality these emotions allow the action that calculation and logic alone could not produce; only the emotional part of rationality can make us feel sure enough about the future to make action seem feasible. Having, then, either expelled emotion or absorbed and renamed it, capitalist instrumental rationality can rest on a comfortable, but ultimately unsustainable, illusion that reason prevails. Indeed it is precisely this failure to distinguish between backgrounded and foregrounded emotion that creates the conviction that emotion endangers the pursuit of rational action.

Emotions must be considered as significant in the constitution of social relationships, a powerful source of human actions. Emotions matter because they produce action always within the context of particular social arrangements in specific societies.

Because language is central in the communication of emotion, Reddy—adapting J. L. Austin's theory of speech acts—coins the term "emotive" to capture the idea that when a person claims to be experiencing an emotion, the very claim is self-exploratory and self-altering. Because the effect of making such a claim may either intensify or attenuate the state claimed, these emotional utterances (emotives) have some of the qualities of a performative—the very utterance effects an outcome. Or, in Reddy's terms, "emotives do things to the world"; they are "instruments for directly changing, building, hiding, intensifying emotions"—2001, 105. They are instruments for trying to organise and shape goal activations which, because they are never fully contained, delimited, or under control, always require conscious attention. The form this effort takes will constitute a normative style of emotional management that is particular to the actual political, social, and cultural regime within which it takes place.

Named emotions then will be universal to the extent that they are socially significant in many—though perhaps not all—cultures but particular in their social inflection and salience—where and when they should be revealed or concealed. In short, exploration of emotions in the production of social action entails recognition that these processes will reproduce differences in cultural practices. It is wrong to assume that everyone will react in the same way to the same experiences and that the same reactions will be culturally appropriate for members of different ethnic groups.

Memory and emotions

Autobiographical and personal memory can be prompted by what Tulving terms "synergistic euphonry" —Tulving, 1983—whereby the emotion or the memory is evoked or revived by means of a stimulus such as a sound, or a photograph. Often aided by the context of the recall, a writer for instance, through placement of arte-facts or words in spatial relationship can create the circumstances which connect with the narrative—of a memory trace, event, object etc.

Signs represent the present in its absence; they take the place of the present...when the present does not present itself, then we signify, we go through the detour of signs.—Derrida, 1973.

Management of Emotions

Ashforth and Humphrey—1995—suggest that there are four overlapping means that regulate the expression of emotions. These include neutralising, buffering, prescribing, (which includes suppressing emotions) and normalising them, so that they conform to the norms of rationality. The aim of neutralising emotions is to prevent their emergence. Buffering attempts to encapsulate and segregate potentially disruptive emotions; prescribing specifies acceptable means of expressing emotions, while suppressing requires the masking of emotions that potentially disrupt role performance; and normalising requires diffusing unacceptable emotions, or reframing the meaning of the emotional outburst.

Emotional display: Emotional display, on the other hand, refers to the discouragement or encouragement of certain types of emotional display, potentially involving physical appearance, demeanour, facial expression or style of language. Such display rules indicate the expectation of showing or hiding emotion, and if violated, can result in serious sanctions being applied to the rule breaker.

Emotions are complex and seldom susceptible to precise definition or the drawing of distinct boundaries; some emotions —shame, for example—are also generally held to be more socially focused than others.

Resentment is one of the many emotions said to arise out of "real, imagined, or anticipated outcomes in social relationships"—Kemper 1978, 43. Often characterised as reaction to a moral offense—derived from a moral belief that one has been treated wrongly—it is also described as "an emotional apprehension" that "acceptable, desirable, proper, and rightful outcomes and procedures" permitting access to capabilities, entitlements, and desirable social outcomes have not been followed—Barbalet 1998, 138. In these terms it has been strongly argued that resentment is the key emotion that moves people to claim their social and legal rights—Barbalet 1998; Solomon 1990.

Resentment has also been seen as an emotional apprehension that others are receiving undeserved advantage. Individuals "gain" and "lose" face in particular circumstances and contexts but not in terms of a "one-dimensional continuum" equating loss or gain with success or failure in social performance. The mechanics of gaining face are different from those of losing it, and the two processes do not carry the same social implications.

One might say that shame is the deeply felt and highly motivating experience of the fear of being judged defective. It is the anxious experience of either the real or anticipated loss of status, affection or self-regard that results from knowing that one is vulnerable to the disapproving gaze or negative judgment of others. "It is a terror that touches the mind, the body, and the soul precisely because one is aware that one might be seen to have come up short in relationship to some shared and uncontested ideal that defines what it means to be a good, worthy, admirable, attractive, or competent person, given one's status or position in society."—Shweder 2003, 1115.

Emotional intelligence: Emotional intelligence is considered a potential for learning skills based on "...self-awareness, motivation, self-regulation, empathy and adeptness in relationships" Goleman, 1998, p. 28. Mayer and Salovey—1997—view it as a multi-dimensional construct of four factors: verbal and non-verbal appraisal and expression of emotion; using emotions to assist in problem-solving; regulating one's own, as others' emotions; and promoting intellectual and emotional growth using emotional knowledge.

Sinclair—1998—coins the phrase 'emotional toughness', which is expected from men, as being part of 'heroism' that manifests as stoicism, stamina, and self-reliance, although this type of behaviour has been recently questioned, now considered undesirable and unhealthy Lupton, 1998, 113. This assumes that it is pathological to suppress and deny emotions, particularly negative ones such as anger, frustration and guilt. There is a considerable literature detailing the effects of denying emotional expression—Salovey, 2001—demonstrating that illnesses such as cardiovascular disease, asthma, digestive disorders, skin diseases and cancer may occur in some individuals. Note also that in terms of emotional intelligence, Salovey—2001—suggests that effective regulation of emotions is 'most relevant to physical health'—p. 172.

Emotional susceptibility: Emotional susceptibility is defined as a stable tendency to feel distressed, inadequate, and vulnerable to perceived threats—Caprara, 1982; Caprara *et al.*, 1983; Caprara, Renzi, *et al.*, 1986. Caprara—1982—hypothesised that emotional susceptibility reflects a propensity to experience negative affect and a tendency to become upset and defensive when confronted with personal attacks and insults.

Impulsivity: "Impulsivity is defined as the extent to which individuals are unable to control their thoughts and behaviours". The relative inability to control one's behaviour is thought to stem from deficits in the self-regulation of affect, motivation, and arousal as well as in working memory and higher order cognitive functions that ordinarily give rise to hindsight, forethought, anticipatory behaviour, and goal-directed action —Barkley, 1997. Barratt—1994—suggested that highly impulsive individuals are characterised by a "hair-trigger temper"—p. 71— and by the lack of self-control that they need to refrain from aggressive behaviour after being provoked. McCrae and Costa —1985—reported that impulsivity is positively correlated with Neuroticism but uncorrelated with Agreeableness. Shafer—2001—and Netter *et al.*—1998—corroborated the positive correlation between impulsivity and Neuroticism—Aluja, Garcia, & Garcia, 2002.

Dissipation–Rumination: Dissipation and rumination are considered opposite ends of a continuum; dissipaters tend to get over feelings of anger and hostility rapidly following provocation, but ruminators tend to maintain and exacerbate their feelings of anger and hostility for prolonged periods of time—Caprara, 1986. The tendency to ruminate refers to the rehearsing of experiences of provocation and thoughts of retaliation. Because of their tendency to perseverate over provoking incidents, high ruminators—low dissipaters should be more likely than high dissipaters—low ruminators—to behave aggressively following provocation.

Factors Influencing Emotional Response

1. Biological
   a. Innate temperament (basic foundation of personality)
   b. Hormone levels
   c. Fatigue
   d. Physical health
2. Psychological
   a. Beliefs (about self, others, the experience or stimuli)
   b. Evaluation of past experiences
3. Socio-cultural
   a. Expectations of one's cultural/ethnic group
   b. Level of conformity to expectations
   c. Impact of being a member of a minority group (e.g. racial, ethnic, sexual orientation)

Expression of Emotions

A. Verbal

1. Actual meaning
2. Hidden meaning

B. Non-verbal
1. Facial expressions
2. Body language
3. Spatial-physical distance between people

Stress

A. Types of Stress
1. Eustress—positive stress
2. Distress—negative stress

B. Common Stressors—any stimulus that produces a stress response

C. Reaction to Stress
1. Individual (i.e., fatigue)
2. Personality

Coping Behaviour to Handle Stress

1. Healthy resolutions
   a. Relaxation techniques
   b. Support groups
   c. Support system
   d. Time management
   e. Exercise
   f. "Time out" or detachment
   g. Other
2. Self defeating choices
   a. Withdrawal
   b. Procrastination
   c. Substance abuse
   d. Violence

PERSONALITY

The term personality refers to a psychic phenomenon. It is neither organic nor social but is an emergent from a combination of the two. The unity of the self does not come easily. It is threatened on all sides by new and often hostile elements which must be either warded off or assimilated. His security is threatened not so much by physical injury as by unpredictability and misunderstanding, particularly in his social relations.

The assimilation of the outer world depends upon a constant but purely subjective interpretation which creates an inner world.

Immersed in an environment which he does not and cannot understand, the individual is forced to create a substitute world which he can understand and in which he puts his faith. He acts in consistency with that conception, derives his standard of value from it, and undertakes to alter it only when convinced by further experience that it fails to serve the goal of unity. Since this self-made scheme of life is his only guarantee of security, its preservation soon becomes a goal in itself. He seeks the type of experience which confirms and supports the unified attitudes, and rejects experiences which seem to promise a disturbance of this attitude.

Conflict is thus a necessary factor in personality development. All human behaviour can be interpreted as motivated by the need for unity. One individual differs from another in his degree of integration. He also differs quite apart from integration, in the kind of traits that are incorporation into his psychic system.

Personality is defined as "a dynamic organisation, inside the person, of psychophysical systems that create the person's characteristic patterns of behaviour, thoughts, and feelings".

Although the term *aggression* refers to a wide spectrum of behaviours, in the psychological literature, it is defined as any behaviour intended to harm another individual who is motivated to avoid being harmed—Baron & Richardson, 1994; Coie & Dodge, 2000; Green, 1990, 1998a, 1998b. Aggressive behaviour is distinguished from high levels of trait aggressiveness; the latter identifies people who are prone to hostile cognitions and angry affect as well as a readiness to engage in physical and verbal aggression—Buss & Perry, 1992.

Hans Eysenck, has proposed that there is a connection between "extrovert personalities" and criminal behaviour. According to Eysenck, extroverts are personality types who "act impulsively...crave excitement...take risks" and so forth. They argue that such personality types are more predisposed to behave in ways that lay them open to criminal sanctions.

Thus, the extrovert personality could quite easily find ways of behaving that are quite socially acceptable—such as in the business world, for example, where the extrovert entrepreneur may well be an admired figure.

John Bowlby, has argued that the failure of the mother to satisfy her child's "basic human need" for emotional security can result in the production of a psychopathic personality. The psychopath is seen as an individual who acts without a sense of guilt or recognition of the rights of others. Psychopaths cannot be deterred from criminal behaviour because they have no sense of right and wrong—they merely follow their own sense of personal need.

The five-factor model—Costa & McCrae, 1992, a prominent theory of personality dimensions, is useful for understanding the link between personality and aggressive behaviour—Jensen-Campbell & Graziano, 2001; Miller *et al.*, 2003. The major personality dimensions in the five-factor model are Neuroticism, Extraversion, Conscientiousness, Agreeableness, and Openness to Experience; each dimension is represented by six facets.

Buss and Perry—1992; Anderson & Bushman, 2001; Berkowitz, 1993—defined trait aggressiveness as a propensity to engage in physical and verbal aggression, to hold hostile cognitions, and to express anger. Tiedens—2001—theorised that the tendency for those high in trait aggressiveness to make hostile attributions may increase anger and create a vicious cycle of hostility and negative affect.

Trait Irritability: The definition of irritability includes being angrier, in general, and taking offense to the slightest provocation; a positive relation between trait irritability and aggressive behaviour under both neutral and provoking conditions.

Trait anger: It has been defined as the tendency for some individuals to feel anger more intensely, more often, and for a longer period of time than others—Deffenbacher *et al.*, 1996. Also, people who are high in trait anger are predisposed toward responding angrily when they are unfairly criticised, treated unjustly, or treated badly—van Goozen, Frijda, & van de Poll, 1994; Spielberger, Jacobs, *et al.*, 1983. van Goozen, Frijda, and van de Poll—1994—noted that people who are high in trait anger focus on a target that they see as blameworthy and act to correct the provoking action; they can do this in either constructive (e.g., assertive) or destructive (e.g., aggressive) ways. Trait anger is positively correlated with Neuroticism and Antagonism—low Agreeableness.

Type A Personality

Similar to narcissism, the Type A personality profile is characterised by feelings of inadequacy with regard to self-worth —self-esteem; Price, 1982. These fears of inadequacy often result in the need for Type A individuals to prove themselves through personal accomplishments—Glass, 1977; Mutaner *et al.*, 1989; Price, 1982. When confronted with a threat or challenge to either their control or their competence, Type A individuals become angry, irritated, and impatient—Brunson & Matthews, 1981; Glass, Snyder, & Hollis, 1974; R. A. Martin, Kuiper, & Westra, 1989; Rosenman, 1978. Thus, higher levels of Type A personality appear to be associated with a greater vulnerability to threats to self-competence and a propensity to experience anger in the presence of threat—Strube *et al.*, 1984.

Narcissism

Narcissists have an inflated sense of self-worth and self-love without a strong set of beliefs that support this sense of superiority—Kernberg, 1975; also Freud, 1917/1966. Because narcissists have unstable self-esteem, they are extremely sensitive to personal slights, such as insults and criticism. These people are characterised by a vulnerability to threats to the self-concept, and thus, when ego-threatening situations occur, narcissistic individuals tend to behave aggressively—Baumeister, Bushman, & Campbell, 2000; Baumeister, Smart, & Boden, 1996; Bushman & Baumeister, 1998. Emmons—1987—linked narcissism to extreme emotional liability and strong reactions, which could include anger and rage—Kernis, Grannemann, & Barclay, 1989; Rhodewalt & Morf, 1995.

•••

6

OUR SENSES AND TV IMAGES

Children and adults remain completely immobile while viewing the idiot box. Most viewing experiences are both quiet and non-interactive. Children absorb millions of images from the television set in just one afternoon's viewing session. And what are they watching? If the child's television has access to cable, his choice can range from 10 to 70 different channels—all of them showing different programmes.

Well-guided television viewing also increases the general vocabulary of your child and provides opportunities for him to learn about various things, which help him in making choices regarding his areas of interest.

Television, when viewed selectively, along with parents can provide immense scope for learning. Channels like Animal Planet, Discovery Channel, Splash and others have interesting programmes which can be beneficial even for young children. Parents can discuss the subject with their children while they watch these programmes together so that the child finds it more interesting and learns better.

When children watch television, they are not playing with shapes and blocks, or getting fresh air, or feeling the three-dimensional figures, or listening to the sounds of the neighbourhood.

HISTORY

The Greek orators and rhetoricians, before the alphabet had been handed down, developed an elaborate form of artificial memory, described so fully in Yates' *Art of Memory*: "...a series of *loci* or places. The commonest, though not the only type of mnemonic place system was the architectural type .... We have to think of the ancient orator as moving in imagination through his memory building whilst he is making his speech, drawing from the memorised places the images he has placed on them"—Yates, 1966. Thus it could be claimed the first movies were a conceptual model made by the Greek rhetoricians. As he moved in his imagination through the *loci* contained by the imaginary building, in the mind's eye they were encountered as wide shots, tracking shots, panning, tilts, close-ups and flashbacks. Like the visual language of cinema developed in the 20th Century, this could be regarded as the very first 'classic' film narrative.

A crime in a cartoon, in a police series, or in a sequence of televised news, does not carry the same weight or have the same effect on the viewer—if relatively speaking, it is considered that the viewing is done in more or less the same type of situation. A violent image seen by young children, unaccompanied by parents, without commentary by a third party and without being reframed through an inter-subjective relationship, has a more traumatic impact than one seen in an environment allowing exchange and a different focusing.

The place that our society gives to our senses is of paramount importance. Without being a sociologist, an ethnologist or a psychologist, and basing myself only on my intuition and my experience, I have the feeling that I am living in a world which builds every social relation on sight and on hearing and relegates thus touch, smell and taste to the sphere of intimacy, or even makes them taboo: socially, physical contacts are reduced and strictly coded, the critical distances are very large, body odours are repressed and concealed. On the other hand, the most perfect relation between two human beings, love—between partners, between parents and children, between friends—the things that pass through touch, smell and even taste are more important than the things that pass through hearing and especially sight which is the least important of our senses in this respect. Sight and hearing are the two coldest senses and are, therefore, the most appropriate to objectify reality. This is how an illusionary search for objective truth is maintained, to the detriment of affective, emotional truth.

The three other senses were definitely banished. People who create works of fiction or creative documentaries know how much work is required to provoke true emotions in the audience while working only with images and sounds. In contrast, images broadcast during the news on television are often served brutally, in order to inform us as objectively as possible, which is undoubtedly a praiseworthy objective. The journalist behind the screen does not give off the same things that a live storyteller, a member of my family telling me a story or an actor on a theatre scene or in a movie would give off.

Through this allegedly objective information, reality arrives amputated. First, the context, the explanations, which are necessary to understand properly what is being shown, are missing. During the television news, we are hit by short clips with little informative value—as they were shot after the event—and which are merely the support of a commentary that has generally only a vague relevance to the images. In the case of investigative reports, we are forced to listen to a voiceover which explains the images, their meaning and also indicates what should be thought about them, instead of letting us understand and feel on our own. In both cases, our freedom and intelligence are violated. As another consequence, reality arrives to us without the essential part of its emotional charge—of its soul. The news reporters using cameras mention the surprising protection given to them by the eye of the camera on the very terrain of horror: seen through the lens, the suffering becomes immediately easier to watch. The most unbearable part of reality does not cross this filter. Censorship strikes more eagerly against violence—or sex—when the images in question stimulate reflection and questioning than when they are a mere commercial ingredient, gratuitous and eye-catching.

Retinal shock

An entire Hollywood tradition is based on the symbolic cinema experience of watching bodies being injured, and physical and mental violence being inflicted; shocking scenes are aimed at the viewers' mind and have an impact not just on the retina but on the emotions, too.

Reaction to TV images

The late physicist, Frank Oppenheimer once said: "We don't live in the real world. We live in a world we made up." How media construct our reality is the first principle of media literacy. We can choose to make up a world that glorifies violence—or reinforces peace.

The word image is based on the word "image". The effort to change our images is the first step in the creation of a caring culture.

Violence on the television news send us back, whether we want it or not, to painful situations and often traumatising personal experiences. Later we are able to stand back and reflect coolly upon it. But at the time, we are often submerged by anger or helplessness. Our words express clumsily what these images of suffering bring up in us. We hesitate between embarrassment and revolt.

These words that we speak under our breath let us, maybe, rediscover first our relation to the suffering of others; buried memories, badly controlled fears, self-protective rejections. A few key words: embarrassment, denunciation, refusal, commitment. This is the reason why this relation to violence in the television news is experienced as a personal hurt. Hurt, as when we learn about a tragedy and are overwhelmed by a feeling of helplessness.

We ask ourselves an unsettling question: why am I more affected by this suffering person rather than by that one? The answer contains some mystery, but has also roots in our private history. I can feel close to a suffering person, because it is easy for me to identify with her:—she is of my age, she has the same background, the same values, but the opposite may be true as well: the other is foreignness affects me because I don't share his or her reference points or defenses and I am, therefore, more able to perceive his or her unacceptable condition.

But why are we affected, touched? Most of the time, when we actually receive the information, we are in a situation which already makes us receptive and available. We do not expect *a priori* the unbearable to explode on the screen in the middle of our usual environment. The relation of trust is heightened by our familiarity with television as the preferred medium in many households. It is fair to say that if the TV news is my main source of daily information.

In one of his articles, ElisÈo VÈron describes this startling effect, which links us to the newscaster, an intercessor between the event and the audience, who looks at us straight in the eyes. Many theorists have tried to identify and to describe these devices, this imaginary realm that we construct along with the media. One way of approaching it is to unveil the media is hidden functions, which serve to satisfy our desires. Even without reviewing the theories of reception of the media, we know that the concept of audience generates various and opposing definitions. Elihu Katz expresses this state of affairs in a humorous, *albeit* severe, way. One side proves that the TV audience is ill-informed, indifferent, anomic, alienated and vulnerable. The other side proves that the viewer is attentive, informed, integrated in a community of interpretation, with a critical attitude towards the media, capable of influencing public opinion.

In the 50s, Jean Stoetzel based his analysis of our confusing relationship with the media on the imaginary of the written press. His approach is still valid for the other media: reading newspapers, watching television programmes, going to the cinema—all these actions affirm our belonging to a community. They are proof of sociability. I belong to a group, I belong to a given moment in the history of the world. The media establish a link between me and the realities of my time. News items, gossip or ads columns are the staple of everyday conversations. By keeping myself informed, I am in contact with my community, I avoid being marginalised, or even excluded. Let us remark here that the media allow today an extreme variety of ways in which we can relate to the world; the press, the television, the Internet allows me to belong in an original way, in harmony with my sensitivity and options.

Do we get rid of our violent tendencies when we see actors on film breaking taboos and laws? I project out of me anything I may not or cannot accomplish. I also identify with characters of my choice. Mostly through haircuts and styles, fashion retains all that these mechanisms provoke by mimetic conduct.

Therefore, the concept of catharsis, as suggested by Aristotle, is not easy to define. It has quite a few dark areas. Most of the time, catharsis is said to have two functions; Purgation and Purification. Purgation makes it easier to adapt to the environment, to the reality of living in a community. Purification points to a journey, to an interrogation about the meaning of life, featuring for instance, rites, meditative silences, prayers, singing. In the case of the suffering of others, we could interpret it as an attempt to assume control over the emotions. Theatre becomes then an excuse for an attempt at self-knowledge, but with safeguards and no danger.

In the *Gutenberg Galaxy*, Marshall MacLuhan describes how the telephone, the radio, the television are modifying our relation to the world and suggested the concept of the global village. Ubiquity and immediacy: the media project us in a new imaginary zone, where I can potentially learn everything of the world. Nothing here is foreign to me; therefore I am not scared of anything. The spectacle of the world explodes suddenly, catching me unprepared. We live in a permanent proximity to the unknown, to the distant through television and the radio. In a strange sensation of reality, the media mobilise our senses. This impression of reality is reinforced–the strange feeling of being present and taking part in the action. Immediacy, following life unfolding with me and which prevents me from turning the television off, which suggests that I continue the experience, just like in my everyday life. This contact with a world in arm's reach is lived, practised for around three hours every day by the average Western viewer. Today, we learn of the world mostly through the media.

In the translations of reality they offer, suffering figures have an obsession place. Therefore, the strong reactions of rejection, sometimes compassion, often indifference. From time to time, a barely whispered question touches gently the conscience: what can I do? This question requires that we identify the words of this feeling of helplessness always present in the confrontation with the violence of the news stories. The simplicity of these words (guilt, urgency, compassion) sends us back to a question which is part of the history of humanity. Each great philosophy has given specific answers, propositions of action and commitment.

But the knowledge that we were acquiring yesterday used to be constructed differently. The nature of the relation to information was different. First, the pace is new. Nowadays, one image covers another; genocide follows up upon a massacre or comes up between a commercial break and a world record. Then, the link which allowed the construction of meaning by the dialogue (within a community or a family) is now mainly maintained by the media. It makes no difference whether we regret or welcome it. But getting the measure of this upheaval avoids looking gullibly at things and thinking that knowing the world is enough to transform it.

No image is unacceptable in itself; television takes away its reality and meaning and makes it a part (sometimes unintentionally) of its permanent spectacle. For, if we look closely enough, television uses violence only so that it can de-materialise it. It conceals, silences, masks real violence. Fictional —and over-abundant—violence in the television is tool in eliminating the reality of death. Contrary to popular belief, television shows hardly anything of the violence in our world. The wars—Iraq, Yugoslavia, Afghanistan—are less real on the screen than the politically correct fictions based on them.

Violence Image Impact

It is one of the recurring questions of our times: do the media sustain and nourish violence, especially among the young? There are different types of media: teenagers are eager consumers of television, video games, and the Internet. They rarely read the newspapers. It is commonplace to say that the written forms of expression are in decline to the benefit of images. Of course, there are also different types of image. Peaceful or varied images are different from brutal and explicit images of violence. Do the latter, short listed as the cause, by mimetism, of some episodes of real violence, have the effect attributed to them by the complacency of common sense, which can often deceive and conceal the laziness of intuitions leading to hasty generalisations?

Recently in the news there was a series of murders committed by very young people, who had copied the *modus operandi* from a movie in which the murderers wore masks. More generally, it is alleged that violent images, omnipresent in the media, create the conditions for their being acting out. But other theories have it that, on the contrary, on-screen violence is a sort of catharsis—purgation—and that it allows for emotions, resentments to be discharged, thus reducing the potential for violence.

In order to understand the problem, it may be useful to start at the other end: what allows us to overcome, to civilise our internal violence, to delay its urgency, or even eliminate it in the long run? Starting in childhood, any frustration generates a risk of violence: when we do not get what we want, we are strongly tempted to use violence whenever it is possible. Violence is the great tempter. If I have the power to get what I want by forcing the other or the others, in short, without their agreement, I will have to be very virtuous to avoid using this power. On the other hand, violence will not be used, at least if we are able to think clearly, when the balance of power is not in our favour. But what is the value of a non-violent behaviour, which in the end is the product of powerlessness? In *Leviathan*, Thomas Hobbes gives a positive value to fear of violent death, which creates the desire for peace. But peace, because we are afraid of losing the war, is a very fragile thing. In order for the negation of violence to become durable and affirm itself in the middle of the thousand frustrations of everyday life, we must work on it internally, which is neither natural nor easy to accomplish. People who are ready to use violence when a conflict or a dispute arises do use it, most of the time, because they are convinced—or have convinced themselves—that they are completely in the right, and that this right is being called into question. And this indignation, this feeling of falling prey to terrible injustice, this self-victimisation, make them almost insane while making them lose the plot, i.e. they tear down the fragile dams built in us by civilisation to domesticate the instinct. Someone who believes themselves to be absolutely in the right may give in to violence with a sort of good conscience which gives backing to all of his or her current and future excesses. Now, bad conscience is one of the main ingredients of not acting out violence. There is a complex alchemy between the adrenaline rush and the conviction that we are right to get angry.

The fact is that most of the time the faults and wrongs are everywhere and we are inclined to show some modesty or tolerance when we realise than we need to take care of ourselves as well. However, this realisation does not occur automatically. We should not think naively that there is symmetry between the recognition of other's faults and the acceptance of our own. The child has been described by Piaget as fundamentally egocentric: it begins by accusing the world, the other, of anything that happens to it. It manages to de-centre itself, i.e. see itself in a critical way, only by a fragile maturation process. At that moment, the adult—actual or future—will be equipped with the first virtue of any discussion: fairness. First, it is discussion that replaces violence. If it fails, only the legitimate violence of the State and of its justice will be able to resolve the problem. This self-distancing process, this ability to put ourselves in the Other's place and to judge ourselves with exactly the same criteria that we apply, assumes the capacity to argue reasonably. It is an illusion to believe that this capacity is the most common quality on earth. Human relations are generally affected by small (or big) paranoiacs, be it at the level of individuals or at the level of groups—nations, ethnic groups, religious communities, etc.

However, assuming the Other's point of view—de-centre oneself—implies a capacity to argue much less widespread than is generally thought. This means, in fact, a commitment to submit oneself to the strength of the best argument, whatever the identity of the person who speaks it. The problem is that argumentation, in its abstraction, belongs to texts, to chains of reasoning. It supposes that the person we are arguing with is able to listen, to read and to think. And here lies the main problem: the image, since Plato, has to be domesticated by the discourse. If it subordinated to the latter, it allows the person presenting an argument to give it a specific content for a pedagogical purpose by providing an example. However, if the image acquires autonomy, if it leaves the framework of the discursive activity, what will happen? The discussion becomes impossible again. We know that the image, because of its specific and singular character, provokes an effect of reality: the people who speak with Socrates are often prisoners of such an illusion and make confusion between the example and the essence, which is the abstract definition of the concept under consideration.

To illustrate this point, let us go back to Plato's famous Allegory of the Cave in Book VII in the *Republic*. Prisoners in chains look at the back wall of a cave which is illuminated by a fire burning outside. Men walk by and events take place between the light source and the entrance to the cave. The prisoners believe that the shadows projected on the wall by these events are reality itself: since they have never looked back, and are not able to leave the cave, they do not know that they are looking at shadows, reflections ñ images ñ and not at true reality, which is outside, out of their field of perception. One day, they are freed by the philosopher and they walk out of the cave. He shows them the real world, which is infinitely richer —in colors, sounds, smells, movements, etc.—than the shadows of the cave. New horizons seem to open up for them: they left the restricted world of the appearance—the shadow shows of the cave. It is restricted because the shadows account for only a part—which in fact is very abstract—of the reality in its complexity. So, what happens next? Do the prisoners thank profusely their liberator for the possibilities of happiness he gave them? On the contrary, they want to go back in the cave.

The external world dazzles them, it is too rich, too complex and, on top of that, they are not spectators anymore: they have to act, with all the responsibilities it implies.

Who cannot fail to see the relation between Plato's Allegory of the Cave and our media system, based on entertainment—in the ordinary meaning as well as in the meaning of Pascal? Why do the former prisoners prefer the cave to reality? Because, on the one hand, the images in the cave are simpler, poorer, more reassuring: it is, *mutatis mutandis*, the pleasure that we get from reading simplistic superhero cartoons. On the other hand, in the cave, we are only spectators of the events: the world unfolds in front of us with its tragedies which we do not take part in, which we contemplate from the outside in a simplified form. In the real world, we constantly have to weigh the alternatives, make choices, argue and think. It is a complex universe where nothing is totally clear and where we can never be certain that we made the right choice: an anxiety-inducing world, where, as Sartre used to say, we have been given no promises. In the imaginary world, everything is simplified, there is Good and Evil, the guilty and the innocent, a clear division between what is fair and what is not. The image takes away responsibility, at least when it is not in a subordinated position assigned to it by the discourse and the thought. The image is immediate; there is no need for words to make it appear, it gives itself to us, in a nearly hallucinatory manner. It is a drug which inhibits lucidity. The arguments had primacy; the image depended on them and was produced by them in me. Today, though, at least in some cases, the text does not come before the image: there is no internal image that is freely and personally constructed; the image is first, everywhere and nowhere, omnipresent. The confrontation between the image-from-text and the given image, which would disappoint me and would push me to prefer mine therefore, the book—has progressively disappeared and the image has taken the power, so to speak.

Another element highlights the distance between the two periods. People would be bored quite often then: when the television was becoming popular, it would be located in the living room and was controlled by the parents. Children in their rooms had to do something in order to avoid the anxiety of nothingness—of idleness. At the time, there were certainly many ways to entertain one-self, i.e. to forget oneself, to escape into an activity the only purpose of which was to lose time. But the reign of the Image had not yet begun. Today, one needs only to switch on the television, put a videocassette or a DVD in the appropriate device, log on the Internet or—soon—the mobile phone data services and a stream of images comes rushing to fill the void and make the risk of boredom disappear—for a time at least. However, according to Heidegger, boredom is the veil of Being: it makes us break up the flow of everyday agitation and come back to ourselves.

The domination of the Image means not only a return to the cave and the defeat of philosophy, but also the end of boredom. Today we have images that create an effect of reality and distract us from our existence. When we talk of entertainment, we should use both meanings of the term: first, as Pascal would define it,—I entertain myself when I escape the possibility of returning to myself, my difficult choices, my responsibility—, then the common meaning—I entertain myself when I watch Channels when I come home after a day of wearying and meaningless work. This second meaning is quite respectable: it is understandable that we may need sometimes to get our minds off our problems, the day at the office, the anxiety of falling ill and getting old, or the death of our loved ones. But if the escape becomes too organised, as it is by the enormous entertainment system of the media universe,—which is often our only point of access to a reality which is external to our restricted field of direct perception—, then we will never find ourselves and a general lack of responsibility will take over.

Media Violence and Active Audiences

Researchers like David Buckingham in the U.K. and Henry Jenkins in the U.S. add another dimension to the debate. They argue that rather than focusing on what media do *to* people, we should focus on what people do *with* media.

As Jenkins writes, media images "are not simple chemical agents like carcinogens that produce predictable results upon those who consume them. They are complex bundles of often contradictory meanings that can yield an enormous range of different responses from the people who consume them".

From this perspective, people don't just passively absorb messages transmitted through the media; they choose which media to consume and are actively involved in determining what the meaning of the messages will be. And that process doesn't occur in a social vacuum. Personal experiences affect what we watch and how we make sense of it. Our class position, our religious upbringing, our level of education, our family setting, and our peer groups all have a role to play in how we understand violent content.

Jenkins draws a different lesson from the shooting in Littleton: "Media images may have given—the Columbine shooters—symbols to express their rage and frustration, but the media did not create the rage or generate their alienation. What sparked the violence was not something they saw on the internet or on television, not some song lyric or some sequence from a movie, but things that really happened to them.... If we want to do something about the problem, we are better off focusing our attention on negative social experiences and not the symbols we use to talk about those experiences."

The Result

Violence dominates television news and entertainment, particularly what we call "happy violence"—cool, swift, painless, and always leading to a happy ending in order to deliver the audience to the next commercial message in a receptive mood.

The Cultural Indicators Project has found that heavy viewers are more likely to overestimate their chances of involvement in violence; to believe that their neighborhoods are unsafe; to state that fear of crime is a very serious personal problem; and to assume that crime is rising, regardless of the facts.

Heavy viewers express a greater sense of insecurity and mistrust than comparable groups of light viewers. They are more likely to be dependent on authority and to support repression if it is presented as enhancing their security.

Reason for more violence

The world is violent. In conjunction with free access to information, we have quantitatively more violence. The first reason is obvious: the technical possibilities and, therefore, the very short reaction time allow TV crews to be on the site of the event very quickly. Many people have portable cameras and the odds of getting live images of the events have never been as high as now. The quantity of available violent images is certainly larger than it used to be. Fifteen years ago, the media would try to have more eyewitnesses, more opinions leading to understanding; today rawer images of violence only.

The quantitative increase of violence is noticeable on the local level, because acts of violence are on the rise there as well. Violence in schools, for example, is a recent topic.

And even if there are not any images of the events, the stories that are broadcasted contain a lot of tension. There is actual violence that society imposes daily upon women, men, children, and families and about many fiction programmes that show hundreds of sadistically appalling acts of violence and desensitise the viewers to their atrocity.

The TV news programmes become thus a formidable instrument for the denunciation of injustices, and for the advancement of democracy. Conflicts, wars, racial hate, social injustice and daily violence have all been given a face—Thanks to the TV news programmes. We have to live with it, since we manage to live with ourselves.

There is no more violence than before, but there are more reporters and cameramen to film it and bear witness to it. No channel would report isolated acts committed by unbalanced people, even if we know that it would attract some viewers. The news programme has to be the most authentic reflection of this society violence—an important element of life in society. The image as spectacle has in principle no place in a news programme, unless it conveys information. Channels respect human dignity. Showing in close-up the victim of an accident covered in blood is not in the values of any country's culture. However, in the name of the respect one owes to the person, to her parents, to the sensitivity of the viewers.

TECHNIQUES FOR INTERPRETING THE CONTENT OF MEDIA

Outlined below are four main approaches to media interpretation:

1. Semiological
2. Marxist
3. Psychoanalytic
4. Sociological

Table 1: Factors believed to have influenced the level and intensity of press coverage*

	Case																
Factor	A	B	C	D	E	F	G	H	I	J	K	L	M	N	O	P	Total
Victim age (very Young/old					✓				✓	✓		✓				✓	5
Victim background	✓	✓						✓	✓	✓	✓	✓		✓			8
Possible motive			✓				✓										2
Severity of the offence								✓	✓	✓						✓	4
Location of offence			✓			✓		✓	✓	✓			✓	✓	✓		8
Time of day													✓				1
Time of year	✓											✓		✓			3
Campaign of local Paper +															✓		1
Confirmed link with other offences							✓										1
Other similar offences in area (not linked)	✓													✓			2
Similar offences Reported at same time not in locality (not linked)												✓					1
Type of press appeal														✓			1
Other factors not Specified above													✓			✓	2

* Interviewees could mention as many factors as they wished. In all but one case, the factors identified were thought to have increased the level press activity.

\+ A press campaign related to the circumstances of the offence but running before the offence took place.

SEMIOLOGICAL ANALYSIS

Semiology—the science of signs—is concerned, primarily, with how meaning is generated in texts—films, television, and works of art. It deals with what signs are and how they 'work'.

Modern semiological analysis is generally seen to have begun with two men—Swiss linguist Ferdinand de Saussure—1857-1913 and American philosopher Charles Peirce—1839-1914.

Saussure's book, Course in General Linguistics—1915—deals with the division of the sign into two components, the signifier, or 'sound-image' and the signified, or 'concept', and his suggestion that the relationship between signifiers and signified is arbitrary was of crucial importance for the development of semiology. Peirce, on the other hand, focused on three aspects of signs—their iconic, indexical and symbolic dimensions. semiological analysis has spread throughout the world. It has been applied to film, theatre, medicine, architecture and a number of other areas that involve or are concerned with communication and the transfer of information.

Peirce argued that interpreters had to supply part of the meaning of signs. He wrote that a sign—"*Is something which stands to somebody for something in some respect or capacity.*"

A central point in understanding semiology is that it is not a word or a picture or even a language that is important but relationships. Thus, as an example, a meal can be seen not just in terms of steak, salad, baked potato and apple pie, but rather as a sign system conveying meanings related to matters such as status, taste, sophistication, nationality, gender, age and so on.

It was Saussure who argued that concepts have meaning because of relations and the basic relationship is oppositional. Thus 'rich' doesn't mean anything unless there is 'poor' or 'happy unless there is 'sad'. It is not content that determines meaning, but relations in some kind of system. Nothing has meaning in itself.

When thinking about oppositions we need to remember that the opposing concepts must be related in some way. There is always some topic—not always mentioned—that they deal with. For example: rich/WEALTH/poor.

So, at this point you should have grasped:

1. Semiological analysis is concerned with meaning in texts
2. That meaning stems from relationships, and, in particular:
3. Meaning derives from relationships among signs.

SIGNS

A sign, according to Saussure, is a combination of a concept and a sound-image, a combination that cannot be separated. These two parts of the sign are designated the signified and the signifier. The relationship between the two is arbitrary—there is no logical connection between a word and a concept. For Saussure the difference between a sign and a symbol is that a symbol has a signifier that is never wholly arbitrary. If the relationship between a signifier and signified is arbitrary, the meanings these signifiers hold must be learned somehow, which implies that there are certain structured associations, or codes we pick up that help us interpret signs. We learn associations and carry them around with us. However, in life, these associations are never completely fixed, they can change. Signifiers can become dated and change their significance. In this sense everybody is a practising semiologist and pays a great deal of attention to signs.

If signs can be used to tell the truth they can also be used to lie and deceive.

LANGUAGE AND SPEAKING

Texts (collections of signs) are like languages. In the same way as language, texts allow us to communicate information feelings, ideas, by establishing rules that people must learn. And just as there is grammar for writing and speaking, there is a grammar for various kinds of texts, and for different media.

We need to distinguish between language and speaking. To understand this difference as that between the words we use —language—and the meaning we create—speaking—whether we intend to speak as we do, or not. Language is a social institution that enables us to communicate with each other. We can speak to each other if we know the code of the language.

What is obvious is that people are speaking—creating meaning for themselves and others—all the time, even when not actually articulating words. Our hairstyles, glasses, clothes, facial expressions, posture, gestures etc are all signs.

THE SYNCHRONIC AND DIACHRONIC

These terms refer to different ways of reading texts. Synchronic means analytical and diachronic means historical. So a synchronic study of a text looks at the relationship that exists between its elements, in particular the pattern of paired opposites. A diachronic study looks at the way the narrative—story—evolves, the chain of events.

Another way of describing diachronic analysis is syntagmatic analysis. A syntagm is a chain, and thus syntagmatic analysis looks at it as a sequence of events that form some kind of narrative. An important discovery of this approach is the extent to which many narratives are based on formulas.

The alternative term for synchronic analysis is paradigmatic analysis. This involves searching for a hidden pattern of oppositions that are buried in the text and that generate meaning. Levi-Strauss argues that a syntagmatic analysis of a text gives the text's manifest meaning and a paradigmatic analysis of a text gives its latent meaning. The manifest structure involves what happens and the latent structure involves what a text is about.

INTERTEXTUALITY

This term refers to the use in texts—consciously or unconsciously—of materials from other, previously created texts. Parody is a good example of the conscious use of materials from a text. Parody being the humorous imitation of a text. There can also be parodies of style, and genre parodies in which the basic plot structure of soap operas or westerns, for example, can be parodied. In some films directors create scenes which we can recognise as being 'quotations' from other films.

METAPHOR AND METONYMY

These are important ways of transmitting meaning. Metaphor works through analogy. Metonymy works through association.

Metaphor	**Metonymy**
Chaplin eats shoelaces like spaghetti (The Gold rush)	red suggests passion
Simile: important sub-categ which comparison is made part stands for the whole	Synecdoche: important sub-categ is made in which
using "like" or "as".	or whole for a part.
"No man is an island...."	Uncle Sam stands for USA
long thin objects seen as Phallic	"bowler" implies Englishman cowboy hat implies American

CODES

Particularly with concepts such as metonymy it is obvious that people carry around highly complex patterns of associations around in their heads. These complex associations are termed Codes. We learn these highly complex patterns of associations from our given society and culture. These codes affect the way we interpret signs and symbols found in the media and the way we live. To be socialised and be given a culture means, in essence, to be taught a number of codes, most of which are quite specific to a person's social class, geographical location, ethnic group, and so on. Codes tell us what to do in particular situations, and what certain things "mean".

Thus it is possible for misunderstandings to arise between those who create media images and those who view them. Eco calls these misunderstandings, aberrant decoding, and argues that such decoding is the rule in the mass media. This is because people bring different codes to a given message and thus interpret it in different ways.

Codes are difficult to see because of their characteristics—they are all-pervasive, specific and clear cut—which makes them almost invisible. However, if you consider specific situations, it is possible to unravel their codes. Sociologists refer to these phenomena as norms—guides to action. Think of the codes embedded in popular culture; the formulae in spy stories, detective stories, westerns, science fiction etc. Similarly, consider the ritual aspects of situations such as drinking in bars, gift giving, watching TV, supermarket shopping, behaviour in lifts, doctor's surgeries, churches etc.

SEMIOLOGY AND TELEVISION

An interesting semiological aspect of TV is the kind of camera shots employed in the medium. Television, because of its small screen is a "close up" medium better suited to revealing character than capturing action. Below are some of the more important kinds of shots which function as signifiers, and suggests what is signified by each shot.

Signifier (shot)	definition signified (meaning)
Close-up face only	intimacy
Medium shot most of body	more personal relationship
Long shot	setting and character context, scope
Full shot full body of person	social relationship

We can carry out a similar analysis for camera work and editing.

Signifier definition signified
Pan down camera looks down power, authority
Pan up camera looks up smallness, weakness
Dolly in camera moves in observation, focus
Fade in image appears on beginning
Fade out image screen goes blank ending
Cut switch from one image simultaneity,
To another excitement
Wipe image wiped off screen imposed conclusion

The above represents a kind of grammar of television. We all learn the meanings of these phenomena as we watch television and they help us to understand what is going on. Other matters that should be considered are—lighting techniques, the use of colour, sound effects, music and so on.

MARXIST ANALYSIS

Marxist thought is one of the most powerful and suggestive ways available to the media analyst for analysing society and its institutions. The easiest way to grasp the power of Marxist analysis is to understand some of its fundamental ideas, these are alienation, materialism, false consciousness, class conflict and hegemony.

MATERIALISM

The Marxist use of the term materialism indicates not a craving for money, or material goods, but a conception of history. A conception of history that centers on how societies organise themselves to produce those items that enable people to live. Among the items produced by a society are the ideas and beliefs that people hold. These ideas are not then our own but a product of our particular society, and in particular, the way that economic life is organised. Indeed Marx divided the organisation of any society into two—the base and the superstructure. The base is the economic organisation of a society, and the super-structure, which includes such institutions as education, the legal system, are influenced by the economic base of society.

Given the above, there are a number of questions that can be asked from the Marxist perspective:

1. What social, political, and economic arrangements characterise the society whose media is being analysed?
2. Who owns, controls, and operates the media?
3. What ideas, values, concepts and beliefs are spread by the media. What ideas, concepts etc are neglected?
4. How are writers, artists, actors and other creative people affected by the patterns of ownership and control of the media?

FALSE CONSCIOUSNESS

The consciousness of people—how they view the world—has important social, economic and political implications. For Marxists, it is the ideas that people hold that enables certain groups of people to disproportionately benefit from the social arrangements in a society. Hence, through the control of ideas the wealthy can maintain their privileged position in society.

Marx argued that in every historical period it is the ideas of the ruling class that are the ruling—dominant—ideas; that the class which has the means of material production—economic— in its control also is the dominant intellectual—ideas—force. These dominant ideas tend to support the organisation of society, and the distribution of its privileges and honours, on the basis of its existing distribution. These ideas justify, and legitimate the situation as it exists now. Clearly the ideas of the ruling class work in its own interest. So according to Marxists, the ruling class propagates an ideology that justifies its status and makes it difficult for the ordinary people to recognise that they are being exploited and victimised.

This notion—that the masses of people are being manipulated and exploited by the ruling class—is one of the central arguments of modern Marxist cultural analysis. Quite obviously the media and popular culture are centrally important in the spread of false consciousness. The media then are tools of manipulation.

CLASS CONFLICT

For Marx, history is based on unending class conflict. The two classes in capitalist society are the bourgeoisie who own the means of production, and the proletariat who own nothing except for their labour power. The bourgeoisie, according to this theory, avert class conflict by indoctrinating the proletariat with "ruling class ideas", such as the notion of the "self-made man", or that society is meritocratic, or that existing social arrangements such as gender roles or the distribution of wealth in a society are "natural" and inevitable.

The media perform their job of distracting people from the realities of their society—poverty, sexism, racism etc. Generally speaking the media are seen to either mask class differences or to act as apologists for the ruling classes in an effort to avert class conflict and changes in the political order.

ALIENATION

The word "alienation" suggests separation and distance; the notion of a stranger in a society who has no connections to others. This idea is central to marxist analysis. To be alienated is to be cut off from our "true" nature as humans. Because of the nature of capitalism—the pursuit of profit—people become estranged from their work, their friends even from themselves. For example, people become detached from their work. Work holds no intrinsic pleasure, it is just something performed for instrumental reward.

In this situation the media play a crucial role. They provide momentary gratifications for people. They distract them from their misery, and with advertising they stimulate desire, leading people to work harder, because if they don't work harder they cannot enjoy the rewards held out by advertising.

THE CONSUMER SOCIETY

It is consumption that maintains the capitalist economic system. People have to be persuaded to consume. Advertising generates anxieties, creates dissatisfactions, and, in general feeds on the alienation present in capitalist societies to maintain consumer culture. Advertising diverts people's attention from social and political concerns into narcissistic and private concerns. Individual self-gratification becomes an obsession.

HEGEMONY

Hegemony at its simplest means domination. It is a complicated intermeshing of forces of a political, social and cultural nature. Hegemony is a saturation of the whole process of living with a particular view of the nature of reality and of humanities' place within that reality. Hegemony constitutes our world; it could be described as "that which goes without saying", the commonsense reality of the world.

PSYCHOANALYTIC ANALYSIS

Psychoanalytic analysis is concerned with the interaction of conscious and unconscious processes. What follows here is a selection of some of Freud's most important concepts—concepts that can be applied to the media to aid understanding of how they work.

One of the keystones of psychoanalytic theory is that of the **unconscious.** We are not aware of everything that is going on in our minds, indeed we are aware of only a very little that is going on in our minds. Only a small portion of our mental life is accessible to us.

This means we are not in complete control of ourselves all the time, we are affected in ways we cannot comprehend, and do things for reasons we do not understand. In short we are not completely rational creatures who act only on the basis of logic and intelligence; we are vulnerable to emotional and non-rational appeals.

Freud argued that we repress much of the material in our minds. We repress it because we do not want to be conscious of it, perhaps because it would cause us pain or guilt.

Motivation research tries to discover the unconscious and, it is assumed, the real reasons that people do things so that manufacturers and others can better shape people's behaviour.

SEXUALITY

Freud described the "force" by which the sexual instinct is represented in the mind as the libido. It should be understood broadly and not as being restricted to sexual relations. That is, libido refers to various kinds of sensual pleasures and gratifications we can obtain.

THE OEDIPUS COMPLEX

This concept represents the core of neurosis for Freud, and is a concept that is thought to explain a great deal. According to psychoanalytic theory we all pass through a stage in which we desire our parent of the opposite sex—all of this at an unconscious level.

One of the ways that children deal with their oedipal anxieties is by listening to fairy tales. In The Uses of Enchantment, Bruno Bettleheim argues that fairy tales help children resolve their problems through the stories. Children identify with the heroes and heroines of these stories and learn important things about life as well.

Fairy tales, and other texts which are very much like—they may be, in truth, modernised—fairy tales, have important functions as far as our psyches are concerned.

ID, EGO AND SUPEREGO

The id, ego and superego are parts of what is usually referred to as Freud's structural hypothesis about mental functioning. In An Elementary Textbook of Psychoanalysis, Charles Brenner offers the following brief description of these three phenomena:

> We may say that id comprises the psychic representatives of the drives, the ego consists of those functions which have to do with the individual's relation to his environment, and the superego comprises the moral precepts of our minds as well as our ideal aspirations.

In essence the structural hypothesis sees the psyche in constant warfare, as the id and superego war against each other. In this war the ego tries to mediate between our desires for pleasure and our fear of punishment, between our drives and our consciences.

We can use these concepts to understand texts. In certain texts, characters may be seen as primarily id figures or ego figures or superego figures. Ego figures tend to represent pure rationality, superego figures tend to dictate what gets done—decision making—and id figures tend to be rather emotional. Villains are nearly always id figures, whilst heroes can be more diverse, for example Superman is a superego figure but Indiana Jones is perhaps more id and ego than superego.

We can also look upon genres in terms of the Freudian structural hypothesis. Certain kinds of films and television programmes, such as news shows, interviews and documentaries can be classified as essentially ego texts. Others featuring the police or, for example, religious television shows are superego texts. Soap-operas and television programmes and films involving sexuality tend to be id texts.

SYMBOLS

Symbols are things that stand for other things, many of which are hidden or at least not obvious. Conventional symbols are words we learn that stand for things. Accidental symbols are personal and private and connected to someone's life history. For example, if you fall in love for the first time in Grimsby, you may well retain Grimsby as your accidental symbol for love. Finally there are universal symbols, in which the relationship between the symbol and what is symbolised is rooted in the experience of all people.

A comparison can be made between dreams and mass-media productions. Dreams tend to be visual, so they are best compared with media such as film, television, and comics. And just as dreams can be interpreted, by analysing their symbolic content, so can mediated dreams such as we find in the cinema or on the TV screen. In both cases we ask the same questions: What is going on? What disguises are there? What gratifications do we get? What do the various symbolic heroes and heroines tell us about ourselves and our societies?

DEFENCE MECHANISMS

These are techniques employed by the ego to control instincts and ward off anxiety. All of us make use of the mechanisms at one time or another, although we are seldom conscious of what we are doing. It is possible to analyse characters portrayed by the media in terms of defense mechanisms. That is their behaviour makes more sense to us when we can relate it to the defenses people use to maintain their equilibrium. Below are some of the more important mechanisms:

Ambivalence: a simultaneous feeling of love and hate or attraction and repulsion toward the same person or object.

Avoidance: a refusal to become involved with subjects that are distressing because they are connected to unconscious sexual or aggressive impulses.

Denial: a refusal to accept the reality of something that generates anxiety by blocking it from consciousness or by becoming involved in a wish-fulfilling fantasy.

Fixation: an obsessive preoccupation or attachment to something, generally the result of some traumatic experience.

Identification: a desire to become "like" someone or something in some aspect of thought or behaviour.

Projection: an attempt to deny some negative or hostile feeling in oneself by attributing it to someone else.

Repression: unconscious instinctual wishes, memories, desires, and so on are barred from consciousness, or repressed. This is considered the most basic defense mechanism.

Suppression: a decision is made to put something out of mind and consciousness; this is the second most basic defense mechanism.

Rationalisation: the offerings of logical and rational reasons and excuses for behaviour that is generated by unconscious and irrational determinants.

Regression: the return to an earlier stage in life development when one is confronted with a stressful or anxiety provoking situation.

These concepts can provide us with a greater understanding of human motivation and moreover, with insights that enrich our ability to analyse the media.

AGGRESSION AND GUILT

Freud suggests that aggressiveness is instinctual. In Civilization and Its Discontents, he writes:

"Men are not gently creatures, who want to be loved, and who at the most can defend themselves if they are attacked; they are, on the contrary, creatures among whose instinctual endowments are to be reckoned a powerful share of aggressiveness."

This aggression threatens to disrupt or even destroy society, so powerful a force is brought into play. This force is guilt, which is, Freud explains, aggression turned back on itself. Freud argues that sometimes we feel so guilty that we become overwhelmed and forfeit our sense of happiness. This is where humour comes in. Humour is a means we have evolved to allow us to enjoy certain kinds of aggression by masking them and evading guilt feelings.

Erik Erikson: *Theories of Child development:*

Identity versus Role Confusion—adolescence

Identity diffusion: excessively self-conscious, overly concerned with sexuality

Identity foreclosure: problem of unfulfilled expectations

Negative identity: objected to by others—rebel to be noticed

Mead states that while we are each conscious, thinking individuals, the way in which we choose to behave is conditioned by the social context of that behaviour. In particular, Mead argued that our behaviour as individuals is conditioned by two aspects of our self-awareness—that is, the ability to "see ourselves" as others see us.

a) The "I" aspect which largely consists of spontaneous actions and

b) The "Me" aspect which consists of an awareness of how other people expect us to behave at any given moment and in any given situation.

The "I" and the "Me" are parallel parts of what Mead called "The Self" and it is the ability of human beings to develop a "self-concept" that, Mead argued, makes us different to the vast majority of animals.

If someone accidentally puts their hand into a fire, the "I" aspect of the self is expressed by such things as feeling pain, pulling your hand out of the flames quickly and so forth.

The "Me" aspect of the self, however, will condition how the person who has burnt their hand will react.

This reaction will be conditioned by such things as:

1. Who we are (social factors such as gender, age and so forth).
2. Where we are (at home, in public and so forth).
3. Who we are with (family, friends, people we don't know, alone and the like).

SOCIOLOGICAL ANALYSIS

Much of the debate about media in contemporary society has a sociological dimension. There are three main areas to look at: the basic concepts sociologists use, a focus on how people use the media and the gratifications it offers, and finally the standard sociological technique content analysis.

BASIC CONCEPTS

Alienation: this means literally "no ties" and refers to a feeling of estrangement. We can use the concept of alienation to understand the behaviour of characters in texts, and of social groups and sub-cultures.

Anomie: this word is derived from the Greek word nomos, meaning norms. A person who rejects the norms of a given society is described as anomic.

Bureaucracy: as society becomes larger and more complex, it becomes increasingly difficult to regulate. Bureaucracies are collections of more or less anonymous people who follow fixed rules and routines in running organisations. There is usually a hierarchy of authority, impersonal handling of problems and a great deal of red tape.

Class: a class is a group of people with something in common. When used sociologically, class refers to socio-economic class, and it refers to a person's work situation.

Deviance: this refers to behavioural patterns that are different from typical or conventional ones. Deviance generates anxiety in people because it forces us to consider how valid our practices are and how correct our attitudes are about what is normal behaviour.

Ethnicity: conventionally understood to mean groups that share certain cultural traits and traditions that distinguish them. Ethnic groups are often stereotyped in the media.

Race: usually taken to mean a category of people with a common genetic heritage.

Role: the concept of role is similar to the roles played in a play. It refers to certain kinds of behaviour that we learn, that relate to expectations people have of us, that are connected to specific situations, and that are determined, in part, by our place in society.

Sex—gender: sex is an important concept when it is linked to roles. Many critics argue that the media have given women destructive sex roles, or images.

Socialisation: this refers to the process by which people are taught the rules, roles, and values of their society. It is a form of indoctrination that is achieved informally through institutions such as the family, and schooling.

Status: status involves the position a person has in some group or organisation and the prestige that is connected with this position.

Stereotype: a group shared image of another group or category of people; stereotypes can be very dangerous because they present oversimplified images.

Values: this refers to attitudes people have relative to what is desirable, good and bad. Our values affect our behaviour.

USES AND GRATIFICATIONS

There has been a considerable amount of interest in the ways that people use media and the gratifications media offer to people. Below is a list of some of the possible offerings of the media:

To be amused

to see authority figures exalted or deflated
to experience the beautiful
to have shared experiences with others
to satisfy curiosity and be informed
to identify with the deity
to find distraction and diversion
to experience empathy
to experience, in a guilt free situation, extreme emotions
to find models to imitate
to gain an identity
to gain information about the world
to reinforce our belief in justice
to believe in romantic love
to believe in magic, the marvelous, and the miraculous
to see others make mistakes

to see order imposed on the world
to participate in history
to be purged of unpleasant emotions
to obtain outlets for our sex drives in a guilt free context
to explore taboo subjects with impunity
to experience the ugly
to affirm moral, spiritual, and cultural values
to see villains in action

When a text is analysed from use's and gratification's standpoint, an attempt is made to determine which uses and gratifications are most important and which are secondary.

CONTENT ANALYSIS

Content analysis is a research technique based upon measuring—counting—the amount of something—violence, women etc—in a random sampling of some forms of communication. The basic assumption implicit in content analysis is that an investigation of messages and communication gives insights into the people who receive these messages.

The advantages of content analysis are:

It is inexpensive

It is usually relatively easy to get material

It is unobtrusive

It yields data that can be quantified

It can deal with current events or past events, or both.

The difficulties are:

It is hard to be certain that the sample is representative

It is often hard to define a topic being studied (what counts as violence?)

It isn't easy to find a measurable unit

VIEW TOWARDS CRIME

There are many reasons and theories as to what causes crime in society. Many argue that crime is a biological response, and others argue that crime is explained through psychological reasoning. However, crime is a balanced mixture of all aspects including but not limited to: psychological, sociological, and biological causes.

From the beginning of time crime has been influenced by the environment that one lives in. Environment is the most influential in determining crime occurrence. For example, theories based on blocked opportunity, which state that crime occurs within members of communities who cannot obtain the "American Dream" and, therefore, resort to crime in order to earn social status and/or to supposedly better themselves. This type of behaviour is best portrayed in inner cities with the concept of gangs.

Moreover, crime is also influenced strongly by sociological influences that can manipulate criminals to commit certain crimes. For example, many teenagers and children today commit crimes mainly because of pressure from other peers. This committing of crimes by teenagers could be considered as an escape or reaction formation in order to escape the pressure and demands in the daily life of many teens and children. Likewise, adults fall to the pressure of society by engaging in criminal behaviour in order to provide an escape from the "measuring rod" of society.

The age-old saying suggests that most criminals are "born into crime", is true to a certain extent. Freud's theory of the *id*, *ego*, and *superego* suggests that these three components of personality counteract with each other and determine what action is taken by the individual. In a criminal's mind, however, the urge of the superego strongly influences the criminal to take actions that a normal person could restrain and/or avoid.

The criminal mind depicted in literature

Literature has a rich tapestry of criminal identities, and is particularly good at depicting the guilty conscience. In *Hamlet*, the Prince of Denmark has a play about a murder performed to see if Claudius will betray his guilt, which he does. Similarly, Macbeth strains out loud under the burden of his heavy conscience. And, of course, we have Dostoevsky's portrayal of Raskolnikov's eventual unburdening of his guilt ridden conscience in *Crime and Punishment*.

Raskolnikov's confession comes after a series of interviews with the psychologically astute prosecutor Porfiry. In the most striking of those sessions, the young, intellectual murderer explains his distressing theory that great men—presumably including himself—are above the law and that they have the moral right to take the lives of others. Merely to be exposed to that theory is to glimpse how the mind of a criminal works in distorted ways.

No one theory explains the variety of the criminal mind. Robert Louis Stevenson gave the world *Dr. Jekyll and Mr. Hyde* and thereby tried to show that all human beings are simultaneously made up of good and evil. In Hugo's *The Hunchback of Notre Dame*, the sexually repressed priest Claude Frollo vents his passions: "when one does evil it's madness to stop halfway. The extremity of crime has a certain delirium of joy; an evil thought is inexorable and strives to become an action"—Victor Hugo, *The Hunchback of Notre Dame* 173–174; Lowell Bair, trans. Bantam Books, 1981. In *The Stranger*, Albert Camus depicts how the criminal mind may simply be alienated. In Balzac's *Père Goriot*, Vautrin is an articulate, intelligent escaped convict, full of practical experience and honourable to his own code.

Equally important in explaining the literature-crime link is our ambivalence about criminals and the allure of evil. On the one hand, we occasionally, if paradoxically, admire those who break the law and, on the other, we often loathe them. One way to minimise the conflict is to endow criminals with virtues such as greatness or goodness. Robin Hood is a virtuous outlaw. The criminal can sometimes be attractive simply because he is an individual at odds with society, one against the many. And the successful criminal may, by definition, have superior mental or other powers, may be an evil genius. Arthur Conan Doyle had Sherlock Holmes respectfully call his nemesis Professor Moriarty the "Napoleon of Crime". A criminal may often have an outsized, unusual, and interesting, if warped, personality. The villains in many of Ian Fleming's James Bond books, such as Dr. No, Auric Goldfinger, and Ernst Blofeld, fit this description. Glamour may even be attached to an elegant rogue.

Another way to reduce the psychological tension is repression, whereby we bar from consciousness our admiration for criminals and replace it with loathing. But such apparent loathing is just another form of fascination, which can lead to obsession. The self-appointed censor who obsessively reviews books, magazines, and films for obscenity falls into this category, as does Victor Hugo's dogged fictional policeman Javert in *Les Misérables*.

Reading about crime is a good thing for a society. Reading is not doing, although some have argued that a culture's portrayal of crime and violence in literary works—or on film or television—can breed more crime and violence. But this argument, so well portrayed in *The Seven Minutes*, Irving Wallace's 1970 novel about a rape-obscenity trial, ignores not only freedom of expression but also how much the experience of literature can serve as a psychological safety valve. Most people slake their thirst for crime vicariously.

Crime in literature helps us better understand crime in life. "A crime is, in the first instance, a defect in the reasoning powers," wrote Balzac in *Cousin Bette*, and that mid-nineteenth century literary insight is both piercing and fruitful—Honore de Balzac, *Cousin Bette* 422; James Waring, trans. "Everyman's Library", 1991. Much of crime can be explained by Balzac's theory—by reason losing control—with a few illustrations drawn from the vast body of crime literature. Other assaults on rationality that can cause crime are extreme political, social, or religious causes, and an inordinate need for power.

• • •

7

9/11

The September 11, 2001 attacks on the World Trade Center in New York and on the Pentagon near Washington, D.C. were shocking global media events that dominated public attention and provoked reams of discourse, reflection, and writing. These media spectacles were intended to terrorise the U.S., to attack symbolic targets, and to unfold a terror spectacle Jihad against the West, as well as to undermine the U.S. and global economy. The World Trade Center is an apt symbol of global capitalism in the heart of the New York financial district, while the Pentagon stands as an icon and center of U.S. military power.

Terror Spectacle

The term "terrorism" is one of the most overloaded and contested terms in contemporary political vocabulary. First used to describe the "reign of terror" following the radical phase of the French Revolution, the term was used in the 19th century to describe the violent activities of Russian revolutionaries. By the late 1960s, the Nixon administration was using the term "terrorism" to describe a wide range of activities and groups. It established a Cabinet Committee to Combat Terrorism in 1972 and subsequent US administrations continued to develop agencies and task forces to fight "terrorism", which became a widespread designation to label groups that the US government or their allies were fighting. But during this era, the US was also widely accused of crimes against civilians in Vietnam and elsewhere, as well as using violence to intervene in other countries' politics, so the term "state terrorism" began to emerge, a term also frequently applied to Israel —see Herman 1998.

Hence, "terrorism" was highly constructed and contested with one group's "terrorists" another group's "freedom fighters". Varied political groups labeled "terrorists" have long constructed media spectacles of terror to promote their causes, attack their adversaries, and gain worldwide publicity and attention. There had been many major terror spectacles before, both in the U.S. and elsewhere. Hijacking of airplanes had been a standard form constructing spectacles of terror, but the ante was significantly upped when in 1970, the Popular Front for the Liberation of Palestine, hijacked three Western jetliners. The group forced the planes to land in the Jordanian desert, and then blew up the planes in an incident known as "Black September" which was the topic of a Hollywood film. In 1972, Palestinian gunmen from the same movement stunned the world when they took Israeli athletes hostage at the Munich Olympic Games, producing another media spectacle turned into an academy award winning documentary film.

In 1975, an OPEC (Organisation for Petroleum Exporting Countries) meeting was disrupted in Vienna, Austria when a terrorist group led by the notorious Carlos the Jackal entered, killing three people and wounding several in a chaotic shootout. Americans were targeted in a 1983 terror campaign in Beruit Lebanon, in which 243 U.S. servicemen were killed, orchestrated by a Shiite Muslim suicide bomber that led the U.S. to withdraw its troops from Lebanon. U.S. tourists were victims in 1985 of Palestinians who seized the cruise ship Achilles Lauro, when

Leon Klinghoffer, 69, a crippled Jewish American, was killed and his body and wheelchair were thrown overboard.

In 1993, the World Trade Center was assaulted in New York by Islamist radicals linked to Osama bin Laden, providing a preview of the more spectacular September 11 attack. An American born terrorist, Timothy McVeigh, bombed the Alfred P. Murrah Federal Building in Oklahoma City, killing 168 and wounding more than 500. And the bin Laden group had assaulted U.S. embassies in Africa in 1998 and a U.S. destroyer harboured in Yemen in 2000. Consequently, terror spectacle is a crucial part of the deadly game of contemporary politics and the bin Laden group had systematically used spectacle of terror to promote its agenda. But the 9/11 terror spectacle was the most extravagant strike on U.S. targets in its history and the first foreign attack on the continental U.S. since the war of 1812.

In a global media world, extravagant terror spectacles have been orchestrated in part to gain worldwide attention, dramatise the issues of the groups involved, and achieve specific political objectives. Previous Al Qaeda strikes against the U.S. hit a range of targets to try to demonstrate that the U.S. was weak and vulnerable to terrorist attacks.

The earlier 1993 World Trade Center bombing in New York, the embassy assaults in Kenya and Tanzania in 1998, and the strike on the USS Cole in 2000 combined surprise with detailed planning and coordination in well-orchestrated, high concept terror spectacle.

Spectacle of terror thus uses dramatic images and montage to catch attention, hoping thereby to catalyse unanticipated events that will spread further terror through domestic populations. The September 11 terror spectacle looked like a disaster film, leading Hollywood director Robert Altman to chide his industry for producing extravaganzas of terror that could serve as models for spectacular terror campaigns. Was

Independence Day—1996—the template for 9/11 in which Los Angeles and New York were attacked by aliens and the White House was destroyed? The collapse of the WTC indeed had resonances of The Towering Inferno—1975—that depicted a high-rise building catching on fire, burning and collapsing, or even Earthquake—1975—that depicted the collapse of entire urban environments. For these two Hollywood disaster films, however, the calamity emerged from within the system, in the case of the first, and from nature itself in the second. In the September 11 terror spectacle, by contrast, the villains were foreign terrorists obviously committed to wreaking maximum destruction on the U.S. and it was not certain how the drama would end or if order would be restored in a "happy ending".

The novelty of the September 11 terror spectacle resulted from the combination of airplane hijacking and the use of airplanes to crash into buildings and destabilises urban and economic life. The targets were symbolic, representing global capital and American military power, yet had material effects, disrupting the airline industry, the businesses centered in downtown New York, and the global economy itself through the closure of the U.S. and other stock markets and subsequent downturns of the world's markets. Indeed, as a response to the drama of the terror spectacle, an unparalleled shutdown occurred in New York, Washington, and other major cities throughout the U.S., with government and businesses closing up for the day and the airline system canceling all flights. Wall Street and the stock market were shut down for days, baseball and entertainment events were postponed, Disneyland and Disneyworld were closed, McDonald's locked up its regional offices, and most major U.S. cities became eerily quiet.

Post 9/11 Media Spectacle

The 9/11 terror spectacle unfolded in a city that was one of the most media saturated in the world and that played out a deadly drama live on television. The images of the planes hitting the World Trade Center towers and their collapse were broadcast repeatedly, as if repetition were necessary to master a highly traumatic event. The spectacle conveyed the message that the U.S. was vulnerable to terror attack, that terrorists could create great harm, and that anyone at anytime could be subject to a violent terror attack, even in Fortress America. The suffering, fear, and death that many people endure on a daily basis in violent and insecure situations in other parts of the world, was brought home to U.S. citizens. Suddenly, the vulnerability and anxiety suffered by many people throughout the world was also deeply experienced by U.S. citizens, in some cases for the first time. The terror attacks thus had material effects, attempting to harm the U.S. and global economy, and psychic effects, traumatising a nation with fear. The spectacle of terror was broadcast throughout the global village, with the whole world watching the assault on the U.S. and New York's attempts to cope with the attacks.

The live television broadcasting brought a "you are there" drama to the September 11 spectacle. The images of the planes striking the World Trade Center, the buildings bursting into flames, individuals jumping out of the window in a desperate attempt to survive the inferno, and the collapse of the Towers and subsequent chaos provided unforgettable images that viewers would not soon forget. The drama continued throughout the day with survivors being pulled from the rubble, and the poignant search for individuals still alive and attempts to deal with the attack produced resonant iconic images seared deeply into spectators' memories. Many people who witnessed the event suffered nightmares and psychological trauma. For those who viewed it intensely, the spectacle provided a powerful set of images that would continue to resonate for years to come, much as the footage of the Kennedy assassination, iconic photographs of Vietnam, the 1986 explosion of the space shuttle Challenger, or the death of Princess Diana in the 1990s provided unforgettable imagery.

The September 11 terror attacks in New York were claimed to be "the most documented event in history" in a May 2002 HBO film In Memoriam which itself provided a collage of images assembled from professional news crews, documentary filmmakers, and amateur video-graphers and photographers who in some cases risked their lives to document the event. As with other major media spectacles, the September 11 terror spectacle took over TV programming for the next three days without commercial break as the major television networks focused on the attack and its aftermath.

There followed a media spectacle of the highest order. For several days, US television suspended broadcasting of advertising and TV entertainment and focused solely on the momentous events of September 11. In the following analysis, I want to suggest how the images and discourses of the US television networks framed the 9/11 attacks to whip up war hysteria, while failing to provide a coherent account of what happened, why it happened, and what would count as responsible responses. In an analysis of the dominant discourses, frames, and representations that informed the media and public debate in the days following the September 11 attacks, the mainstream media in the United States privileged the "clash of civilisations" model, established a binary dualism between Islamic terrorism and civilisation, and largely circulated war fever and retaliatory feelings and discourses that called for and supported a form of military intervention. Such one-dimensional militarism could arguably make the crisis worse, rather than providing solutions to the problem of global terrorism. Thus, while the media in a democracy should critically debate urgent questions facing the nation, in the terror crisis the mainstream U.S. corporate media, especially television, promoted war fever and military solutions to the problem of global terrorism.

Many commentators on U.S. television offered similarly one-sided and Manichean accounts of the cause of the September 11 events, blaming their favourite opponents in the current U.S. political spectrum as the source of the terror assaults. Hence, broadcast television allowed dangerous and extremist zealots to vent and circulate the most aggressive, fanatic, and sometimes lunatic views, creating a consensus around the need for immediate military action and all-out war. The television networks themselves featured logos such as "War on America," "America's New War," and other inflammatory slogans that assumed that the U.S. was at war and that only a military response was appropriate. Few cooler heads appeared on any of the major television networks that repeatedly beat the war drums day after day, without even the relief of commercials for three days straight, driving the country into hysteria and making it certain that there would be a military response and war.

Radio was even more frightening. Not surprisingly, talk radio oozed hatred and hysteria, calling for violence against Arabs and Muslims, nuclear retaliation, and global war. As the days went by, even mainstream radio news became hyper-dramatic, replete with music, patriotic gore, and wall-to-wall terror hysteria and war propaganda. National Public Radio, Pacifica, and some programs attempted rational discussion and debate, but on the whole talk radio was all propaganda, all the time. There is no question concerning the depth of emotion and horror.

Bush Family Media Spectacles

War itself has become a media spectacle in which successive U.S. regimes have used military extravaganzas to promote their agendas. The Reagan administration repeatedly used military spectacle to deflect attention from its foreign policy and economic problems. And two Bush administrations and the Clinton administration famously "wagged the dog," using military spectacle to deflect attention from embarrassing domestic or foreign policy blunders, or in Clinton's case, a sex scandal that threatened him with impeachment—Kellner 2003a.

The Gulf War of 1990-1991 was the major media spectacle of its era, captivating global audiences, and seeming to save the first Bush presidency, before the war's ambiguous outcome and a declining economy helped defeat the Bush presidential campaign of 1992. In the summer of 1990, the elder Bush's popularity was declining, he had promised "no new taxes" and then raised taxes, and it appeared that he would not be re-elected. Bush senior's salvation seemed to appear in the figure of Saddam Hussein and his August 1990 invasion of Kuwait that allowed Bush to organise a military intervention to displace him.

On March 19, the media spectacle of the war against Iraq unfolded with a dramatic attempt to "decapitate" the Iraqi regime. Large numbers of missiles were aimed at targets in Baghdad where Saddam Hussein and the Iraqi leadership were believed to be staying and the tens of thousands of ground troops on the Kuwait-Iraq border poised for invasion entered Iraq in a blitzkrieg toward Baghdad. The media followed the Bush administration and Pentagon slogan of "shock and awe" and presented the war against Iraq as a great military spectacle, as triumphalism marked the opening days of the U.S. bombing of Iraq and invasion.

The Al Jazeera network live coverage of the bombing of a palace belonging to the Hussein family was indeed shocking as loud explosions and blasts jolted viewers throughout the world. Whereas some Western audiences experienced this bombing positively as a powerful assault on "evil," for Arab audiences it was experienced as an attack on the body of the Arab and Muslim people, just as the September 11 terror attacks were experienced by Americans as assaults on the very body and symbols of the United States. While during Gulf War I, CNN was the only network live in Baghdad and throughout the war framed the images, discourses, and spectacle, there were over twenty broadcasting networks in Baghdad for the 2003 Iraq war, including several Arab networks, and the different TV companies presented the war quite diversely.

A great debate emerged around the embedded reporters and whether journalists who depended on the protection of the U.S. and British military, lived with the troops, and signed papers agreeing to a rigorous set of restrictions on their reporting could be objective and critical of their protectors. From the beginning, it was clear that the embedded reporters were indeed "in bed with" their military escorts and as the U.S. and Britain stormed into Iraq, the reporters presented exultant and triumphant accounts that trumped any paid propagandist. The embedded U.S. network television reporters were *gung ho* cheerleaders and spinners for the U.S. and UK military and lost all veneer of objectivity. But as the blitzkrieg stalled, a sandstorm hit, and U.S. and British forces came under attack, the embedded reporters reflected genuine fear, helped capture the chaos of war, provided often vivid accounts of the fighting, and occasionally, as I note below, deflated a propaganda lie of the U.S. or U.K. military allegedly confirmed by a Pentagon source to the Fox TV military correspondent who quickly spread it through the U.S. media—BBC was skeptical from the beginning. The embedded and other reporters on the site provided documentation of the more raw and brutal aspects of war and telling accounts that often put in question official versions of the events, as well as propaganda and military spin. But since their every posting and broadcast was censored by the U.S. military, it was the independent "unilateral" journalists who provided the most accurate account of the horrors of the war and the Coalition of Two military mishaps. Thus, on the whole the embedded journalists were largely propagandists who often outdid the Pentagon and Bush administration in spinning the message of the moment.

The dramatic story of "Saving Private Lynch" was one of the more spectacular human-interest stories of the war that revealed the constructed and spectacle nature of the event and ways that the Pentagon constructed mythologies that were replicated by the TV networks. Private Jessica Lynch was one of the first American POWs shown on Iraqi TV and since she was young, female, and attractive, her fate became a topic of intense interest. Stories circulated that she was shot and stabbed and was tortured by Iraqis holding her in captivity. Eight days after her capture, the U.S. media broadcast footage of her dramatic rescue, obviously staged like a reality TV spectacle. Soldiers stormed the hospital, found Lynch, and claimed a dramatic rescue under fire from Iraqis. In fact, several media institutions interviewed the doctors in the hospital who claimed that Iraqi troops had left the hospital two days before, that the hospital staff had tried to take Jessica to the Americans but they fired on them, and that in the "rescue" the U.S. troops shot through the doors, terrorised doctors and patients, and created a dangerous scene that could have resulted in deaths, simply to get some dramatic rescue footage for TV audiences.

Comparing American broadcasting networks with the BBC, Canadian, and other outlets during the opening weeks of the U.S. war against Iraq showed two different wars being presented. The U.S. networks tended to ignore Iraqi casualties, Arab outrage about the war, global antiwar and anti-U.S. protests, and the negative features of the war, while the BBC and Canadian CBC often featured these more critical themes. On the whole, U.S. broadcasting networks tended to present a sensitised view of the war while Canadian, British and other European, and Arab broadcasting presented copious images of civilian casualties and the horrors of war. U.S. television coverage tended toward pro-military patriotism, propaganda, and technological fetishism, celebrating the weapons of war and military humanism, highlighting the achievements and heroism of the U.S. military.

Other global broadcasting networks, however, were highly critical of the U.S. and U.K. military and often presented highly negative spectacles of the assault on Iraq and the shock and awe high-tech massacre. Subsequent images of looting, anarchy and chaos throughout Iraq, however, including the looting of the National Museum, the National Archive that contained rare books and historical documents, and the Ministry for Religious Affairs, which contained rare religious material, created extremely negative impressions. For weeks after the fall of the Iraqi regime negative images continued for circulation of clashes between Iraqis and the U.S. forces, gigantic Shia demonstrations and celebrations that produced the specter of the growing of radical Islamic power in the region, and the continued failure to produce security and stability. The spectacle of Shia on the march and taking over power in many regions of the country created worries that "democracy" in Iraqi could produce religious fundamentalist regimes. This negative spectacle suggests the limitations of a politics of the spectacle that can backfire, spiral out of control, and generate unintended consequences.

Media spectacles can backfire and are subject to dialectical reversal as positive images give way to negative ones. They are difficult to control and manage, and can be subject to different framings and interpretations, as when non-U.S. broadcasting networks focus on civilian casualties, looting and chaos, and U.S. military crimes against Iraqis rather than the U.S. victory and the evils of Saddam Hussein. In a mediated world in which only a few–and increasingly, fewer–media corporations control the broadcasting and print media the Internet provides the best source of alternative information. It offers a wealth of opinion and debate, and a variety of sites that presents material for a better-informed public and the organisation of political alternatives to the current U.S. regime—Kellner 2001 and 2003b.

Dream journals being kept by students in a college psychology class have provided researchers with a unique look at how people experienced the events of 9/11, including the influence that television coverage of the World Trade Center attacks had on people's levels of stress.

Reported in the April 2007 issue of the journal *Psychological Science*, the study data finds that for every hour of television viewed on Sept. 11—with some students reporting in excess of 13 hours watched—levels of stress, as indicated by dream content, increased significantly. In addition, the study found that time spent talking with family and friends helped individuals to better process the day's horrific events.

"What distinguishes these findings is that they occurred in 'real-time,'" adds co-author, Robert Stickgold, PhD, a sleep researcher in the Division of Psychiatry at Beth Israel Deaconess Medical Center and Associate Professor of Medicine at Harvard Medical School. "Because we have the students' pre-9/11 dreams with which to compare, we can draw more reliable conclusions about our post-9/11 findings."

People's dreams can function as a measure of how much distress they are feeling and how well or poorly they are coping. If, in your dreams, you are still seeing specific traumatic images—buildings collapsing, fire burning, people jumping—then it means that these stressful events are not being adequately processed. But, if you're seeing tangential events in your dreams—for example, a hurricane rather than the specific 9/11 images—it indicates that your brain is trying to make sense of the trauma and that you are coping successfully. Repeated viewing of horrific images may result in increased levels of stress and trauma in the general population.

Dreams are not only measurable for the individual distress they convey, but also, indirectly, the impact of mediatisation of the catastrophy.

The horrors of September 11th are the latest and one of the most atrocious reminders of the fact that humans have the sad monopoly of using violence for any purpose. Animals will defend themselves, attack if hunting and fight over females. Humans probably started this way but then kept adding new reasons for violence: punishment, torture, wars of aggression or for "defending national honour", genocide and other types of group extermination, and, of course, terrorism. Today's humans then more violent than their ancestors. They have lost inhibitions as a result of a culture showing violence in reality and fiction as something perfectly normal. Moreover, they have at their disposal means and knowledge that used to be much more difficult to access.

To cope with this new situation it would appear that traditional roots of violence—poverty, injustice, intolerance and discrimination, hate campaigns—must be more effectively tackled.

•••

8

TV VIOLENCE AND RESEARCH

"When television is good, nothing—not the theatre, not the magazines or newspapers—nothing is better. But when television is bad, nothing is worse."

Violence Concerns

TV violence concern made its official debut in 1952 with the first of a series of congressional hearings. That particular hearing was held in the House of Representatives before the Commerce Committee—United States Congress, 1952. The following year, in 1953, the first major Senate hearing was held before the Senate Subcommittee on Juvenile Delinquency, then headed by Senator Estes Kefauver, who convened a panel to inquire into the impact of television violence on juvenile delinquency—United States Congress, 1955a; 1955b. Senator Kefauver established the model hearing by inviting several panels of experts or interested parties to discuss TV violence. In the typical hearing, there would be a panel of parents and teachers to testify about their concerns about television violence. The next panel was a group of experts from the criminal justice system or general field of social science, followed by a panel of TV executives.

In one of the early hearings, a developmental psychologist, Eleanor Maccoby—1954—who was—and is still—a Professor of Psychology at Stanford University, and Paul Lazarsfeld—1955—, who was a Professor of Sociology at Columbia University, testified on the effects of television violence. Both of those social scientists noted that, while we really did not have much information on the impact of television—because social scientists were not studying that issue—we did know something about the way films influence children and we could make some suggestions about television. That early testimony initiated a series of congressional hearings on television violence and set a pattern for congressional hearings that have been held to this date. The most recent congressional activity in this area was the February 2, 1995, Children's Media Protection Act of 1995 introduced by Senator Kent Conrad.

There have been many hearings since the 1950's, but there has been only limited change—until recently—because this is a difficult issue. TV violence reduction is fraught with legal complications, with policy pitfalls, with social scientists arguing with each other. Nevertheless, our knowledge base has changed over time and there have been some significant changes in research and landmark reviews of that research.

There were many hearings, but the landmark events that map out where we have been and what we need to do have moved forward from those 1950's hearings. The National Commission on the Causes and Prevention of Violence was a presidential commission—established by President Johnson in response to the assassinations of John Kennedy, Robert Kennedy, and Martin Luther King—to assess the role violence plays in our society. This was a broad-ranging national commission, sometimes referred to as the Eisenhower commission because it was chaired by Milton Eisenhower. The Eisenhower Commission issued its report in 1969—actually, a bookshelf full of reports, there were about nine or ten staff report volumes. One of those volumes was devoted to media violence, not just television, but media violence. The sections that related to television violence reviewed the research that was available up to that date. The pace of research began to pick up speed in the 1960's with some early studies, which I will describe in a moment. Yet, there was a research base to review in the 1960's, and the conclusion of the National Commission on the Causes and Prevention of Violence was, and I paraphrase: Yes, from the research that we have, although it is thin and limited, we do know that there is reason for concern about violence in media, particularly violence on television, and particularly the violence on television that is seen by children—Baker & Ball, 1969.

The next landmark event occurred at this point. A very influential Senator, John Pastore from Rhode Island, who was chair of the Senate Subcommittee on Communications, held another hearing. This hearing differed slightly from any of the prior hearings because Senator Pastore included more than the usual parents, teachers, social scientists, and network executives. He added a wrinkle by inviting the Surgeon General of the United States to attend the hearing. When the various panels had testified, he asked the Surgeon General to make some comments. The Surgeon General's Office had just concluded the first reports on smoking and health. At this point, you have to cast your minds back to the mid 1960's. There was quite an outcry over the first Surgeon General's report on smoking and health, because it indicated that there might be some link between smoking and lung cancer. So, it was this same health officer, the Surgeon General, who was asked to comment on what had been presented at the hearing. And, the Surgeon General responded by placing the TV violence controversy in the same context as the smoking and lung cancer controversy—a public health context.

Now, that was the first time that TV violence had ever been framed as a public health issue. The Surgeon General suggested that he would approach the issue by establishing a panel of scientists and representatives from the industry to review the evidence and to develop a consensus report. And, he got his wish.

A 12-member panel was appointed with distinguished social scientists, professionals in psychiatry and child development, political scientists, and two representatives of the industry. Thomas Coffin, a psychologist who was Vice President for Research at NBC, and Joseph Klapper, a sociologist who was Director of the Office of Social Research at CBS, were among the industry representatives. Senator Pastore did not get his report in one year; it took longer, things always do. But, the funding established 60 research projects around the country, and it took three years to conduct the research and write the report. The report, released in 1972, concluded that violence on television does influence children who view that programming and does increase the likelihood that they will become more aggressive in certain ways. Not all children are affected, not all children are affected in the same way, but there is evidence that TV violence can be harmful to young viewers —Surgeon General's Scientific Advisory Committee on Television and Social Behaviour, 1972; Murray, 1973.

The next landmark report was the 1982 study from the National Institute of Mental Health—1982. This review was a ten year follow-up to the Surgeon General's report. The conclusion: Now with 10 years of more research, we know that violence on television does affect the aggressive behaviour of children—and adults for that matter—and there are many more reasons for concern about violence on television. "The research question has moved from asking whether or not there is an effect to seeking explanations for that effect."—National Institute of Mental Health, 1982, p. 6.

The next report was in 1992 from the American Psychological Association Task Force on Television and Social Behaviour—Huston, *et al*, 1992—which concluded that 30 years of research confirms the harmful effects of TV violence. These conclusions were reaffirmed by the American Psychological Association Commission on Violence and Youth—1993; Eron & Slaby, 1994.

Identification with aggressor

"Identification with aggressor"—Freud, 1946—or "defensive identification"—Mowrer, 1950, whereby a person presumably transforms himself from object to agent of aggression by adopting the attributes of an aggressive threatening model so as to allay anxiety, is widely accepted as an explanation of the imitative learning of aggression.

The effect of television violence may depend largely on the person's present cognitive state. If a person is already aroused, further television violence may cause no more arousal, however if the violence is related to what originally aroused them, the arousal may be greater.

The second effect that violence can have on its viewers is that of dis-inhibition. This is based on the idea that if we watch a lot of violence, we come to see it as "a permitted or legitimate way of solving problems or attaining goals"—Gross 1992:456.

The third effect that can occur in viewers who watch a lot of violence on television is de-sensitisation. In a sense this is linked to dis-inhibition as viewers who are prone to seeing too much violence on television, become used to it and therefore accept it as being part of our everyday life. The repeat exposure to it reduces our emotional response to it, increases acceptance and makes us more tolerant towards any subsequent violence that we see.

The final effect that occurs when watching violence on television is imitation. This is when the viewer is likely to imitate what they see on television; re-enact the behaviour observed. This is particularly likely to occur with young children who are unaware of behaviour that is correct and behaviour that is wrong. It is sometimes known as observational learning —Gunter and McAleer 1990:103. A real example of this is the Jamie Bulger case where the toddler was killed. It is believed that the two youngsters that killed him had been watching the film 'Child's Play 3' and had then imitated the violence they had seen in the film. This consequently killed Jamie Bulger. If this theory is correct, it would appear that imitating violence from television can have some harmful effects.

It has, therefore, been established that these four effects namely arousal, de-sensitisation, dis-inhibition and imitation can occur when watching violence on television. Other factors, however, may come into play that would mean that the results could not be conclusive evidence of television violence causing violent behaviour. The first of these is age. The more mature an individual is, the less likely it appears they would be affected. The level of comprehension an individual has is, therefore, vital. Younger children are less able to understand what they should and should not do and what the harmful effects is that may occur from watching television.

Another variable that could cause disruption in the results is gender differences. It is generally believed that less violent behaviour occurs in women than it does in men. Eron—1980— believed that this was largely due to there being fewer aggressive female models and, therefore, there was less possibility for imitation effects to occur. He then, however, found that the activity that the model was engaging in was more important than the actual gender of the model. Boys and girls were both found to be more aggressive after viewing a male model, perhaps suggesting that girls identify better with a male model than a female one. Eron concluded that susceptibility to violent behaviour begins at the age of three although by the age of eight he thought that girls had found other interests, learnt other ways of behaving and were, therefore, less affected—Van Evra 1990:85.

Singer and Singer—1984—believe that the more an individual watches the television, the more likely they are to be aggressive, restless and have little belief in a 'scary' world — Van Evra 1990:90.

Amount of viewing is also linked with socio-economic levels. It has been found that heavy viewers tend, in general, to come from more disadvantaged homes and have a high incidence of behavioural problems—Gernstein and Eisenberg. Van der Voort—1986—also suggested that these lower socio-economic people show more enjoyment and approval of violence, are more likely to identify with the television characters and have low achievements in school—Van Evra 1990:91. These factors make them more susceptible to being influenced by television violence.

Parental influence on a child's viewing may also determine how affected they are by violence on television. Those parents, who are not concerned about the effects of television, will allow their children to actively watch whatever programme they want. This allows them to be more susceptible to violence as they may well choose violent programmes and consequently encourage their own violent behaviour—Van der Voort 1986—Huston-Stein and Friedrich—1975—however, found that when parents disapproved of violence on television and limited the child's viewing of it, it did actually cause a decrease in the amount of violent behaviour occurring in the child.

Mean World Syndrome, suggests that children or adults who watch a lot of violence on television may begin to believe that the world is as mean and dangerous in real life as it appears on television, and hence, they begin to view the world as a much more mean and dangerous place.

"If it bleeds it leads"

The disproportionate prominence of gore and violence on daily TV news broadcasts—following the "if it bleeds it leads" formula—inflates the public's fears for personal safety. Crime is often a factor when deciding whether to move from Baltimore City to the suburbs, which are perceived as safer.

"Most crimes are not newsworthy," Dr. Miller said at the press conference. "A considerable proportion of crime stories are follow-ups about crimes committed weeks before. These stories are a highly charged, visceral experience for viewers. We're riveted. You get a deep and stubborn impression of danger concentrated in the city, even though the crime might have been committed far away."

The TV news content analysis found that crime coverage dominates the available news time, followed by human interest and "soft" news, and then weather and sports. Politics, education, the environment and business rate, on average, just seconds of attention.

The Public Agenda poll revealed that 60% of area residents believe TV news is an accurate reflection of reality. Most of them say they are frightened of the city; 84% fear criminals will harm them or their loved ones. This concern seems driven both by personal experiences and by media coverage. Interestingly, however, 92% of respondents reported they feel safe in their own neighborhoods, where they get first-hand information about things going on.

At the beginning of the 20th Century, about the time the movies were invented, our visions of the future were transformed from utopian dreams into urban nightmares.

Many factors were at work. But it's likely that the new visual media played an important role in this shift. Film and later television producers found it easier to visualise a world of surrealistic decay than to laboriously shape entertainment that, as Gloria de Gaetano, media literacy author from Redmond, Washington, puts it, "shows people negotiating conflict and resolving it through communication, understanding and empathy".

Media creators must also face up to their own responsibility for moulding our hopes and dreams. But it's up to all of us—as teachers, parents and caring citizens—to demand and work for a culture in which "blood and gore, horror and the basest of human instincts are not the driving storyline of prime-time entertainment and talk shows," DeGaetano.

Psychologists and social critics are beginning to understand that traditional therapy breaks down when it tells people to "adjust" to a pathological society. In the same way, media that merely "reflect" a troubled society are not providing the hope and new ideas we need. We need not just the "politics of meaning," but a "media of meaning".

Concerns about the impact of TV violence on children have been addressed in social and behavioural science research for almost 50 years—Murray, 1973, 1980; Pecora, Murray, & Wartella, 2006. Three main classes of behavioural effects that have been demonstrated over this half-century of research are increased aggression, desensitisation, and fear—Murray, 1998, 2000. Behavioural studies have demonstrated that TV violence, in combination with the associated fast action and excitement, holds attention to the screen and is emotionally arousing for children and adults Bandura, 1994; Berkowitz, 1984; Huston *et al.*, 1992. Studies with children—Ekman *et al.*, 1972—have shown that children's expression of emotional arousal or interest while viewing video violence was related to higher levels of aggression in subsequent play interactions.

There are three main areas of research into media:

1. The content of the mass media
2. The effects of the mass media
3. The process of media production

The edge television has over other media due to its multi-sensorial appeal and its ubiquitous existence has made researchers probe its mesmeric hold on people across the world—especially pre-teen children, considering their impressionable developmental stage.

In many Indian homes today, with both parents away at work, the urban, middle-class Indian is increasingly seeing children being brought up with television as the new baby-sitter; even when parents are at home, watching television is still the favoured family pastime.

A study has confirmed that kids who watch a lot of television are less likely to play imaginatively. It is also said that big-time viewing seems to sap energy that might otherwise be spent making up games and stories. Watching television is a passive event.

Children and adults remain completely immobile while viewing the idiot box. Most viewing experiences are both quiet and non-interactive. Children absorb millions of images from the television set in just one afternoon's viewing session. And what are they watching? If the child's television has access to cable, his choice can range from 10 to 70 different channels; all of them showing different programmes.

Before the age of eighteen, the average American teen will have witnessed eighteen thousand simulated murders on TV. While staggering in number, more disturbing is the effect this steady diet of imaginary violence may have on America's youth.

Watching television is one of a number of important factors affecting aggressive behaviour.

However, research indicates that the popularity of a TV show depends less on content and more on scheduling. As Gerbner points out, "... violence as such is not highly rated. That means it coasts on viewer inertia, not selection. Unlike other media use, viewing is a ritual; people watch by the clock and not by the program."

WASHINGTON—Two-thirds of parents said they are very concerned about sex and violence the nation's children are exposed to in the media, and there would be broad support for new federal limits on such material on television.

Today, in addition to entertaining and informing, television serves as background noise, as babysitter, as safe haven from mean streets, and as a way to avoid social interaction.

Researches warn that the risks of viewing the most common depiction of television violence includes learning to behave violently, becoming more de-sensitised to the harmful consequences of violence and becoming more fearful of being attacked.

Viewing a lot of violence on television does not necessarily cause a child to act more violently, but it can contribute to promoting a view that violence is common place in everyday life. It could also create a heightened fear of being assaulted on the street.

A moderate amount of television may be beneficial for young children, depending entirely on the type of programmes the child is watching and the kind of supervision it is getting from the parents. Quality television can teach children about the world around and the different people that they may not have access to by other means. There are quite a few interesting as well as informative programmes on history, literature, Nature, current affairs, art and culture of various countries and so on.

Well-guided television viewing also increases the general vocabulary of your child and provides opportunities for him to learn about various things, which help him in making choices regarding his areas of interest.

Television, when viewed selectively, along with parents can provide immense scope for learning. Channels like Animal Planet, Discovery Channel, Splash and others have interesting programmes which can be beneficial even for young children. Parents can discuss the subject with their children while they watch these programmes together so that the child finds it more interesting and learns better. When children watch television, they are not playing with shapes and blocks, or getting fresh air, or feeling the three-dimensional figures, or listening to the sounds of the neighborhood.

Kids need parents. They need your time and attention. They also need to interact with you and require that you read out to them. They need time to explore and have no time to be bored. The best way for kids to develop physically, mentally and emotionally is for a caring adult or sibling to hold them, talk to them, play with them, and provide a rich interactive experience.

Cultivating intelligent viewing implies that you encourage your child to carefully choose the programmes, restrict viewing time and help them to find fun things to do when the set is turned off.

American Studies

The first American studies, in the 1970s, revolved more around the notion of frustration. The theory was that the improvement of social conditions for the middle classes makes them more desirous than before of new consumer goods. The sheer volume of television advertising and its exhibition of desirable objects increases the frustration of dissatisfied consumers and, therefore, generates social violence (minor delinquency, theft). Accumulated frustration leads to an increasing number of individual acts—here it is not even necessary to consider if violent images have been screened. Later studies centred on the form of the aggressivity which precedes the actual expression of social violence.

Filming in a laboratory the excitement felt by an individual watching violent images does not allow the inference that in a real situation this stimulation would be transformed into violent behaviour against a third party. The same applies for the opposing hypothesis, that of catharsis. This model rests on the idea that viewing violent scenes releases built up frustration, thus reducing the temptations of violent behaviour and, because the tension has been relieved, leading to greater peaceful behaviour. Therefore, television, having a calming effect, leads to a reduction in social violence. Yet this model, first defended by Aristotle in order to explain the social role of Greek tragedies —first the examples of the public representation of very violent scenes—whilst being intellectually seductive, and verifiable in the laboratory, has never been confirmed on a macro-sociological level, in other words, in a real situation involving a large number of spectators.

Increased consumption of violence can have diametrically opposed effects. It can lead some viewers to have a skewed perception of reality and to overestimate the place of violence in society. They believe they are living in a universe of crime where criminals are waiting on every street corner, and accordingly adopt a security conscious state of mind—demands for the toughening of punitive judicial sentences, wishes for the strengthening of police infrastructure, desires for strong political government.

One type of study tries to show a link between heavy television consumption and the learning abilities of young people. Youths watching the most television are also those with the most educational failures, which it is argued leads to their having bad social etiquette, progressively internalised, leading to social disengagement and, therefore, to crime. If and when victimised they will be more inclined to imitate deviant models found on the television and to reassure themselves by following negative examples, those marginalised like themselves in the world of television.

The first debates on this tele-visual monster-making sprang up at the time of the Vietnam war when a sequence was sent around the world showing a young twelve-year old girl running along a road, naked and terrified, in order to escape aerial bombardment. In the 1970s it was Stanley Kubrickís film *Clockwork Orange*—for a long time banned from television screens in numerous countries—which raised questions concerning violence in works of fiction broadcast to the homes of people who hadn't taken the explicit step of going to the cinema to see the film. The debate again flared up with intensity, first in America and then in France, when Oliver Stoneís *Natural Born Killers* was considered responsible for the criminal behaviour of certain young people who had wanted to reproduce for real the murderous trajectory of the film's heroes.

A recent study carried out by American psychologists, who appeared in March 2002 in the prestigious journal *Science*, finally provided proof that consuming television is directly linked to the degree of young people's social aggressivity. The researchers followed 700 young adolescents for eighteen years. According to the inquiry, 5.7% of young people who spend less than an hour in front of the television had committed acts of violence, whilst 28.8% who watch more than three hours had carried out criminal acts. In the middle of those who watch between one and three hours, 22.5% found themselves in a similar situation. Laurent BËgue, a French psychologist, adds that 10% of this delinquent behaviour was directly linked to violence seen on the television or at the cinema.

A violent image has no value in itself, but only takes on meaning at its point of enunciation and consumption. If the violence seen is reframed by the family, and if the spectator's psychological state is positive, he will not give in to negative influences. It is not, therefore, a question of an effect which is inevitable, but of effects of identification which can be activated when the viewing environment is unfavourable.

One study stated the stress stimulated by the violent images is not inevitably transformed into traumatism. Children have a number of means of managing the stress of violent images: words—the violent images made them talk much more than the non-violent images; internal scenarios which consist of images that the children willingly talk about and through which they represent themselves in the same or similar situations—violent images bring about many more such scenarios than non-violent images; and finally non-verbal expressions in the mimicking of gestures—violent images lead to many more non-verbal expressions than non-violent images. The fact that these non-verbal expressions are always consistent with the language and the internal scenarios which the children evoke verbally shows that there exist three complementary methods at the children's disposal to manage the effects of stress and avoid them being transformed into traumatism: words, images and sensory-motor expressions. The stress caused by the violent images also leads to a greater development of hard mentality on the part of the children: the children who had seen the violent images more easily gave up their individual characteristics and were quicker to align themselves with the decisions of the group, and notably those of their leader.

The book 'Moving Images: Understanding Children's Emotional Responses to Television' by David Buckingham on the basis of his research on children stated that children were often upset by factual and news programmes, and did not seem to be desensitised to real-life violence by the fictional violence they had seen. He also found that children did not identify with the 'perpetrators of violence'— their emotional responses related to a 'fear of victimisation'. They developed coping strategies for dealing with material that they found difficult.

People also react to cinematic violence according to the film's genre. Audiences find some representations of violence more upsetting than others. Cartoons, comedy, westerns, science fiction and war films were ranked low, whilst more realistic genres like crime dramas were seen as more alarming.

'Modality'

Researchers have identified the idea of 'modality'. This means the judgements people make about how close to reality a media product is. For example, science fiction or spy thrillers are very clearly perceived as fantasy, whilst crime dramas might be seen as 'more real', though in fact both are fictions constructed according to certain conventions. The conventions of different genres are also clearly understood by audiences.

Does TV affect child aspirations?

'Centre for Advocacy and Research', a Delhi-based media research organisation in Delhi recently undertook an interesting quantitative survey in the national capital to probe the media habits and activities of children in difficult circumstances.

What children aspire for depends largely on what they derive from their environment. Media, in turn, is known for its crucial role in justifying these aspirations. It is widely believed that children in difficult circumstances draw excessively on the media, thereby deriving unrealistic aspirations for themselves.

Observations also revealed that a child could have both realistic, as well as overly ambitious aspirations. Many aspired a realistic job, yet also wished to be rich and famous and several of them did not find any conflict between these two aspirations.

Television has become a part of a child's life today. The amount of time spent in front of it is indicative of how gratifying television can be for the child and how easily it influences his aspirations.

Easy routines, no muss, no fuss

An interesting report on the eating habits of 91 families in neighbourhoods around Washington DC, USA, has revealed a significant set of findings: children belonging to families that watch TV regularly during mealtimes go more for pizza, snack foods and soft drinks laced with caffeine, and less for fruits and vegetables. The study also reveals that television mealtime habits are found more in families with less educated mothers.

Socialisation and TV Research

Most of the research carried in the specific area of television viewing and the socialisation of young children shows that children socially benefit from watching educational programming, as well as perhaps suffering from watching violent programming—Anderson 2001: 132. Significantly, these research studies stress the theory that it is not television as a medium that has an influence in children's socialisation, but rather the content of the programming they watch, their active engagement while they watch it and other external issues such as whom they watch television with.

Firstly, what is socialisation? In the given context, DeFleur defines socialisation as a complex, long-term, and multidimensional set of communicative exchanges between individuals and various agents of society that result in the individual's preparation for life in a socio-cultural environment —DeFleur1989: 209. This preparation or induction to social life takes place in the infancy of the individual and derives from different agencies that converge in the child's reasoning, perception and interaction with the surrounding world. These agencies alternate between the parents, family and social groups sphere on one side, to the child's exposure to media on the other.

However, the approaches to socialisation vary from the anthropological point of view to the more Freudian one. The first refers to the process as *enculturation* which consists in the individual's internalisation of 'all aspects of their culture' – DeFleur & Ball-Rokeach 1989: 209—such as traditions, language and common discourses. The media has its importance in this view, for it can teach the child about the nature of his or her social order—*ibid.* On the other hand, psychologists see socialisation as an inner process that one must acquire in order to control inborn drives that 'would lead to socially unacceptable behaviour'—*ibid.* The role of the media in this case can be considered as highly important, for the negative aspects that explicit exposition of adult issues can cause in the child's future development.

Cultivation theory and socialisation

For cultivation theorists, the heavy consumption of media in general and television in particular "leads to the adoption of beliefs about the nature of the social world which conform to the stereotyped, distorted and very selective view of reality as portrayed in a systematic way in television fiction and news" – McQuail 2000: 465. Furthermore, cultivation theorists argue that television has long-term effects, which are 'small, gradual, indirect but cumulative and significant'. Theorists distinguish between 'first order' effects—general beliefs about the everyday world, such as about the prevalence of violence—and 'second order' effects—specific attitudes, such as to law and order or to personal safety—Chandler 1997.

However, there are other theoretical considerations, criticisms and assumptions that arise from the cultivation theory, and which are mainly addressed in the work of Huston and Wright—in MacBeth 1996:38. Cultivation theory needs to rely on other approaches such as the influence of the family, the child's cognitive development, the amount and most importantly the type of television the child views... to fully understand the socialisation development of the subject. Therefore, many different levels of analysis— sociocultural, social institutions, family, and individual—*ibid*: 44—take place along the utilisation of the cultivation theory. Furthermore, other theorists reject the use of these 'intervening variables'—Buckingham 1993:15—in favour of the cognitive capabilities of children, in relation to what has been cautiously noted as 'television literacy'. As children do not submit passively against the fictional—or real—representations seen on television, they process that information and make sense of it on one way or another. Further studies on television literacy link television viewing with academic performance of the viewer and other social habits—see Neuman 1991. This theory concludes that in some cases television viewing acts as a replacement to other activities, while in other cases television acts as an aid to the personal development of the child—Newman 1991:110.

Social Organisation Theory

The other major theory in the study of television as a main agency of socialisation is social organisation theory. As a social group develops through the interaction and socialisation of its members, a series of events are repeated and transmitted from generation to generation. Those events, which can be divided into norms, rules, ranking and sanctions, are the driving motives for the actions of each individual within the social group. Therefore, before the individual takes the initiative towards an action, he or she will be comparing his or her actions to the ones of the fellow members of the group. This equilibrium through the mere imitation of actions is, in very broad terms, the basis of any given social group. Each member of the family has a determined social niche. This is, each member has a role with its significant levels of discourse in accordance to the other members of the group—father, mother, son—working in what DeFleur and Ball-Rokeach call 'a set of specialised and interdependent roles, like the parts of a machine or an organic system'—DeFleur & Ball-Rokeach 1989: 222. Eventually, one piece of that system will replace the other but in the meantime each individual must hold to his or her determined position in the group, just expecting to step further in this invisible hierarchy of the society. The way in which this theory is linked to media studies, television viewing and socialisation is through the proposition that television conveys information regarding rules of social conduct that the individual remembers and that directly shapes overt behaviour—*Ibid*: 225. It has been proved that young viewers internalise norms, role definitions and other understandings of social organisation from what they see on TV screens and mainly thorugh the representation of stereotypes of recognisable portrayals of stable patterns of group life *ibid*: 224.

Cultivation Theory

Cultivation theory—sometimes referred to as the cultivation hypothesis or cultivation analysis—was an approach developed by Professor George Gerbner, dean of the Annenberg School of Communications at the University of Pennsylvania. He began the 'Cultural Indicators' research project in the mid-1960s, to study whether and how watching television may influence viewers' ideas of what the everyday world is like. Cultivation research is in 'effects' tradition. Cultivation theorists argue that television has long-term effects which are small, gradual, indirect but cumulative and significant.

They emphasise the effects of television viewing on the attitudes rather than the behaviour of viewers. Heavy watching of television is seen as 'cultivating' attitudes which are more consistent with the world of television programmes than with the everyday world. Watching television may tend to induce a general mindset about violence in the world, quite apart from any effects it might have in inducing violent behaviour. Cultivation theorists distinguish between 'first order' effects—general beliefs about the everyday world, such as about the prevalence of violence—and 'second order' effects—specific attitudes, such as to law and order or to personal safety.

Gerbner argues that the mass media cultivate attitudes and values which are already present in a culture: the media maintain and propagate these values amongst members of a culture, thus binding it together. He has argued that television tends to cultivate middle-of-the-road political perspectives. And Gross considered that 'television is a cultural arm of the established industrial order and as such serves primarily to maintain, stabilise and reinforce rather than to alter, threaten or weaken conventional beliefs and behaviours'—1977, in Boyd-Barrett & Braham 1987, p. 100. Such a function is conservative, but heavy viewers tend to regard themselves as 'moderate'.

Cultivation research looks at the mass media as a socialising agent and investigates whether television viewers come to believe the television version of reality the more they watch it. Gerbner and his colleagues contend that television drama has a small but significant influence on the attitudes, beliefs and judgements of viewers concerning the social world. The focus is on 'heavy viewers'. People who watch a lot of television are likely to be more influenced by the ways in which the world is framed by television programmes than are individuals who watch less, especially regarding topics of which the viewer has little first-hand experience. Light viewers may have more sources of information than heavy viewers. Judith van Evra argues that by virtue of inexperience, young viewers may depend on television for information more than other viewers do (van Evra 1990, p. 167), although Hawkins and Pingree argue that some children may not experience a cultivation effect at all where they do not understand motives or consequences (cited by van Evra, *ibid.*). It may be that lone viewers are more open to a cultivation effect than those who view with others (van Evra 1990, p. 171).

Television is seen by Gerbner as dominating our 'symbolic environment'. As McQuail and Windahl note, cultivation theory presents television as 'not a window on or reflection of the world, but a world in itself' (1993, p. 100). Gerbner argued that the over-representation of violence on television constitutes a symbolic message about law and order rather than a simple cause of more aggressive behaviour by viewers (as Bandura argued). For instance, the action-adventure genre acts to reinforce a faith in law and order, the *status quo* and social justice—baddies usually get their just dessert.

Since 1967, Gerbner and his colleagues have been analysing sample weeks of prime-time and daytime television programming. Cultivation analysis usually involves the correlation of data from content analysis—identifying prevailing images on television—with survey data from audience research to assess any influence of such images on the attitudes of viewers. Content analysis by cultivation theorists seeks to characterise 'the TV world'. Such analysis shows not only that the TV world is far more violent than the everyday world, but also, for instance, that television is dominated by males and over-represents the professions and those involved in law enforcement.

Audience research by cultivation theorists involves asking large-scale public opinion poll organisations to include in their national surveys questions regarding such issues as the amount of violence in everyday life. Answers are interpreted as reflecting either the world of television or that of everyday life. Respondents are asked such questions as: 'What percentage of all males who have jobs work in law enforcement or crime detection? Is it 1 percent or 10 percent?'. On American TV, about 12 percent of all male characters hold such jobs, and about 1 percent of males are employed in the USA in these jobs, so 10 percent would be the 'TV answer' and 1 percent would be the 'real-world answer'—Dominick 1990, p. 512.

Answers are then related to the amount of television watched, other media habits and demographic data such as sex, age, income and education. The cultivation hypothesis involves predicting or expecting heavy television viewers to give more TV answers than light viewers. The responses of a large number of heavy viewers are compared with those of light viewers. A tendency of heavy viewers to choose TV answers is interpreted as evidence of a cultivation effect.

Cultivation theorists are best known for their study of television and viewers, and in particular for a focus on the topic of violence.

Cultivation theorists argue that heavy viewing leads viewers —even among high educational/high income groups—to have more homogeneous or convergent opinions than light viewers —who tend to have more heterogeneous or divergent opinions.The cultivation effect of television viewing is one of 'levelling' or 'homogenising' opinion. Gerbner and his associates argue that heavy viewers of violence on television come to believe that the incidence of violence in the everyday world is higher than do light viewers of similar backgrounds. They refer to this as a mainstreaming effect.

Misjudging the amount of violence in society is sometimes called the 'mean world syndrome'. Heavy viewers tend to believe that the world is a nastier place than do light viewers. Since on television women are most likely to be victims of crime, women heavy viewers are influenced by the usual heavy viewer mainstreaming effect but are also led to feel especially fearful for themselves as women. The cultivation effect is also argued to be strongest when the viewer's neighborhood is similar to that shown on television. Crime on television is largely urban, so urban heavy viewers are subject to a double dose, and cultivation theorists argue that violent content 'resonates' more for them. The strongest effects of heavy viewing on attitudes to violence are likely to be amongst those in the high crime areas of cities.

Cultivation theorists tend to ignore the importance of the social dynamics of television use. Interacting factors such as developmental stages, viewing experience, general knowledge, gender, ethnicity, viewing contexts, family attitudes and socio-economic background all contribute to shaping the ways in which television is interpreted by viewers.

Media Violence and Children—1993-2000

2000

Sex, Violence and Foul Language on Prime Time Television, 1989 vs. 1999.

The following information is from a comparative study by the Parents Television Council on the increasing prevalence of sex, violence, and foul language in prime time programming in 1989 and 1999. The study concentrates on programming from the first four weeks of the 1989-1990 and 1999-2000 television seasons.

In terms of sexual and violent material and coarse language combined, the per-hour rate almost tripled from '89 to '99.

On a per-hour basis, sexual content more than tripled from '89 to '99.

Overall, material in the sexual subcategories was more than seven times as frequent in '99. The most dramatic increase was in homosexual references, which were more than twenty-four times as common.

Foul language was more than five and a half times as frequent in '99, and the curse words used were, as a group, far harsher in '99 than in '89.

The rate of violent content remained almost unchanged from '89 to '99.

Though still rare in absolute terms, instances where sex was mixed with violence or was graphically depicted went up significantly in percentage terms

One show, UPN's WWF Smackdown!—was responsible for more than 11 per cent of all the combined sex, cursing, and violence in 1999.

Violence in Popular Culture—U.S.

The following information is from *Merchandising Mayhem*, part of a three-part study by the Center for Media and Public Affairs. *Merchandising Mayhem* focuses on the appearance of violence in broadcast and cable TV programs, TV movies, music videos, and Hollywood films. In all, the study examines 573 popular culture products. For the purposes of the study, the definition of violence was as follows: "Any deliberate act of physical force or use of a weapon in an attempt to achieve a goal, further a cause, stop the action of another, act out an angry impulse, defend oneself from attack, secure material reward or merely to intimidate others." Only violence that was shown on-screen or whose immediate aftermath was seen on-screen was coded; discussions or descriptions of violence were not coded.

In broadcast television series, a total of 3,381 acts of violence were identified within 284 series episodes—broadcast, cable, and premium cable TV. Over half of these acts—1,754—could be described as serious violence. Fully 80 per cent of the total violence recorded in the study occurred on broadcast TV.

CBS had nearly five times as much violence in its programming—635 acts total—as the much-criticised Fox network—only 137 acts total:

- Cable networks had noticeably less violence than did broadcast networks. The most violent cable network, USA, had the same number of acts—112—as the least violent broadcast network, ABC

Among the most violent TV series were *Walker, Texas Ranger*—CBS—with 112 violent acts per episode, and HBO's *Oz*, with 76 violent acts per episode. Also particularly violent was *Buffy, the Vampire Slayer*—59 acts per episode—which is featured on YTV and has a large teen and preteen following.

- In most TV series, the violence depicted shows no physical harm—75 per cent—no psychological trauma —90 per cent and no judgment about the morality of the act-87 per cent. Positive and negative motives for violent actions were roughly equal—45 and 55 per cent, respectively. "Good guys" were slightly more likely than "bad guys" to be the instigators of violent activities—46 per cent vs. 41 per cent.
- The total number of violent acts in the movies studied totaled 2,319, with about three-fifths of those qualifying as serious acts of violence. Overall, movies averaged about 46 violent acts per film.
- The most violent film studied, the Second World War drama *Saving Private Ryan*, accounted for 30 per cent of all the serious incidents noted in the study of movies. Of the film's 275 violent acts, almost all were serious —262. However, it should be noted that the film's emphasis was on accurately depicting the atrocities of

war. By contrast, the next most violent film, at 147 acts, was *The Mask of Zorro*, based on a popular 1950's TV series, and aimed at a 'family' audience.

In 188 different music videos, 1,785 separate acts of violence were depicted, nearly one-third of them being serious in nature. However, much of the violence observed was concentrated in relatively few videos. The ten most violent music videos accounted for half of all violence shown within the study sample. The Beastie Boys' *Body Movin'* was the most violent video, with 21 acts of violence.

Baseball and Violent TV—U.S.

According to a study by Minnesota family physician Charles Anderson, annual US baseball championships have become interspersed with TV commercials containing violence.

- Out of 1,550 commercials in 15 playoff and championship games in 1998, 137 contained what he regarded as violence, such as use of a gun and displays of blood.
- Most of the violent ads were promoting TV programs and big-screen movies.

"It continues to be counterintuitive to find such commercials in family-oriented programming and makes it difficult for parents to avoid exposing their children to this form of violence," he said. His study, based on monitoring of network commercials during the Major League playoff and World Series games of 1996 and 1998, is published in the October issue of "Pediatrics", the journal of the American Academy of Pediatrics.

Source: Media Central, October 2, 2000.

Prime-Time Violence—U.S.

- A 32-month study of television violence, commissioned by the National Cable Television Association, found that the level of violent programming stayed about the same for the duration of the study – about 61 per cent.

- The three-year study found that the number of prime-time shows containing violent scenes rose from slightly over half in October 1994, to about two-thirds in June 1997.
- Ninety-two per cent of programs aired by pay cable networks contained violent content.
- Nearly 40 per cent of violent incidents are initiated by "good" characters. The negative consequences, meanwhile, are shown in only 15 per cent of programs.

Source: Study Finds More Violence in Prime-Time TV Shows, CNN Interactive, Apr. 16, 1998.

Violence on U.S. Cable Television

The 1996 U.S. National Television Violence Study reported that 90 per cent of theatrical movies shown on television include violence. Movies are more likely to include blood in violent scenes than any other program type.

Violence is found most frequently on subscription television —85 per cent on premium cable, and 59 per cent on basic cable, followed by 44 per cent on independent broadcast networks. The figure for PBS was 18 per cent.

Eighty-four per cent of violent scenes do not depict any long-term consequences. Perpetrators go unpunished in 73 per cent of violent scenes. By the end of the program, bad characters are punished 62 per cent of the time, but good characters only 15 per cent.

Of the scenes surveyed, 47 per cent of all violent interactions showed no resulting harm to the victims, and 58 per cent depicted no pain.

About 67 per cent of the programs depict violence in a humorous context.

The study on violence found that 76 per cent of typical violent perpetrators are adults, 78 per cent male, and 76 per cent white.

Twenty-five per cent of the violent interactions on television involve the use of a handgun.

Source: National Television Violence Study, produced by Mediascope, February 1996.

Effects of Television Viewing on Children

A Canadian study reports that television violence affects children of varying ages differently:

- As toddlers, children will mimic what they see and hear on television. A number of preschoolers pay greater attention to the TV than toddlers, though most preschoolers can't tell the difference between fantasy and reality—and may not distinguish between commercials and programs.
- Once children reach elementary school age, they begin to stay up late and watch more adult programs.
- Teens prefer adult programs that deal with subjects like growing up, dating, alcohol, drugs and sex. Horror movies, music videos, and X-rated films are also popular with teens. These programs often contain violent pornographic images and scenes of abuse against women. Research has shown that these shows can convey to boys the message that violence against women is OK, and can make teenage girls more afraid.

Source: Television Violence: A Review of the Effects on Children of Different Ages, by Wendy L. Josephson, Ph.D., 1995.

Researchers have identified three potential responses to media violence in children:

- Increased fear—also known as the "mean and scary world" syndrome:

Children, particularly girls, are much more likely than adults to be portrayed as victims of violence on TV, and this can make them more afraid of the world around them.

- Desensitisation to real-life violence:

Some of the most violent TV shows are children's cartoons, in which violence is portrayed as humorous—and realistic consequences of violence are seldom shown.

- Increased aggressive behaviour:

This can be especially true of young children, who are more likely to exhibit aggressive behaviour after viewing violent TV shows or movies.

TV viewing is a sedentary activity, and has been proven to be a significant factor in childhood obesity.

A *Scientific American* article entitled "Television Addiction" examined why children and adults may find it hard to turn their TVs off. According to researchers, viewers feel an instant sense of relaxation when they start to watch TV—but that feeling disappears just as quickly when the box is turned off. While people generally feel more energised after playing sports or engaging in hobbies, after watching TV they usually feel depleted of energy. According to the article, "This is the irony of TV: people watch a great deal longer than they plan to, even though prolonged viewing is less rewarding."

The makers of TV shows follow guidelines that protect kids under twelve from too much TV violence. These guidelines are based on research gathered by experts who have studied children. According to the experts, a child can't tell the difference between real and make-believe until they're around five years old. By the time a kid is eight years old, however, they no longer believe everything they see and hear.

Public Opinion on TV Violence—U.S.

- About 82 per cent of the American public considers movies too violent, 72 per cent finds that entertainment television has too much violence, and 57 per cent thinks television news gives too much attention to stories about violent crime.
- Eighty per cent of Americans think that television violence is "harmful" to society. The number who think it is "very harmful" increased from 26 per cent in 1983 to 47 per cent in 1993.
- Of those surveyed, 53 per cent of Americans believe that viewing portrayals of violence in television, film, books and newspaper stories make people more likely to "do something violent".
- Half of those polled who had children aged 8 to 13 said they have turned the TV off or changed the channel to prevent a child from seeing something on the news.
- Twice as many people are upset about the level of violence in entertainment as are upset about other aspects such as sex, bad language, drugs, crime or nudity.

Source: American Public Opinion on Media Violence, produced by Mediascope, June 1993.

Media violence is notoriously hard to define and measure. Some experts who track violence in television programming, such as George Gerbner of Temple University, define violence as the act (or threat) of injuring or killing someone, independent of the method used or the surrounding context.

VIOLENCE AND CASE HISTORY

Violence and Television: A History

In 1977 Ronny Zamora, a fifteen-year-old, shot and killed the eighty-two-year-old woman who lived next door to him in Florida. Not guilty, pleaded his lawyer, Ellis Rubin, by reason of the boy's having watched too much television. From watching television Ronny had become dangerously inured to violence. Suffering from what Rubin called "television intoxication," he could no longer tell right from wrong. "If you judge Ronny Zamora guilty," Rubin argued, "television will be an accessory." The jury demurred: Ronny was convicted of first-degree murder.

The latest burst of activity around the issue of television violence, culminating in the legislating of the V-chip, can be traced to a night in the mid-1980s when a weary Senator Paul Simon, of Illinois, lying in his motel bed, flipped on the television and saw, in graphic detail, a man being sliced in half with a chain saw—a victim—Simon's staff later surmised, of Colombian drug dealers in Scarface. Appalled that there was nothing to prevent a child from witnessing such grisliness, Simon urged the passage of a law reducing gore on television.

What matters is not so much the raw fact that a violent act is committed on television but who does what to whom.

The result, the 1990 Television Violence Act, was a compromise between the broadcasting industry and those who, like Simon, wanted somehow to reduce the violence on shows that children might be watching. Ordinarily, antitrust laws prohibit broadcast networks from collaborating, but Simon's proposal gave the networks a three-year exemption from the laws so that they could jointly work out a policy to curb violence. Though Simon hailed the announcement of the networks (except Fox), in December of 1992, of a set of guidelines governing television violence, this basically toothless bit of legislation had little effect until it was about to expire, at which point network executives promised that they would place parental advisories at the beginning of violent programs—"Due to violent content, parental discretion is advised". When the act expired, in December of 1993, television was as violent as ever.

After the Television Violence Act expired, Representative Edward J. Markey, of Massachusetts, introduced legislation requiring manufacturers to install the V-chip in all U.S. television sets. President Bill Clinton extolled the V-chip in his State of the Union Address last year, and then signed its use into law as part of the mammoth 1996 elecommunications Act. As of February of next year all new television sets—Americans buy 24 million of them a year—must have the chip. Meanwhile, the broadcasting industry has established a rating system to be employed in conjunction with the chip, age-based like the system used by the Motion Picture Association of America.

• • •

which point network executives promised that they would place parental advisories at the beginning of violent programs—"The following program contains [illegible] parental discretion is advised." When the [illegible] reported in December [illegible] advisories [illegible] however.

After the [illegible] Representatives [illegible]

[illegible]

9

ROLE OF JOURNALIST

To be a reporter today and try to disentangle the story from the facts is to peer into a hall of mirrors. A journalist is a person who practises journalism, the gathering and dissemination of information about current events, trends, issues and people.

Reporters are one type of journalist. They create reports as a profession for broadcast or publication in mass media such as newspapers, television, radio, magazines, documentary film, and the Internet. Reporters find the sources for their work, their reports can be either spoken or written, and they are generally expected to report in the most objective and unbiased way to serve the public good.

Depending on the context, the term *journalist* also includes various types of editors and visual journalists, such as photographers, graphic artists, and page designers.

According to Dan Schiller—1979—objectivity also helped commercial newspapers legitimate their function as watchdogs of the public good. While allowing journalists to be independent from the self-interests of business and politicians, objectivity has also come under attack for thwarting the autonomy of journalism—a critique attached to professionalism itself. While some envision professionalism as the opposite of bias, others charge professionalism with serving as a method of control by management over reporters and editors—a co-opting of labour unrest—that ultimately standardises news content and protects the status quo. In this view, Douglas Birkhead—1984—argues that the professionalisation of journalism is so opposed to independence in favour of business interests as to be "a perversion of the ideal".

Media as a powerful tool

The media is a very powerful tool and the media needs to accept responsibility for the stories they write. Society needs good journalists who will do their research and write stories that will educate and inform society.

Investigative journalism is a kind of journalism in which reporters deeply investigate a topic of interest, often involving crime, political corruption, or some other scandal.

De Burgh—2000—states: "An investigative journalist is a man or woman whose profession it is to discover the truth and to identify lapses from it in whatever media may be available. The act of doing this generally is called investigative journalism and is distinct from apparently similar work done by police, lawyers, auditors and regulatory bodies in that it is not limited as to target, not legally founded and closely connected to publicity."

Only in the twentieth century did journalism attain the status of a profession, with professional schools, organisations, honours, norms, and the means of disciplining transgressors. Early conceptions of the journalist as an objective conduit of facts about the world have given way to more complex models of journalism in which the role of institutional imperatives and individual biases are recognised as highly influential, if not decisive, factors shaping the content of news—Bennett; McManus; Winch.

Various elements of the criminal justice system are among those most likely to influence journalism. Public interest in crime news is generally high, so there is a commercial incentive for newspapers and broadcasters to provide such information. Crimes are usually good stories; they can be told as morality plays, dramatic confrontations, and human-interest stories even when their value as hard news is not high. Demand for crime news produces close relationships between police, judicial officers, and reporters. The information resources controlled by police, such as the identity of suspects, the status of cases, and the evidence assembled, are highly prized by reporters. Attorneys and—less frequently—judges may offer valuable information about ongoing—and even long-past—trials. Reporters do their best to cultivate close and reliable relations with the police, the courts, and the prosecuting attorneys on their beats. If a reporter is not on good terms with these people, he or she risks losing information necessary to tell a coherent or interesting story. A reporter may not be alerted to new discoveries of evidence, new legal strategies, or impending changes in the dates and times of public hearings. Often there is no source of this information other than the police, courts, and prosecutors.

Reporters control resources of their own, prized by the criminal justice system. The threat of adverse publicity can be potent, especially for elected officers of the court and—in some jurisdictions—police chiefs or sheriffs. Truly virulent public attacks on the police or the judiciary are rare, however, since the relationship between journalists and these institutions is ongoing and valuable; no newspaper or broadcast outlet can afford to burn such bridges. Apart from publicity, journalists can enhance the overall legitimacy of the justice system by covering its activities. Public confidence that the police are behaving appropriately or that the judicial system "works" can be maintained simply through routine coverage of crime. Stories that challenge that confidence may be presented as aberrations from an otherwise upbeat routine.

Pritchard and Hughes demonstrate the practical result of these dependency relations. They studied the newspaper coverage of a year's worth of homicides in Milwaukee, Wisconsin, with attention to the factors that determine whether a murder will merit coverage or not. They found that "reporters tended to take cues for evaluations of newsworthiness from race, gender, and age"—p. 52—, information about both victims and suspects usually available from official sources. Deadline pressure seems to encourage reporters and editors to use such attributes to calculate the extent and nature of "deviance" the murder involves. While conventional wisdom describes newsworthiness in terms of "statistical deviance" —i.e., departure from the usual, as in "man bites dog"—Pritchard and Hughes show that "status deviance"—i.e., the death or suspect-status of high status citizens—and cultural deviance—i.e., murder of the "especially vulnerable," such as women, children, and the aged—explains the decision to cover or ignore a homicide—p. 52.

Pritchard had earlier—1986—demonstrated that coverage of homicides in Milwaukee was a strong predictor of whether or not the prosecuting attorney would plea—bargain the case. Murders that received more coverage in the newspapers were less likely to be bargained than low-publicity crimes. Pritchard notes that this finding is consistent with earlier research—Alschuler; Jones— regarding the decision-making of prosecutors that indicated that political considerations—e.g., fear of being seen as "soft on crime"—exercised strong influence on prosecutors' decisions. Further, Pritchard, Dilts, and Berkowitz demonstrated that prosecution of pornography offenses in Indiana in the mid-1980s was influenced by the relative priority of pornography on the agendas of citizens and of the local newspapers.

The cumulative impact of Pritchard and others' work is to illustrate that reporters and editors are most likely to report crimes based on certain attributes of the victims and suspects, and that prosecutors monitor press coverage and choose which crimes to prosecute aggressively based in part on the level of press attention the crime has received. Since the criteria of reporters tend toward coverage of white victims and victims who are either female, very young, or very old—or some combination of those attributes—the least likely crime to be covered is one in which the victim is a black adult male. Thus the least likely crime to be aggressively prosecuted is one committed against a black adult male.

Defendants and defense attorneys are less likely to benefit from these relations of dependency. A guilty criminal defendant has no interest in sharing details of a crime, of course, and innocent defendants have no details to offer. Even if defendants do have valuable information, they are unlikely to have valuable information on a regular basis for years to come, the way police and judicial officers do. Defense attorneys are a bit more likely to be valuable sources in the future, but not nearly as likely as prosecutors. There is much more crime in the world than there is coverage of it, so most defense attorneys most times will not be defending newsworthy clients. But *all* newsworthy prosecutions are performed by a handful of offices, from city attorneys to federal prosecutors. Given a choice between developing close, mutually rewarding relationships with defendants or prosecutors, a working reporter knows where his or her professional future is most safely insured. Robert Shapiro, a prominent defense attorney—and member of O.J. Simpson's "Dream Team"— noted that "[t]he defense lawyer who has never dealt with the press, or has no pre-existing relationship with a particular reporter, is at a severe disadvantage.

In order to overcome this, the lawyer must cultivate a line of communication with the reporter so that the client's point of view can be expressed in the most favourable way"—p. 27.

Many serious crime investigations attract substantial amounts of press interest. If effectively managed, the media can make a significant contribution to investigations by acting as a conduit for information from the general public. Every investigator can recall instances where the press has contributed the vital lead which unlocks an enquiry. The media spotlight can, however, also place major resource demands on investigations at the critical early stage of an enquiry; and in a wider sense, the media play an important role in shaping the public's views of crime, the police service, and the wider criminal justice system. They can drive the fear of crime.

Media management and public relations is very professional

The impacts of public relations cannot be underestimated. In the commercial world, marketing and advertising are typically needed to make people aware of products. There are many issues in that area alone—which is looked at in this site's section on corporate media. When it comes to propaganda for purposes of war, for example, professional public relations firms can often be involved to help sell a war. In cases where a war is questionable, the PR firms are indirectly contributing to the eventual and therefore unavoidable casualties. Media management may also be used to promote certain political policies and ideologies. Where this is problematic for the citizenry is when media reports on various issues do not attribute their sources properly.

Some techniques used by governments and parties/people with hidden agendas include:

- Paying journalists to promote certain issues without the journalist acknowledging this, or without the media mentioning the sources.

- Governments and individuals contracting PR firms to sell a war, or other important issues
- Disinformation or partial information reported as news or fact without attributing sources that might be questionable.
- PR firms feeding stories to the press without revealing the nature of the information with the intention of creating a public opinion—for example, to support a war, as the previous link highlights where even human rights groups fell for some of the disinformation, thus creating an even more effective propaganda campaign.

GUIDING PRINCIPLES FOR THE JOURNALIST

There are three guiding principles for journalists that are particularly applicable to their coverage of crime and victimisation (Black, Steele, and Barney 1995).

1. *Seek truth and report it as fully as possible.*

- Inform yourself continuously so you in turn can inform, engage, and educate the public in a clear and compelling way on significant issues.
- Be honest, fair, and courageous in gathering, reporting, and interpreting accurate information.
- Give voice to the voiceless.
- Hold the powerful accountable.

2. *Act independently.*

- Guard vigorously the essential stewardship role a free press plays in an open society.
- Seek out and disseminate competing perspectives without being unduly influenced by those who would use their power or position to counter the public interest.

- Remain free of associations and activities that may compromise your integrity or damage your credibility.
- Recognise that good ethical, decisions require individual responsibility enriched by collaborative efforts.

3. *Minimise harm.*

- Be compassionate toward those affected by your actions.
- Treat sources, subjects, and colleagues as human beings deserving of respect, not merely as means to your journalistic ends.
- Recognise that gathering and reporting information may cause harm or discomfort but balance those negatives by choosing alternatives that maximise your goal of truth telling.

It has often been said that journalism's role is to afflict the comfortable and comfort the afflicted. Sadly, too many media owners—many of whom have great power—see the role of the media differently: they believe the role of the media is to comfort the comfortable and ignore the afflicted.

One [journalist] commented to us that news reporters were effectively told not to focus on explanation, but to go for eye-catching events like fighting, shooting or riots. As he put it, they had been stopped from doing "explainers"—now it was "all bang, bang stuff".

—*Professor Greg Philo,* An unseen world: how the media portrays the poor, *The Courier, UNESCO, November 2001*

A commentary from Sandy Landau also agrees with the above, saying that the mainstream media often provides world news in the form of "shotgun pellets". That is, there are quick bursts of world news, but often only on certain types of issues such as dramatic disasters, and often without context making it incomplete.

As a matter of fact, the question of the use of images of violence or violent images can be asked in the same terms as the question about the use of any image on television. The journalist needs to answer a few simple questions: how does this scene allow me to illustrate, to show or to demonstrate the given subject? In which way does it add to the information? The journalist is not on his own while performing this evaluation. Television is still based on teamwork: during the shooting of the scene, the reporter can talk about it with his operator; if the images have been sent from abroad, he can talk with his colleagues from the international affairs service; lastly, in nearly all cases, images are edited and, therefore, they are seen and evaluated by another professional.

The selection is based firstly, on the importance of the piece of information, its significance, the contribution of the violent image to the understanding of this piece of information, its informative efficiency. If the first criterion was respected, the—sometimes traumatising—images of accidents, news items etc, which fundamentally do not benefit the viewer, are not broadcasted. The second criterion does not depend only on the sensitivity of the journalist or his colleagues. It depends also on the evolution of the medium. At the time of reality television, with its excesses, violence, voyeurism, and exhibitionism, the viewer's threshold of tolerance, and even maybe, of perception, has probably changed. They are certainly less sensitive to images of violence and even to violent images than they used to be. It is, therefore, tempting to think that we can do more than before.

The real danger is elsewhere, though. It lies in the often blinding quality of the strong image. There is also this impossibility of the reporter to explain the strong image, once it has been used. When he uses strong images—especially violent ones—the TV journalist does his job: he informs using the image. But quite often, the images are not put into perspective and they are not explained. Today, even more than yesterday, we need to be fast, the subjects have to be short, and few programmes devote more than one slot to a problem. Moreover, there are not many who, after having broadcast strong or violent images on a topic, give themselves the time to go beyond the images. The danger of the strong image and, therefore, of the violent image is that it conceals the information that it theoretically should support and that it provokes the confusion between the document and the information, between emotions and reporting. It is clear that this danger sends us to the limits of the medium itself, of this extraordinary tool of knowledge and information and which is often used today to serve purely commercial purposes.

The presence of journalist and crew may sometimes trigger the explosion of violence. Determined groups, whose aggressiveness lies dormant like an apparently sleeping volcano, may become active when they appear. There have been many times have demonstrators turned into rioters when camera appeared? The phenomenon of television as mirror may explain this attitude. These groups need to be seen, recognised, to give meaning to their behaviour. Even if they absurdly risk being identified and prosecuted; this is the reason why we try so hard to anticipate, to reduce, and even to eliminate the danger of becoming involved in incidents. Every reporter and camera operator is made aware of the measures to adopt to avoid affecting the situation. First, in the case of a confrontation between the young and the police, journalists are taught to take the time to evaluate the situation before unpacking the camera. It is unthinkable to turn up without preparation at any more or less aggressive gathering. Then the journalist needs to be certain that the fact does indeed require coverage in our news programmes. Sometimes, journalist drives around in an unmarked vehicle to take the measure of the situation. TV crews often play the role of catalysts of emotions, be they aggressiveness, joy or pride.

Some elements that would explain the change of the relationship to violence along with other current tendencies in the media—the first element is the role of economic considerations. In a democracy, the journalist is under a double constraint: the respect of his mission to exercise freedom of expression in the name of the public and the profitability of the company that he or she works for. Public service would traditionally create a space devoid of competition. The decision regarding which violent images go on air is determined by two elements. On the one hand, the feelings brought up by these images are a factor in attracting the viewer and take part in the process of generating good ratings. On the other hand, the ethical limit that the journalist uses in his or her judgment is influenced by what the journalists belonging to other channels do. In this respect, the deontological initiatives of some channels, which defined internal codes specifying what may be and may not be broadcast, are outflanked by the practices of the competitors. If a given image was broadcast by another channel without reaction or sanction, the limit is implicitly pushed out and further away. The production and circulation of images from armed conflicts and, even more often, from news items, increases the stock of violent images. From an information point of view, the value of these images is extremely negligible, which indicates that they are shown only for their sensationalistic qualities. Violence in television has no value in itself, in what it says about the world, but in its morbid power to fascinate as a spectacle.

Factors such as camera angles, the type of shot, including use of close-ups, plus the sensitivity and collusion of the team members and the journalist all play a role in determining whether or not the reporting of an event is hard to take but still presentable or something appalling, even un-nameable.

As regards public Newsmakers, whether political big-shots with their legions of spin doctors or members of the public hungry for their fifteen minutes of fame, are basing their behaviour on calculations of what's in it for them when the media show up.

Journalists are brought up to "tell it how it is". Reporters are supposed to report the facts, but experience at the news face shows that facts, far from being accomplished independently before they arrive to cover them, are increasingly created for them to cover, serving an agenda far removed from quaint notions of informing the public.

There is no role as "merely observers" left—we are always already participants whether reporter likes it or not.

Participants in stories alter their behaviour to provide facts for journalists to report. The deployment of news resources always already conditions the occurrence, emergence, selection and presentation of those facts. The reproduction of hidden narratives resting on binary oppositions makes journalism receptive to propaganda, especially as time-honored rhetorical techniques, central to the Doctrine of News itself, have the effect of camouflaging perspective. The illusion of objectivity is over—it is time for journalism to take responsibility for its influence on events. How would news discharge that responsibility, while remaining news? The Peace Journalism Option elaborated on a suggestion by Professor Galtung that constructing binary oppositions in reporting conflicts, "mapping a conflict as a zero-sum game between two parties," were the chief symptom of a condition he diagnosed as War Journalism.

War journalism focuses on violence as its own cause—explained as expressing atavistic urges. At the BBC some years ago, there was a certain Middle East Correspondent whose reports, according to wags in the London newsroom, could be aired with the same informative content and much less running time expended, by reducing them to a simple formula: "Arabs and Jews hate each other's guts. They always have. They always will; Correspondent BBC News, in the Middle East." In advocating a focus on the underlying causes of violence, peace journalism does not seek excuses for it, but to replace this species of explanation, as the expression of innate and unalterable enmities, with a mission to identify and commentate upon processes which perpetuate the culture of violence.

In place of "strategic" assessments of military options, as proffered when violence is on the agenda by the likes of former army "experts".

"Just reporting the facts" amounts to an undeclared theory of journalism which no longer fits the evidence about how it actually works.

An example of "lop-sided" reporting of West Asian/Middle Eastern affairs can be gauzed by the fact that those Arabs who killed civilians are routinely referred to as "terrorists.... But when an Israeli slaughtered 29 innocent Palestinian worshippers in a Hebron mosque, the US media called the murderer a fanatic, an extremist, or, in a new and popular word found increasingly in the American press, a zealot.

Why is news so receptive to binary oppositions and why are they such an effective form of propaganda? Not because journalists are corrupt pawns—or even naive dupes—of the system, but because they perform an essential task for news itself. They find a ready reception in news precisely because they divert us from looking at the story and encourage us to believe we are looking through it to independently accomplished facts above, beyond or behind it—the central contention of the Doctrine of News. A rhetorical strategy based on reproducing binary oppositions, therefore, puts us off our guard and reinforces the most basic underlying statement of the Doctrine of News—that a story merely expresses or reflects the facts.

By offering such deeply familiar explanations for things, it encourages us to believe we are looking through the story to a previously existing reality, not at "the story"—that shorthand term for a tangle of overlapping interests—and the process it is carrying out in selecting and framing the reality or even causing —some of—it to occur.

CAMOUFLAGING PERSPECTIVE

At the same forum, an international gathering of forty journalists, editors, programme-makers and analysts carried out a close textual analysis of coverage, by the Times and Sunday Times of London of the entire African embassy bombing episode of 1998, from the reports of the initial blasts in Nairobi and Dar es Salaam to the American missile strikes on Sudan and Afghanistan.

It proved a case study in time-honored techniques of the Doctrine of News, which have the effect of camouflaging favoured perspectives and making them seem, not perspectives active in selecting and framing reality but common sense expressions of previously accomplished fact.

"In the world's television studios, peace journalism urges a consideration of the likely damage to structure and culture if violence is adopted as a means of settling disputes. Invariably this means evaluating the long term deterioration of relations and taking this into account when judging whether violence is a wise course. How far does the incipient cold war with the Islamic world have to go before we reach a new view on the wisdom of Operation Desert Storm in 1991? How might it affect our assessment of follow-ups like Operation Desert Fox in 1998?

Perhaps the most important recommendation of the Peace Journalism Option, and certainly the most resonant for this broader discussion of today's newsgathering milieu and its special demands, is to develop techniques for outflanking the client relationship of news with the Official Sources industry.

NEWS AND CHANGE

The resources of news are deployed in clusters around Official Information Sources—the established institutions of power. These define themselves by the limits they set down on what can be debated and what can be changed. Anyone who works within them can be treated as part of the 'Self'—those who reject the limits belong to the 'Other'. It follows that the Official agenda—setting machinery works by perpetually reproducing binary oppositions—a rhetorical strategy to which news, for reasons of its own, is highly receptive. News, in turn, validates the self-definition of Official Sources by making binary oppositions seem natural and obvious, concealing the construction of the 'Self' behind the doctrine that stories express or reflect previously existing facts. A doctrine entrenched by rhetorical techniques which camouflage perspective. Many individual journalists set out to question specific aspects but their very deployment sustains and reproduces the key binary oppositions which define Official Sources as the 'Self'.

NEWSWORTHINESS

The media glorifies gangs & actually makes them feel empowered. Newsworthiness' is itself a function of 'periodicity' —the degree to which an event's cycle corresponds to a medium's publication cycle—and the 'consonance'—the extent to which an event corresponds to existing themes in the news. The development and news coverage of road rage incidents is a good example of consonance in crime reporting.

Media researchers have coined the term 'newsworthiness' as the criterion by which news producers or gatekeepers (editors and sub-editors—select events which are to be presented to the public as news—Surette, 1998. Research into the reporting of crime in British newspapers found that on average almost 13 per cent of 'event-oriented' news was about crime—Williams and Dickinson, 1993—while international research has shown serious crime to be disproportionately well covered by the media. In one US study, murder cases were found to account for around one quarter of all stories carried in newspapers but only 0.2 per cent of all recorded crime—Graber, 1980, cited in Surette, 1998.

One of the consequences of the high levels of news coverage of serious crime is that the public develops a distorted view of the prevalence of certain types of offending behaviour, as well as the criminal justice system's response to it—Hough and Roberts, 1998.

Recent UK research indicates that broadcast media devote even more attention to crime than newspapers. Just over one-fifth of news items carried on independent radio news were about crime, more than any other medium—Cumberbatch *et al.*, 1995. There are, however, important qualitative differences between crime coverage by different media: newspapers generally have more analysis compared to both television and radio.

According to a British survey, 70% of violence is found in news programmes and 20 % in fiction programmes.

'Location' is a particularly complex factor. Places that were perceived to be relatively free of crime, at least during the daytime, attract particular attention, although certain serious offences attract publicity because the pattern of offending conforms to the perception of an area. In addition, several respondents stated that simple logistical factors, that is the ease with which journalists and television crews can get access to the scene or senior investigator can play an important role in determining the level of press interest. The proximity of major news centers to crime scenes can, therefore, be an important factor in determining the level of coverage.

Editors are increasingly driven to consider how they can serve up news with sufficiently obvious relevancy to keep their viewers awake, definitions of "significant change," as the very touchstone of news, have been formulated, where before they could be left unspoken to seep through the walls of the morning planning meeting and out on to the road.

One of these, the mantra of ABC executive Av Westin during the "vanishing" years of the early 1990s, as network viewing figures plummeted, posed three key criteria of newsworthiness:

1. Is my world safe?
2. Are my city and home safe?
3. If my spouse, children and loved ones are safe, what happened in the past 24 hours to shock them, amuse them or make them better off?

These questions frame their own responses and produce television that is titillating but ultimately pacifying, even numbing.

For journalism to avert its gaze, even for some of the time, from the official agenda and engage with this discourse, might prove more effective in bringing audiences where the prospects for significant change are located, in areas like the safety of their homes, their cities and even their gardens.

In newsgathering, what is the boundary between the "legitimate" and the "deviant"? By treating political action originating outside the normal sphere of "legitimate controversy" —the charmed circle of the Official Sources Industry—as raising important, serious political issues, a radical practice in news can simultaneously rehabilitate the "deviant" and interrogate the "legitimate".

To reinforce the boundary between the legitimate and the deviant, the Doctrine of News allots two roles for speakers outside the charmed circle of Official Sources—"victims" and "vox pops". This creates a framework of understanding in which it makes sense to ask them "how do you feel?" but never "what do you think?" By using specific techniques to transgress this boundary, a radical newsgathering and reporting practice can create its own framework of understanding in which it makes sense to overturn this also. Transgressing a boundary such as that dividing the "legitimate" from the "deviant" automatically destabilises the categories on either side of the line.

Newspapers emerged in an age of information scarcity, often read out loud by the only literate person in the room. Today we live in an age of information glut. It is a daily task to remove from the mailbox the latest items of junk mail Add in the potential offered by the Internet and it makes the point—the achievement of putting a package of information on the doorstep every day is now less impressive and less useful than at any time since newspapers were invented.

The notion that news is based on "reporting the facts" is undermined by evidence that "facts" are provided for reporters to report. More evidence is at hand in the bureaucratic structure of news, and the evolution of an Official Sources Industry, imbricated into that structure, to take the provision of facts in the service of a prior agenda to ever more sophisticated levels.

Doctrine of News

A disparity of esteem for suffering sustains the key distinction of identity and alterity—the "Self" and the "Other". To challenge this distinction, a new, radical practice in news could take newsgathering and rhetorical strategies conventionally turned on "Others" and turn them on the "Self". Among these is to invoke international standards as upheld by agencies such as the UN—a convenient fig-leaf for Official Sources when denouncing—or indeed justifying the bombing of—recalcitrant "rogue states", but altogether more awkward when focused on events within the "home" jurisdiction.

On television, at least, news is one of a category of programmes which models its audience as essentially passive, but this is by no means the only category. Elsewhere, the medium is already accustomed to—and good at—pointing viewers to the next step they would take if they wanted to act on the information they'd just received from the broadcast. No self-respecting producer of cookery or travel programmes, for instance, would embark on a new series without panoply of free fact sheets and, these days, a website at the ready, providing the bridge from viewer interest to viewer action. Indeed, the much-mocked phrase, "don't try this at home," was coined precisely because to do so is many viewers' natural inclination.

LINGUISTIC THEORY

As an undeclared theory of journalism, the Doctrine of News also contains an unacknowledged theory of language. According to this theory, identifying "the facts", only then translate them into language to express intentions, which remain identical with themselves. Journalism requires a new theory of language.

Modern conditions at the news-face are increasingly reminiscent of the most famous one-liner in linguistic theory—"il n'y a pas dehors le texte". Jacques Derrida's dictum is usually translated as "there is nothing outside the text", but its relevance to news is better understood by considering its other accepted rendering—"there is no outside to the text". "Facts" taken as arising independently, before the text was even a twinkle in the reporter's eye, turn out, on closer examination, to have been textual long before s/he arrived to cover them—in the mind, for example, of the newsmaker whose behaviour constitutes "the facts". This behaviour was, perhaps, conditioned by the knowledge that reporters will pick up certain kinds of facts—knowledge gleaned from a reading of previous texts in newspapers and on radio and television.

The first to theorise that words do not work by being pegged, by some inherent quality, to particular meanings, was the French philologist Ferdinand de Saussure. His basic proposition, that language is a closed system in which meaning is generated by internal differences, not by expressing anything outside itself, formed the basis for a crucial inversion of what had previously been taken as 'common sense'. In the words of one influential interpreter of modern linguistic theory, the Oxford English Professor Terry Eagleton, "cat is cat because it is not cap or bat", not because of something inherently cat-like about the word, "cat".

Saussure divided language into "sign"—the word on a page or in speech—and "referent"—the external thing which we agree it to signify within the closed system of language. In a further subdivision, the actual combination of letters is a "signifier," which is attached to a particular "signified", the concept, or what we take it to mean in a given context. This, in turn, bears its own relation to the "referent".

The importance for journalism is the notion that they can look through a text to extract the meaning of a previously existing reality of which it is a reflection or expression. Meaning is never "identical with it—self," but dispersed along a chain of signifiers, a play of differences within and between texts which is out of control as soon as a journalist speaks or write. Languages does not express or reflect meanings arrived at before it began—it constructs them by virtue of what it is not—a potentially infinite category or "sprawling limitless web" as Eagleton puts it.

In the Doctrine of News model, meaning springs from the reporter's experience of the facts, guaranteed by his or her honesty in relaying it without fear or favour to the audience. But experiences, even of interiority, are themselves textual. Propaganda is present in our daily media picture.

CRIME VICTIMS AND THE "PACK MENTALITY"

The constituency most affected by the news media's coverage of violence and victimisation is crime victims. While sensitive coverage of victim's cases can be helpful and, in some cases, even healing, media coverage that is sometimes viewed as insensitive, voyeuristic, and uncaring can compound victims' emotional and psychological suffering.

Most crime victims have never before dealt with the news media. They are thrust, often unwillingly, into a limelight they do not seek and do not enjoy solely because of the crimes committed against them. Many victims describe the initial assault from the perpetrator, a secondary assault from the criminal justice system, and a tertiary assault at the hands of the news media. As ABC News and Political Analyst Jeff Greenfield explained in 1986, "What weighs in the scale is not simply the desire of a victim for privacy... but the prospect of further victimisation beyond the involuntary thrust into the public arena. And this is something that the journalism community must begin to consider in its daily business."

In high profile cases, where either the victim or the alleged or convicted offender is a well-known person, the victim is often thrust unwillingly into an excessive and excruciating limelight that he or she neither asked for, nor desires. The "pack mentality" that can result from a combination of mainstream and tabloid media competing for the same scoops, under the same deadlines, can be devastating to victims.

The question of where a society's right to know ends and an individual's right to privacy begins is one of journalism's thorniest ethical dilemmas—Thomason and Babbili 1988.

In addition to privacy protections, the National Center for Victims of Crime has identified fourteen significant concerns that crime victims and service providers have in regard to the news media's coverage of crime and victimisation—Seymour and Lowrance 1988, 5-7.

- *Interviewing at inappropriate times.* "Inappropriate times" for interviewing victims include immediately following a crime, at funerals, in hospital settings, and during trials when the judge or prosecutor has issued a gag order to witnesses. It is during these periods that a victim's trauma and distress tend to be extremely high; dealing with the news media can create a secondary victimisation that compounds the victim's tragedy caused by the violent crime.
- *Using euphemisms to describe victims and offenders.* Euphemisms are often utilised by journalists and, in particular, newspaper headline writers to capture the essence of a violent act in a brief, memorable manner. However, in doing so, the identity of the victim can be demeaned and even lost. Most Americans remember the notorious "Preppie Murder" in Central Park in the 1980s, but how many people can recall the name of the victim, Jennifer Levin?
- *Glamourizing the offender.* The following words were used at various times to describe a well-known criminal: "handsome", "intelligent", "rape crisis center volunteer", and "law school student". The man who was so described was Ted Bundy, one of our nation's worst serial murderers. While such descriptions may be essential to a news story, what often adds insult to the victim's injury is the lack of such detail in describing the victims of such heinous criminals.

- *Exhibiting aggressive behaviour toward victims, survivors, and their advocates.* The pressure to obtain a news story, often under a tight deadline, can lead some journalists to be overly aggressive to victims, their loved ones, and victim service providers. A television photographer illuminated this problem when he noted:

I think at times we don't take into consideration what these people have been through. There is pressure there, someone breathing down your back to go out and get that story, get that interview. We should be more sensitive to these people's feelings. Sometimes I think we're a bit too aggressive —Grotta 1986, 7.

- *Ignoring victims' and survivors' wishes.* The issues of control and decision-making are essential to a victim's reconstruction following a crime. Since victims do not choose to be victimised, their ability to make decisions and have some degree of control over their lives following a violent crime is very important. Crime victims' wishes relevant to the news media's coverage of their cases should be respected and followed.
- *Filming and photographing scenes with bodies, body bags, and blood.* Many victim service professionals believe that the steady diet of gory crime scenes, often involving murdered victims, body bags, and blood, portrayed in broadcast and print media contributes to individual and collective desensitisation to violence and the personal tragedy it wreaks on victims and survivors of crime.
- *Repeatedly using crime scene footage as a "lead-in" to newscasts.* When a broadcast medium chooses to show crime footage as the "lead-in" prior to a newscast, it can re-victimise anybody who was involved in that specific crime. One victim told of watching the evening news and seeing a body bag containing her husband:

There was no warning to the family that this was upcoming. You look up and there's his body. That's offensive. You can't be any more offensive than that (Grotta 1986, 7).

- *Reporting hearsay.* The "double-edged sword" wielded by the media who cover crime is often evident when victims, their loved ones, and law enforcement officials refuse to be interviewed for reasons including the need for privacy, or to preserve the sanctity of the criminal investigation or case. In such cases, some media rely on interviews with third parties, including neighbours and people who may, or may not, have known the victim, to obtain details about the victim and/or alleged perpetrator. However, such hearsay interviews often cannot be relied upon for accuracy and can invoke additional trauma for victims.
- *Interfering in police investigations.* The need for cooperation among law enforcement, other criminal justice officials, and the news media is essential to criminal investigations and prosecutions. Often, details that journalists consider key to a good story are also details that must be kept confidential in order to successfully complete a criminal investigation.
- *Referring to drunk driving crashes as "accidents".* The public awareness generated over the past two decades by Mothers against Drunk Driving, Remove Intoxicated Drivers, and other victim advocacy organisations has successfully educated citizens about the dangers of drinking, drugging, and driving. There is nothing "accidental" about a person who chooses to drink and drive, resulting in a crime that injures or kills another human being. Many journalists have begun referring to such tragedies as "crashes" or

"crimes", which more accurately describes the criminality of driving under the influence of alcohol or other drugs.

- *Failing to cover a crime at all.* Societal biases in America are sometimes reflected in news reporting. The length of news copy and scope of broadcast coverage tend to vary based upon the victim's race, where they live, socioeconomic status, and other factors that have nothing to do with the crime committed against them. These issues were elaborated upon in an article by the associate editor of a large metropolitan daily newspaper:

When city editors get calls from the crime reporter, often the first question asked is "Where did it happen?" The news team's reaction to the crime is often predicated on where the crime occurred.

- *Identifying child victims.* The criminal justice system goes to a great length to protect the privacy of child victims, recognising that any public identification of children's emotional, physical, or sexual assaults can have devastating consequences. The media should similarly respect the privacy rights of child victims, and should avoid all reporting that in any way contacts or identifies victims of child abuse. In cases of incest allegations or convictions, journalists should not identify perpetrators if the child victim is in any way at risk of also being identified.
- *Attempting to interview survivors of homicide victims prior to official death notifications by law enforcement.* In homicide cases, the news media should always ascertain whether or not surviving family members of the victim have been notified of their loved one's murder. One victim recalled driving his car on a Florida freeway and hearing a radio report of his brother's

brutal murder at the hands of a high-profile, and yet unidentified, killer. The shock and grief associated with the news media's reporting of violent deaths prior to sensitive death notification comprise a second tragic victimisation that can easily be avoided with communication and cooperation between law enforcement and the media.

- *Inaccurate reporting*. Accurate media coverage of details of a crime, however minute, are very important to crime victims and survivors. For example, inaccurately reporting of the age of a homicide victim can have traumatic consequences on that victim's surviving family members. Factual reporting of all details associated with a crime is critical not only to the media's underlying philosophy of accuracy, but also to a victim's efforts to reconstruct his or her life following a crime.

Guidelines for Victims Who Choose to Deal With the Media

YOU HAVE THE RIGHT TO:

1. Say "no" to an interview.

2. Select the spokesperson or advocate of your choice.

3. Select the time and location for media interviews.

4. Request a specific reporter.

5. Refuse an interview with a specific reporter even though you have granted interviews to other reporters.

6. Say "no" to an interview even though you have previously granted interviews.

7. Release a written statement through a spokesperson in lieu of an interview.

8. Exclude children from interviews.

9. Refrain from answering any questions with which you are uncomfortable or that you feel are inappropriate.

10. Know in advance the direction the story about your victimisation is going to take.

11. Avoid a press conference atmosphere and speak to only one reporter at a time.

12. Demand a correction when inaccurate information is reported.

13. Ask that offensive photographs or visuals be omitted from broadcast or publication.

14. Conduct a television interview using a silhouette or a newspaper interview without having your photograph taken.

15. Completely give your side of the story related to your victimisation.

16. Refrain from answering reporters' questions during trial.

17. File a formal complaint against a journalist.

18. Grieve in privacy.

19. Suggest training about media and victims for print and electronic media in your community—Seymour and Lowrance 1988, 7-10.

Guidelines for Television Talk Shows and Crime Victim Guests

Recognising the need for accountability from television talk shows, the National Center for Victims of Crime—NCVC 1994—developed guidelines for talk shows and crime victim guests that promote victim sensitivity and reduce opportunities for "re-victimising victims".

- Television talk shows should use only those victims who have had the benefit of counseling and guidance from a trained victim counselor, professional, or advocate.

- Crime victims should not appear in the immediate wake of their victimisation, particularly if they have not had the advantage of counseling by professional victim advocates and service providers.

Child victims should not be guests.

- A professionally trained victim advocate or crisis counselor should be on hand at all times.
- Crime victims should be treated with dignity and respect at all times.
- Crime victims should always be fully informed about the format of the show; how their story will be told; who else will appear—in person or otherwise such as from a remote location—and what subjects will be discussed with each guest. Whenever possible, victims should be provided with copies of the producer's notes on each guest.
- If an offender—any offender—is to be physically present in the studio or elsewhere in the facility, the victim should be given notice of the specific facts and asked what arrangements can be made in the studio to make the victim feel comfortable and safe if he or she chooses to be a guest. Every precaution should be taken to prevent the offender and the victim from "crossing paths" before, during, and after the show.
- Victims should be offered the opportunity to get comfortable with the set by allowing them to arrive early, or even the day before the actual taping.
- Victims should always have the right to view pictures, video/audio tapes, and graphic or other depictions that will air as part of the show.

- Victims should be informed in advance of the option to protect their anonymity by whatever means are necessary such as silhouette screens, disguises, electronic voice alteration, pixel and fog screening, etc.
- When the victim desires, no information should be presented that would disclose the location of their home, place of work, or whereabouts.
- Victims should have the right to request that their show must not air in certain markets if there are safety concerns.
- Victims should have the opportunity to request that disclosures which compromise their anonymity or safety be edited from the broadcast program.
- Victims should be informed of when the original show will air and when the show will be re-broadcast.
- Victims in the viewing audience may experience a crisis reaction while watching a show about crime victimisation experiences. It is strongly advised that producers provide a disclaimer at the beginning of the show cautioning viewers of the content.

MEDIA AND GANG

A gang that has made headlines in newspapers and the television news also contributes to gangs. Gang members feel that they have done something that has greatly made them known to society. When a minor gang crime has been mentioned in the news, that gang feels they must top that crime with a broader crime so that they become known.

Another factor that contributes to gangs are gang prevention programs. When gangs see that they are trying to be stopped, they become stronger, larger and richer by impacting more communities, selling major money, drugs and exerting more control than prevention units that try to stop them. Gangs take their reputation seriously and thus highly motivated in ensuring control over their territories and reacting to exterior forces.

CRIME AND LAWYER

The news media wield a "double-edged sword" in their coverage of crime and victimisation relevant to the "public's right to know" versus "the victim's right to privacy". Victim service providers play crucial roles in protecting victims' privacy rights, and helping victims cope with media coverage immediately following a crime, during the trial, and following verdicts. Advocates must possess knowledge of who the media are, how they operate, and victims' needs pertinent to dealing with the media.

Media reporting of crime and victimisation, in both print and broadcast formats, has far-reaching effects on a number of populations and special interests.

However, the past fifteen years have also witnessed an increase in media professionals who seek sensitivity training from crime victims and advocates so that they can accurately cover crime stories with the least amount of trauma to the victim. Today, crime victims and service providers offer training programs to newsrooms, professional journalism associations, and university-level journalism classes about media sensitivity in addressing violence and victimisation.

Journalists who cover crime beats are also affected by the scope and demands of their jobs. Those who cover the horror and degradation of violence on a regular basis have few outlets for the personal trauma they must endure. As such, there is high demand for a protocol to "debrief" journalists whose assignments include regular coverage of violence.

MEDIA VIOLENCE AND LAW

Laws are norms defined and enforced by governments: Use of the wide variety of available technological controls, household media rules and other private sector efforts are a much better alternative to government regulation to address concerns about children's exposure to violence on television. Lawmakers should be wary of policies that could be struck down in court as unconstitutional, thus restrictive alternative and away from broad, government-imposed censorship is a better policy.

Numerous tools and methods, both technical and non-technical, which can be used to control what media content children are exposed to in the home, include private ratings systems, V-chips, personal video recorders, controls provided by cable and satellite providers, and formal or informal household media consumption rules.

Concerned parents and others can work with third parties to gather information and even work within the media marketplace to influence what fare is shown on broadcast and cable television, by making use of ratings and reviews provided by independent organisations and the many educational efforts aimed at teaching adults about parental controls available for all types of media, including television, movies and games.

But if, for whatever reason, some parents are not taking advantage of these tools and options, their inaction should not be used to justify government regulation of programming as a surrogate for household/parental choice.

Police and TV Crew

Media handling in serious crime investigations is a complex issue. On the one hand, the media can be an important mechanism for generating valuable information from the general public. On the other hand, dealing with the media can take up valuable time and resources during the critical early stages of an investigation. Consequently, media handling has been acknowledged as a critical skill of the Senior Investigating Officer (SIO).

Public attitudes toward police are generally positive (Huang and Vaughn, 1996). However, there are few studies that examine the media's influence on public ratings of police effectiveness. Much of the literature focuses on media portrayals of police officers and findings reveal two conflicting views. Some researchers argue that the police are presented favourably in the media, while other research suggests that the police are negatively portrayed in the media.

Presentations of police are often over-dramatised and romanticised by fictional television crime dramas while the news media portray the police as heroic, professional crime fighters —Surette, 1998; Reiner, 1985. In television crime dramas, the majority of crimes are solved and criminal suspects are successfully apprehended—Dominick, 1973; Estep and MacDonald, 1984; Carlson, 1985; Kooistra *et al.* 1998, Zillman and Wakshlag, 1985. Similarly, news accounts tend to exaggerate the proportion of offenses that result in arrest which projects an image that police are more effective than official statistics demonstrate—Sacco and Fair, 1988; Skogan and Maxfield, 1981; Marsh, 1991; Roshier, 1973. The favourable view of policing is partly a consequence of police's public relations strategy. Reporting of proactive police activity creates an image of the police as effective and efficient investigators of crime— Christensen, Schmidt and Henderson, 1982. Accordingly, a positive police portrayal reinforces traditional approaches to law and order that involves increased police presence, harsher penalties and increasing police power—Sacco, 1995.

In addition, a number of researchers suggest that a symbiotic relationship exists between news media personnel and the police. It is suggested that the police and the media engage in a mutually beneficial relationship. The media needs the police to provide them with quick, reliable sources of crime information, while the police have a vested interest in maintaining a positive public image—Ericson, Baranek, and Chan, 1987; Fishman, 1981; Hall *et al*, 1978.

Other researchers argue that the police are not portrayed positively in the news media. For example, Surette—1998—claims that docu-dramas and news tabloid programs represent the police as heroes that fight evil, yet print and broadcast news personify the police as ineffective and incompetent. Likewise, Graber—1980— claims that the general public evaluates police performance more favourably compared with courts and correction. Nevertheless, Graber—1980—states that the media provides little information to judge police and that the news media focus on negative criticism rather than positive or successful crime prevention efforts. In essence, most media crime is punished, but policemen are rarely the heroes—Lichter and Lichter, 1983.

Police effectiveness, fear of crime and punitive attitudes are important aspects of public attitudes toward crime and justice. First, police strategies reflect departmental values, which reflect community values. Negative or positive attitudes towards the police may influence police policy making and strategy. Second, citizen attitudes toward the police may influence decisions to report crime. Third, both fear of crime and punitive attitudes may influence policy making and law making by government agencies, as public support or opposition may determine policy.

A TV crew is never perceived neutrally by police. Police goes to great lengths to remain in the role of observers and to avoid becoming actors of the events. But police acknowledges that their mere presence has an influence over the events, which is a serious paradox in itself for Reporters.

Many serious crime investigations attract substantial amounts of press interest. If effectively managed, the media can make a significant contribution to investigations by acting as a conduit for information from the general public. Every investigator can recall instances where the press has contributed the vital lead which unlocks an enquiry. The media spotlight can, however, also place major resource demands on investigations at the critical early stage of an enquiry; and in a wider sense, the media play an important role in shaping the public's views of crime, the police service, and the wider criminal justice system. They can drive the fear of crime.

MEDIA AND PUBLIC INTEREST

Media interest in serious crimes: In general, investigations into serious crime such as murder and rape attract a substantial amount of press interest, particularly in the first few days of an enquiry. Thereafter, interest will tend to diminish although some particularly newsworthy offences will sustain national media interest for some time. The factors that determine the level of press interest will vary from case to case and depend partly upon the coverage of other news events. For the cases examined, the age and background of the victim and location of the offence were most frequently perceived as influencing the level of media coverage. Not all offences, however, attract the desired level of press interest, and in these cases the challenge for any strategy is to gain and enhance media coverage.

The demands on the investigation: Where press interest is high, one of the main problems arising from media handling in serious crime investigations is the demands placed on the resources of the investigative team. Most police investigating officers estimated that they spent between 20 and 40 per cent of their time dealing with the media in the first two days of an enquiry.

The disclosure of information: Investigations have to effectively resolve tensions around the hold-back or disclosure of information about the offence. The investigative team's judgment about whether or not to disclose a piece of information should be influenced by a mature assessment of the likely *consequences* of that decision. In certain instances, providing more detailed information to the general public can increase the likelihood of generating additional valuable information.

The timing of disclosed information: Interviewees placed particular importance on when initial contact is made with the press, and the timing of subsequent press releases and press conferences. Getting information out allowed the investigation to take the lead in press handling at an early stage, while allowing the rest of the investigation to progress. Furthermore, it was argued that early initial communications with the press limits the degree to which they formulate their own accounts of what happened and begin their own 'investigations'.

The objectives of media appeals: Finding 'unknowing witnesses' was the most frequently stated objective for press appeals. Three cases attempted to use the media to achieve more specific investigative objectives, such as putting pressure on an offender to admit the offence.

Dealing with the generation of information: Appeals can generate substantial amounts of information from the general public. Two main issues were raised regarding the practical consequences of public appeals: First, the need to deal with the immediate response to an appeal by arranging sufficient phone lines and briefed operators. Secondly, the impact on the investigation of having to respond to a potentially large number of new messages entering the system. The extent to which the public will contribute new information in the wake of an appeal is likely to depend on four key factors:

- the size of the potential population who might be able to contribute information;
- the extent to which the potential population can be targeted by particular media;
- how the disclosed information can be packaged to *appeal* to the public to come forward; and,
- the degree to which the information required can be made *specific*.

The ability of the investigation to assess the quality of incoming information will depend on the quality of information residing in the enquiry at the time of the appeal.

General relations with the press, victims, victims' relatives and communities

An important part of effective press handling relies on understanding the media context in which any investigation will be conducted. Respondents identified several areas that influence the context within which a serious crime investigation is reported and which can affect reporting style and the dialogue with the press.

These included:

- general relations between the local/regional press and the police service;
- the variation in relations with different media outlets in the same force area;
- the nature of media boundaries and catchments;
- any general themes or campaigns adopted by local media; and,
- the experience of crime reporters covering major investigations and their understanding of the legal process.

Media portrayal of serious crime investigations: Although investigators can determine the content and timing of a press release, they are not in a position to determine how that information is portrayed by the media. This was particularly important in terms of the way in which victims or communities were described in the media. The way this information was presented in the press could influence the willingness, for instance, of the victim's family or the general public to co-operate with the enquiry.

Improving media relations: Investigating officer specifically highlighted the importance of explaining to the media the reasons why they could not furnish particular information about an enquiry, or why some investigative tasks took so long. While explaining why operationally sensitive material had to be held back, it was important to provide as much 'non-sensitive' information about the crime and the investigation as possible to the press. The aim is to 'over-provide' information for reporters to discourage 'journalist investigations'.

Legal issues: When an investigation goes into a post-charge phase, the due legal process comes into force. Many times, the activities of some parts of the press can lead to a development that has the potential to jeopardise proceedings. It is seen in many cases which encountered particular problems over the press gaining access to, and then publishing, pictures of a suspect prior to charge or the commencement of the trial.

The role of the media liaison officer: A central feature of the handling of the press in serious crime investigations is the bringing together of the investigating officer and the media liaison officer in the early stages of an enquiry. This was often regarded as a key working relationship at one of the most difficult times of an investigation. Many of the media liaison officers were civilians and had worked as journalists prior to joining the police.

Figure 2: The objective and consequence of disclosing or holding back information

Disclosure of informationfs	Holding back information
objectives	*objectives*
Keep investigation in public eye	information to assist with investigative/evidential strategies
Provides more information to the public and assists their ability to help with investigation	Minimise anxlety among loval community
Minimises journalist speculation	Minimise distress to victim's family
Takes pressure off victim's family	Maximise public response (where victim background / lifestyle may inhibit this)
Reassure community	Avoid the liklihood of copycatting
Induce offender response	Prevent offender destroying evidence
Crime provention advice (e.g. details of the offender's modus operandi)	Avoid offender changing behaviour in subsequent offences (e.g. non-disclosure of DNA samples)
	Information is available to release subsequently to maintain public interest
Possible consequences	***Possible consequences***
Cannot use information in interviews with suspects	May hinder public response to appeals by limiting information in the public domain.
Less information to disclose later on	Increased risk of 'press investigations' and press acquiring information regardless, and using it in a way that either damages the investigation of any subsequent trial
Possibility of copycatting speculation Impact on offender (e.g. destruction of forensis evidence or psychological state of offender)	Increased risk of misinformation and
May damage the possibility of a fair trial (S78 of PACE Act 1984 may be applied)	

Investigating officers training and ability in media handling: The majority of the officers do receive some training in media presentation skills, but relatively little training in how to develop effective media strategies. In spite of the general lack of formal training in this area, several experienced officers develop expert skills in relation to media handling. Their abilities is reflected in a combination of personal charisma, a wide range of experience and a close working relationship with individuals and organisations in the media. They have the ability to *anticipate* the consequences of the media interpretation of a crime, the investigation and any decisions associated with media handling. The balance between disclosure and hold-back.

Table 3: Messages received by four homicide investigations, by source and content.

	Column percentage				
Message referred to:	General public	Victim associate	Police source	Other*	Total
Object found at scene	8	2	13	-	8
Activity at or near scene	39	2	14	18	20
Victim sightings	8	4	3	18	4
Background on victim	17	72	28	24	32
General background	1	4	4	-	3
Suspect names	11	4	19	6	11
Related criminal activity	6	4	8	-	6
Other	15	6	5	33	5
Total	100	100	100	100	100
N	85	54	80	17	236
Row percentage	36	23	34	7	100

The media as an investigative tool

Decisions over the content and timing of communications with the media will in part reflect the need for the investigation to generate additional information from the general public. It is widely acknowledged that the public play an important role as providers of information in the detection of crime — Greenwood, Chaitken, and Petersilia, 1977; Morgan, 1980; Ainsworth, 1995. This is illustrated by the findings from a separate study of the messages recorded in four murder investigations by Greater Manchester Police—Table 3. The data revealed that the general public accounted for more than one-third of messages received. Of these, the majority related to activity at or near the scene—39 per cent—and 11 per cent of messages from the general public offered the enquiry the names of suspects.

The main objectives of media appeal.

A total of thirteen objectives were identified—Table 4—with identifying 'unknowing

Table 4: Objectives of media appeals *	
Objective	No. of appeals with objective
Acquisition of information	
Identify victim	1
Identify suspects +	4
Trace a named suspect	1
Trace history of vehicle involved in offence	1
Trace witnesses to the offence/people near scene at time	9
Locate item stolen in linked offence	2
Establish victim's last movements	4
Get associates of the victim to come forward	3
Find whereabouts of missing person	1
Close down a specific line of enquiry	1
Other investigative objectives	
Put pressure on suspect/suspect's associates to admit the offence	1
Use of non-disclosed information to incriminate offenders	1
To directly address the offender	1

* Most case offered more than one object.

+ Although the provision of suspect names was not often explicitly stated as an objective, in 25 per cent of case, suspect names were contributed to the investigation.

It is important to distinguish between a police *appeal* for information and the more general provision of information to the media about the offence—*publicity*.

A media appeal is of course just one of a number of routes by which the police can try to engage the support of, and receive information from, the general public to assist in the investigation of serious crimes. House-to-house enquiries, leaflet drops, reconstructions and road stop-checks are alternative mechanisms. Each of these has strengths and weaknesses as techniques for acquiring information, particularly in terms of:

- the ability to focus on a particular geographical area or community;
- the speed with which they can be initiated in relation to the offence;
- the extent to which the police can retain 'editorial' control over the request for information;
- the extent to which they can guarantee that target populations have been reached by an appeal;
- the expected volume and quality of information into the enquiry;
- the option for repeated or updated appeals; and,
- the resources required to make the initial appeal, handle the response, analyse it and respond to it.

The use of the media offers a relatively flexible means of acquiring information. Unlike other forms of information collection, the investigative team can alter the detail and the tone of the media message accordingly as the enquiry progresses.

Victims and victims' relatives

The media portrayal of the victims of serious crime is a sensitive area. The way in which the victim is presented in the press can influence the willingness of the victim's family to co-operate with the enquiry. Press coverage of the victim can occasionally be negative and inaccurate, and the editorial or interpretative slant of the press is sometimes not fully understood by those reading newspapers and watching television. Police relations with the victim's family can be strained through a misunderstanding of the relationship between the police message and actual press coverage, and the investigation needs to be aware of this possibility

Victims' relatives and press appeals

There has been much discussion about the use of victims' relatives in appeals for assistance via the media—Chesshyre, 1997. While it is clearly preferable to *manage* press contact with a victim's relatives, it is difficult to prevent relatives commenting to the media if they so wish.

The Right to More Meaningful Crime Coverage

Viewers describe "meaningful" crime reporting as coverage which focuses more on the apprehension of criminals than on the crimes they commit. These viewers feel that local news "glorifies" criminals, making them into inappropriate "heroes" or "role models". They also say that repetitive coverage of the crime itself is negative, doesn't serve any constructive purpose, and can result in "copycat" crimes. Many believe that it would be better for society if more emphasis were placed on the punishment than the crime.

Focusing on the apprehension of the perpetrator is a good way of making a turning an otherwise negative crime story into coverage most viewers see as "positive." It makes people feel as if something is being done to bring closure to the situation. They say it also helps the community and the local Police Department, and makes them feel as if something good is being accomplished. "If there are fugitives out there, we need to know it. The more that's on TV where we can see faces, the quicker they can apprehend these people.... We want to know the effort is on trying to catch the person.... It means—the TV station—is helping out instead of just doing it for ratings.... There's a lot of news, but not much action.... Arrests are positive. We need to see successes, too." Some viewers believe that the sensational, repetitive coverage of crime can actually make it harder to catch criminals; it also impinges on a suspect's right to a fair trial.

Viewers don't need a drama series.... Rather than dwell on what criminals did; to try and catch them is the most important issue. A lot of stories on violent crime don't have any follow-up on the consequences of the act. You never hear about punishment

•••

10

GUIDANCE AND PREVENTION

GUIDANCE

Cultivating intelligent viewing implies that parents encourage children to carefully choose the programmes, restrict viewing time and help them to find fun things to do when the set is turned off.

First and foremost, a child needs to feel safe at home. There is no surer way to start children on the right path in life than to provide consistent, reliable, loving care. How you relate to the children inside your home is perhaps the most powerful tool for protecting them from violence outside the home.

Just being exposed to violence is harmful

When children, even very young children, see a violent act, they are deeply affected by it. This is especially true if the violence involves a family member or someone they know in the neighborhood. What can you do to help? First, allow the children plenty of time to talk about violence they have seen at school, in the neighborhood, or on TV. Encourage them to express their feelings about it. Second, make sure your children get to see many more examples of people dealing with each other in a spirit of friendly cooperation rather than by threatening violence or hurting each other. The children will gradually realise that there are many ways to deal with people and resolve conflicts peacefully, and that violence is not the best way to get what they want.

Handling anger

Everyone gets angry at times. It's part of being human. Anger is a normal feeling that can be helpful, because it signals that change is needed. But anger also can get out of control. Helping children learn to manage anger is a very important part of early violence prevention.

It is hard for very young children to understand and manage their anger. As your young child grows, gradually teach these principles:

- It's okay to be angry.
- There are "okay" ways and "not okay" ways to show your anger.
- It's not okay to hurt anyone, to break things, or to hurt pets when you are angry.
- It's okay to tell someone that you are angry.
- There are ways to calm yourself when you are angry.

Young children get angry for many reasons

Several things stir young children's anger, and they show it in different ways. Here are some typical examples:

- When infants, from birth to about 9 or 10 months, feel bad because they are hungry, sick, or in pain, or when they are startled by a loud noise.they show their anger by crying and thrashing their arms and legs.
- Older babies, up to about 18 months, still show anger with crying and fussing, but the reasons may be

different. This tends to occur when they don't get an appealing object, when they can't be with the person they want to be near, when they are frightened, or when they feel bad because of illness.

- From about age 18 months to 4 years, children are easily frustrated and will aggressively try to get or to keep what they want. They may grab a toy or take a cookie away from a friend, push a child away from the place they want to stand, or hit someone who takes something away from them.
- Children from about ages 4 to 8 years old gradually understand more, and they get angry about what people say, as well as what they do. They get better and better at expressing themselves with words, and their understanding of the world expands dramatically. Their aggression often is aimed at hurting another person, perhaps directly, by hitting or fighting, perhaps indirectly by damaging something the other person cares about.

Children can learn to manage anger

Young children who learn to manage angry feelings are more likely to make and keep friends. Also this skill can help prevent and resolve conflicts at home. Schoolchildren who are constantly arguing and fighting are the ones most likely to have problems in school and to have trouble making friends. And these issues can later lead to quitting school, having problems with the law, and abusing alcohol and drugs.

Importantly, helping a child to control angry feelings begins when you respond to the child's anger in a calm, respectful manner:

- Calm an infant by holding and comforting the infant, as well as removing or changing what caused the fussing.

- Encourage a toddler to use words to tell you what he or she feels, even in simple language. "I mad," or "Want doll," is a reasonable response from a little boy or girl.
- Help preschoolers begin to learn and practise a self-calming method, taking a few deep breaths, sitting down, counting to 10, or repeating, "Be cool, be calm," for example.
- Encourage kindergarten and elementary school youngsters to explain what happened and how they feel. After a child is calm, ask what is wrong and *LISTEN* to the explanation, without interrupting. Help the child think about and tell ways to change the situation that caused the anger.

Social problem solving

Problem solving doesn't just mean doing arithmetic or figuring out how to fix a leaky faucet tap. Many of the toughest problems, some-times involving strong feelings, occur between people. Adults and children who can manage the strong feelings and resolve conflicts reasonably, without hurting someone, have good skills for social problem solving.

Start early to help young children *STOP* and *THINK* about different ways to solve a problem. Help them choose to act in a way that is nonviolent, safe, and fair. Around age 3, children are usually ready to begin simple steps of thinking and making choices which are part of social problem solving.

As children grow, they get better at solving problems. Around age 4 or 5, children can think of more than one way to solve a problem, and they can predict how people will react to their actions.—"If I hit George when he wants my truck, he will hit me back. If we take turns, he won't grab it any more." They also learn to name their own feelings and those of others. —"I am mad because Sandra won't let me on the swing." "Carlos is sad because his balloon popped." Further, they begin to care about other people's feelings and well-being—"Mark, I'm sorry you hurt your knee." "Grandma will be happy when she sees the picture I coloured for her."

Children aged 6 to 8 can understand how others might see a problem differently, and they can talk about a situation more clearly. They also develop a conscience and worry about rules and fairness.

- Be sure to praise a child who does any of these things:
- Calms down
- Tells how he or she feels
- Describes a problem
- Thinks of solutions to a problem
- Acts in a way that is safe, fair, and nonviolent

Make sure that your children understand that it's okay to make mistakes trying to solve problems and that we can learn from our mistakes. Always encourage children to seek help from trusted adults when a problem is too hard for them to handle.

Most of all, remember that children learn by watching you solve problems with respectful words and nonviolent actions. The best way to get children to behave the way you want is to pay attention to them when things are calm and comment on their good behavior. Praise children for sharing a toy with a playmate without being told to do so or for putting their toys away when they are finished with them or for avoiding conflicts with other children. If children get attention only when they misbehave, they repeat the bad behaviour.

Discipline

No child's behaviour is perfect all of the time and some kids are harder to deal with than others. When you must act to stop a child's bad behaviour, your goal should always be to do it with self-control and without violence. The goal of discipline is to teach children self-control, not to punish them.

Discipline is an important job. A young child's constant out-of-control behaviour can:

- Hurt that child or others
- Interfere with the child's learning and making friends
- Damage property
- Lead to school failure
- Create tension and stress at home
- Set the stage for serious problems as the child grows older
- You can teach a child self-control by—
- Setting reasonable limits and rules
- Having consistent, age-appropriate standards for behaviour
- Showing consistent consequences for misbehaving
- Letting the child see good behaviour by your example.

When young children "act up"

- Let children know what you expect, with simple statements. "Please put away your toys right now."
- Give warnings and reminders, without threats. "When you put away your toys, then you can go outside with your friends."
- Tell a child what to do rather than what not to do. "Please use a soft voice," instead of "Stop yelling!"
- Follow through with praise for following instructions or consequences for disobeying.

Sometimes a youngster's bad behaviour can be so frustrating that a parent or caregiver strikes the child without stopping to think. Yet children become confused, scared, and angry when adults hurt them, especially the adults whom they depend on to love and protect them. And continual, harsh punishment can lead a child to become aggressive and out of control just the opposite of what you want to accomplish.

Some discipline methods to try

Ignore some behaviour that is irritating but not dangerous: for example, whining, swearing, or having tantrums. It may be hard to do this, but paying attention to such behavior may just encourage more of it.

Taking away a privilege can help to stop bad behaviour. Once children are old enough to understand, tell them that something they like—riding a bike, playing at a friend's house, watching a favorite TV show will be taken away if they continue to misbehave. This sets up a choice: With self-control, they get what they like; if they continue to behave badly, they don't. This kind of approach teaches that actions have consequences. *When young children are fighting or arguing*, place yourself between them. If possible, kneel to get to the children's eye level. Let them know you understand that they are upset. If they are fighting over a toy or object, hold the object until the problem is settled. Ask each child to tell you what is wrong and listen to what they say. Ask both children to think of ways they might resolve the problem. Help them think about consequences,—"If we do this, then what will happen?". Help them choose a solution that is fair and nonviolent. Watch what happens: If it works, praise them; if not, have them choose another solution and try again.

If one child clearly has been hitting or picking on another, speak to the victim first, allowing him to say what he wants and how he feels. Encourage the victim to face the bully and say how he feels perhaps something like this: "I don't like it when you push me. It hurts and makes me mad!" Be sure that the bully doesn't get more attention than the victim gets.

Timeout is a method that some families use to give children —and adults—a short cooling off period. If you use it, keep the time short and follow these guidelines:

- Choose a safe, supervised place where the child can be quiet and undisturbed.
- Tell the child that at the end of the timeout, the two of you will talk about the troublesome behaviour.
- Tell the child to sit quietly, without talking to anyone, until he or she is calm and ready to have a discussion.
- When timeout is over, keep your promise and talk with the child about what happened.

About spanking

People have a variety of opinions about spanking, but the reality is that hitting or spanking your child sends a confusing message. It says it's okay to hurt someone you love in order to control them or solve a problem. Repeated harshly, over time, it will train children to punish others with force the same way that they were punished.

Media influences

Media especially television, but also videos, movies, comic books, music lyrics, and computer games as well have a strong influence on children. On the one hand, such media offer powerful tools for learning and entertainment; on the other hand, violence in the media is damaging for young children.

Research shows that violence in the media has the following effects on children:

- It gives children violent heroes to imitate.
- It increases mean-spirited, aggressive behaviour.
- It shows children that violence is all right as a way to handle conflict.

- It makes it easy for children to ignore suffering and the bad effects of violence.
- It causes fear, mistrust, and worry—sometimes including nightmares.
- It whets their appetite for viewing more violence, in more extreme forms.
- And, bear in mind that even when the "good guys" win, the effects are the same.

As children get older, those who watch a lot of television also have lower grades, especially in reading. After all, they are substituting TV for homework, study time, reading practice, using their imagination, and interacting with others. Start limiting children's TV viewing while they are young to help prevent later problems in school.

The extent of children's exposure to television violence is stunning. Violence also is a theme in many popular video and computer games for children, and new research suggests that those games may be more harmful than television and movies.

Here are some ways that you can prevent violence in the media from having such a strong influence on your young children:

- Watch TV with your children and talk about what happens in the shows.
- Monitor what your kids watch or play.
- Limit the number of hours your children watch TV or play video games.
- Insist that schoolwork and family responsibilities are done before TV is allowed.
- Prevent the children from watching violent shows.
- Help them select shows that promote learning and positive development.

- Tell babysitters, caregivers, and family members about your rules on TV watching.

Talk with children about violence in the media. In those discussions, you can teach some important lessons:

- Violence in the media is make-believe, not real.
- Real-life violence hurts people.
- Guns, bullets, knives, and other weapons on TV are fake; real weapons hurt or kill people.
- If a show is scary or confusing, talk to an adult about it.
- Also, teach your children that violent toys may seem exciting in "pretend" games, but that real-life violence is not fun. Encourage your children to pretend and play in ways that don't involve violence.

Caution about weapons

A child's curiosity about weapons can be deadly. It is heart-breaking to hear of accidental shootings and serious injuries by children who handle guns or play with them. Teach children to never touch a gun, bullet, or knife. Let them know that if they find one, they should not touch it, but should tell a trusted adult about it.

If you own a gun, never leave it out where a child might get it. Always lock your unloaded guns and bullets separately, in secure places that children cannot reach.

At home and in your community

The daily experiences you provide for young children are powerful, not only for preventing violence, but also for increasing their chances to have a productive, happy life. If you stay at home with your children, have a schedule and plan activities for them and with them. If your children are in a child-care program while you work outside of home, make sure that it offers chances for constructive play and learning opportunities, with well-qualified staff who promote positive social behaviour. Research shows that high quality child-care programs can reduce behaviour problems in later childhood.

Teach your child a sense of community by being part of the community yourself. Participate in activities to keep your neighborhood safe and to prevent violence.

Give your children opportunities to play with other children and to interact with people of all ages.

Give children your time. Play together, eat together, watch their activities, work on projects together, just hang out and share everyday experiences.

As part of a young child's family, you have a critical influence on that young child's development. What you teach children today will make a difference in which they are tomorrow. You are the best person to show a path to nonviolence for the children, for your family, and for your community.

Tips for Picking Good TV Shows

What's the difference between good TV and the bad stuff? Kids' TV expert Karen Jaffe says there are five questions parents should ask before their kids pick up the remote:

Value:

Is the message a valuable one—one that is important and beneficial for the target audience? You know your child and his/her taste. Make recommendations that are consistent with these interests. You can match up genres like science fiction or history or even sports. If your child is a bibliophile, look for shows with literary connections. Then consider whether the objective of the show is worthwhile.

Clarity:

Is the message clearly laid out so that it can be easily comprehended by the target audience? Make sure that the show is appropriate for the age of your child. If the material is age-appropriate, the language and subjects should be clearly understood. Then check to see if the information is presented effectively. Sometimes the format of the show will dictate whether your child can pick up the messages. Magazine-style shows usually include many different stories with separate lessons for each one. Some children will be challenged by too much information while others will thrive on the diversity. Some children will be enchanted by a drama, others fascinated by a documentary.

Salience:

Is the message consistently conveyed and/or an integral element of the program as a whole? There are two ways to look at issue. If you are only interested in exposing your child to an educational show that is specifically designed to inform, then the main thrust of the show—the premise—should have a message that is developed and resolved at the conclusion of the program or series. This is different from a show that is developed primarily for entertainment but which carries educational messages as a sidebar or, as they say in Hollywood, as the secondary story line. These are often important lessons—but they're clearly ancillary to the main topic of the program.

Another example of educational "nuggets" are shows that embed a lesson at the end of the show or even as a short message after the conclusion of the show. With guidance, parents can reinforce these "secondary" lessons and turn these briefer programming messages into an instructional experience.

Involvement:

Is the message presented in such a way that it is engaging and challenging for the target audience? Some shows have terrific content that falls flat in the presentation. Again, some of this depends on your child's response to the material. An animated science lesson will work for some children, while the live-action version makes sense to others. However, the show won't work at all if the format does not present the information in an entertaining manner.

Relevance:

Is the message conveyed in such a way that the target audience can see its usefulness in his/her own life? This is perhaps the most important criteria for parents who want to make television an enriching experience. It's also the most global in scope. A newscast or newsmagazine or even a talk show—which you have determined is age-appropriate—can provide valuable information and place issues affecting your child's life and community in perspective.

Parents' Reaction to TV Violence—U.S.

- A survey by the American Medical Association found that 75 per cent of parents have turned off a television program or left a movie theatre because the show was too violent.
- Of those children surveyed, 79 per cent have set rules in their home regarding when their children can watch television.

Source: American Medical Association Media Violence Survey, Aug. 13, 1996.

Consequences

When you see violence on TV, movies, or video games think about the consequences that would result from this violence in real life. Ask yourself some of the questions below:

Feelings	Responsibilities	Injuries	Results
Who will be sad?	Who will pay for the damages?	Who will have to go to the hospital?	What will happen to the victim's families?
Who will be scared?	Who will clean up the mess?	How long will they stay in the hospital?	Who will be left alone?
Who will be angry?	Who will fix everything that was broken? How much will it cost?	Will they fully recover from their injuries?	How does this affect other people?
Who will be embarrassed?	Who will pay the hospital bills or the fees for the funeral?	Will their lives go back to normal?	If someone dies, who will attend the funeral?
Who will be left out?	Who will pay the	Will their	If someone dies,

Because of the popularity of electronic media, completely eliminating them from your child's life might be difficult. However, following are suggestions for decreasing the negative impact that they might have on your child.

- Monitor all of your child's media consumption—video games, television, movies and Internet.
- With your child, discuss and make decisions on how much your child is allowed to play video games, listen to music or watch TV. Enforce those limits and be consistent.
- Be a good example by limiting your own use of electronic media.
- Take the time to discuss with your children the games they are playing or other media they are watching. Ask your children how they feel about what they

observe in these video games, television programs or movies. This is an opportunity to share your feelings and grow closer with your child.

Share with other parents' information about certain games or ideas for helping each other in parenting.

Half of the children who watch the news say they felt depressed, angry, or sad afterward. This is the unsettling result of a study by the Los Angeles advocacy group, Children Now. Yet concern about the impact of news shows on children has been completely absent from discussions about quality television, the V-chip, and the rating system. We live in a society governed by a democratic constitution. In India, we have freedom of the press, so citizens cannot censor the news. Even if news can be harmful to children, it cannot be subject to TV ratings. But, news has a powerful impact on kids.

We help children deal with disasters, but ignore the daily onslaught.

When the Challenger blew up in 1986 before the eyes of millions of American school children, caring adults rushed to help them cope with this dramatic, and very public, tragedy. After the explosion, experts offering advice for families appeared on television, in newspapers, and in magazines.

The media is increasingly more competitive and carefully packaged stories to attract instant attention. Unfortunately, adults aren't the only ones whose interest is caught. Our children are naturally curious and that makes them susceptible to the gory details of the television news.

Projection—Know your own shadow

The shadow is made of traits we disown—"the part of us we fail to see or know." Projection can also result from denial of our finer traits. Hero-worship and the glorious mystery of falling in love are largely due to projecting our disinherited inner divinity onto another. Ever since we were quite young, we've been learning what characteristics are acceptable—or not—in our particular culture. Civilisation is a great achievement, and diverse. Within various cultures there are various taboos. These are differing social mores. The collective life of a society depends on some structure.

Poet Robert Bly describes the shadow as a long bag we drag behind us. "We spend our lives until we're twenty deciding what parts of ourselves to put in the bag..." the civilising process; "and we spend the rest of our lives trying to get them out again," the humanising, integrating, holistic process. Disowned traits are rattling in an overcrowded closet called the Shadow. In that closet named shadow may be wildness, anger, spontaneity, freedom, sexuality.

Great sophistication and discipline are required to allow a society to ignore or suppress the shadow. Such idealism backfires, however, as spurned demons are not vanquished. They are right here, living in the walls.

As Bly said, we spend our early lives becoming civilised, responsible and productive, usually at great expense to our wholeness, as we stuff more and more into our bag. most of us deal with shadow through the unconscious means of *projection*. Parents commonly project their shadow on to their children.

Much social interaction among supposed equals is vivid with projections. When someone projects a shadow at you, it's likely that your own shadow will jump out in reaction. As Robert Johnson writes, "When your shadow is like a gasoline can wait for a match to fall in it, you are fair game for anyone who wants to irritate you." Hopefully, he continues: "To refuse another's shadow, you don't fight back, but like a good matador you just let the bull go by... to be in the presence of another's shadow and not reply is nothing short of genius. No one has the right to dump his shadow on you, and you have the right to self-protection.

There are plenty of ways to devalue and disown our shadow, and projection is a path of least resistance, an easy way out. But in giving away essential components of our very self, we are thin, superficial, easily manipulated. Others can push our buttons. We are less than whole, less vital.

TV Violence and Brain Activity

Though social and behavioural effects of TV violence have been studied extensively, the brain systems involved in TV violence viewing in children are, at present, not known. In one study, 8 children viewed televised violent and nonviolent video sequences while brain activity was measured with functional magnetic resonance imaging. Both violent and nonviolent viewing activated regions involved in visual motion, visual object and scenes, and auditory listening. However, viewing TV violence selectively recruited a network of right hemisphere regions including precuneus, posterior cingulate, amygdala, inferior parietal, and prefrontal and premotor cortex. Bilateral activations were apparent in hippocampus, parahippocampus, and pulvinar. TV violence viewing transiently recruits a network of brain regions involved in the regulation of emotion, arousal and attention, episodic memory encoding and retrieval, and motor programming. This pattern of brain activations may explain the behavioural effects observed in many studies, especially the finding that children who are frequent viewers of TV violence are more likely to behave aggressively. Such extensive viewing may result in a large number of aggressive scripts stored in long-term memory in the posterior cingulate, which facilitates rapid recall of aggressive scenes that serve as a guide for overt social behaviour.

Thus one can derive five conclusions: TV violence viewing in children—

(a) is emotionally arousing;

(b) leads to activation of a network of regions involved in attention, arousal, and salience;

(c) recruits a phylogenetically-old brain system involved in the detection of fear or threat in the environment;

(d) is accompanied by activation of limbic and neocortical systems likely to be involved in the episodic encoding and retrieval of the environmental context associated with such threat; and

(e) is accompanied by activation of premotor regions possibly involved in the programming of motor plans —fight or flight.

The relevance of these findings resides in the demonstration that though the child may not be aware of the threat posed by TV violence at a conscious level, and may even perceive it as interesting and arousing, a more primitive system within his or her brain—amygdala, pulvinar—may not discriminate between real violence and entertainment fictional violence, suggesting that TV violence may act at a preconscious level. Proof that this may be the case is provided by a recent study—Morris *et al.*, 1999—showing that masked—not consciously seen—fearful faces activate the same right amygdala-pulvinar circuit present in our study. Second, the simple act of viewing TV violence appears to transiently activate a network of right lateralized regions that are hyperactive in the resting state of individuals with impulsive aggressive behaviour—Raine *et al.*, 1997. Moreover, the strong activation of long-term memory systems during TV violence viewing —precuneus, posterior cingulate, hippocampus and parahippocampus, and amygdala—may suggest that the impact of TV violence viewing on brain function may extend in time beyond the simple act of viewing TV violence.

How TV affects your child

There are many ways that television affects your child's life. When your child sits down to watch TV, consider the following:

Time

Children in the United States watch about 4 hours of TV every day. Watching movies on tape and playing video games only adds to time spent in front of the TV screen. It may be tempting to use television, movies, and video games to keep your child busy, but your child needs to spend as much time growing and learning as possible. Playing, reading, and spending time with friends and family are much healthier than sitting in front of a TV screen.

Nutrition

Children who watch too much television are more likely to be overweight. They do not spend as much time running, jumping, and getting the exercise they need. They also see many commercials for unhealthy foods, such as candy, snacks, sugary cereals, and drinks during children's programs. Commercials almost never give information about the foods children should eat to keep healthy.

Violence

If your child watches 3 to 4 hours of non-educational TV per day, he will have seen about 8,000 murders on TV by the time he finishes grade school. Children who see violence on television may not understand that real violence hurts and kills people. Even if the "good guys" use violence, children may learn that it is okay to use force to handle aggression and settle disagreements. It is best not to let your child watch violent programs and cartoons.

Sex

Television exposes children to adult behaviours, like sex. But it usually does not show the risks and results of early sexual activity. On TV, sexual activity is shown as normal, fun, exciting, and without any risks. Your child may copy what he/she sees on TV in order to feel more grown up.

Alcohol, tobacco, and other drugs

Young people today are surrounded by messages that say drinking alcohol and smoking cigarettes or cigars are normal activities. These messages don't say that alcohol and tobacco harm people and may lead to death. Beer and wine are some of the most advertised products on television. TV programs and commercials often show people who drink and smoke as healthy, energetic, sexy, and successful. It is up to you to teach your child the truth about the dangers of alcohol, tobacco, and other drugs.

Commercials

The average child sees more than 20,000 commercials each year. Commercials are quick, fast-paced, and entertaining. After seeing the same commercials over and over, your child can easily remember a song, slogan, or catchy phrase. Ads may try to convince your child that having a certain toy or eating a certain food will make him happy or popular. Older children can begin to understand how ads use pictures, music, and sound to entertain. Kids need to know that ads try to convince people to buy things they may not need.

Learning

Television affects how your child learns. High-quality, nonviolent children's shows can have a positive effect on learning. Studies show that preschool children who watch educational TV programs do better on reading and math tests than children who do not watch those programs. When used carefully, television can be a positive tool to help your child learn.

A word about...TV for toddlers

Children of all ages are constantly learning new things. The first 2 years of life are especially important in the growth and development of your child's brain. During this time, children need good, positive interaction with other children and adults. Too much television can negatively affect early brain development. This is especially true at younger ages, when learning to talk and play with others is so important.

Until more research is done about the effects of TV on very young children, the American Academy of Pediatrics—AAP—does not recommend television for children age 2 or younger. For older children, the Academy recommends no more than 1 to 2 hours per day of educational, nonviolent programs.

TEN THINGS PARENTS CAN DO

As a parent, there are many ways you can help your child develop positive viewing habits. The following tips may help:

1. Set limits

Limit your child's use of TV, movies, and video and computer games to no more than 1 or 2 hours per day. Do not let your child watch TV while doing homework.

2. Plan your child's viewing

Instead of flipping through channels, use a program guide and the TV ratings to help you and your child choose shows. Turn the TV on to watch the program you chose and turn it off when the program is over.

3. Watch TV with your child

Whenever possible, watch TV with your child and talk about what you see. If your child is very young, she may not be able to tell the difference between a show, a commercial, a cartoon, or real life. Explain that characters on TV are make-believe and not real. Some "reality-based" programs may appear to be "real," but most of these shows focus on stories that will attract as many viewers as possible. Often these are stories about tragedy and violence. Much of their content is not appropriate for children. Young children may worry that what they see could happen to them or their family. News broadcasts also contain violent or inappropriate material. If your schedule prevents you from watching TV with your child, talk to her later about what she watched. Better yet, videotape the programs so that you can watch them with your child at a later time.

4. Find the right message

Even a poor program can turn out to be a learning experience if you help your child find the right message. Some television programs may portray people as stereotypes. Talk with your child about the real-life roles of women, the elderly, and people of other races that may not be shown on television. Discuss ways that people are different and ways that we are the same. Help your child learn tolerance for others. Remember, if you don't agree with certain subject matter, you can either turn off the TV or explain why you object.

5. Help your child resist commercials

Don't expect your child to be able to resist ads for toys, candy, snacks, cereal, drinks, or new TV programs without your help. When your child asks for products advertised on TV, explain that the purpose of commercials is to make people want things they may not need. Limit the number of commercials your child sees by watching public television stations—PBS. You can also tape programs and leave out the commercials or buy or rent children's videos.

6. Look for quality children's videos

There are many quality videos available for children that you can buy or rent.

7. Give other options

Watching TV can become a habit for your child. Help your child find other things to do with his time, such as the following:

- Playing
- Reading
- Activities with family, friends, or neighbours
- Learning a hobby, sport, instrument, or an art

8. Set a good example

You are the most important role model in your child's life. Limiting your own TV viewing and choosing programs carefully will help your child do the same.

9. Express your views

When you like or don't like something you see on television, make yourself heard. Write to the TV station, network, or the program's sponsor. Stations, networks, and sponsors pay attention to letters from the public. If you think a commercial is misleading, write down the product name, channel, and time you saw the commercial and describe your concerns. Help in answering your child the following questions:

Who created this message?

What creative techniques are used to attract my attention?

How might different people understand this message differently than I?

What values, lifestyles and points of view are represented in, or omitted from, this message?

Why is this message being sent?

Five Core Concepts:

All media messages are 'constructed'.

Media messages are constructed using a creative language with its own rules.

Different people experience the same media message differently.

Media have embedded values and points of view.

Most media messages are organised to gain points and/or power.

HANDLING GUIDANCE

Everyone gets angry at times. It's part of being human. Anger is a normal feeling that can be helpful, because it signals that change is needed. But anger also can get out of control. Helping children learn to manage anger is a very important part of early violence prevention.

It is hard for very young children to understand and manage their anger. As your young child grows, gradually teach these principles:

- It's okay to be angry.
- There are "okay" ways and "not okay" ways to show your anger.
- It's not okay to hurt anyone, to break things, or to hurt pets when you are angry.
- It's okay to tell someone that you are angry.
- There are ways to calm yourself when you are angry.

WAYS OF SHOWING ANGER

Several things stir young children's anger, and they show it in different ways. Here are some typical examples:

- When infants, from birth to about 9 or 10 months, feel bad because they are hungry, sick, or in pain, or when they are startled by a loud noise.they show their anger by crying and thrashing their arms and legs.
- Older babies, up to about 18 months, still show anger with crying and fussing, but the reasons may be different. This tends to occur when they don't get an appealing object, when they can't be with the person they want to be near, when they are frightened, or when they feel bad because of illness.
- From about age 18 months to 4 years, children are easily frustrated and will aggressively try to get or to keep what they want. They may grab a toy or take a cookie away from a friend, push a child away from the place they want to stand, or hit someone who takes something away from them.
- Children from about ages 4 to 8 years old gradually understand more, and they get angry about what people say, as well as what they do. They get better and better at expressing themselves with words, and their understanding of the world expands dramatically. Their aggression often is aimed at hurting another person, perhaps directly, by hitting or fighting, perhaps indirectly by damaging something the other person cares about.

ANGER MANAGEMENT

Young children who learn to manage angry feelings are more likely to make and keep friends. Also this skill can help prevent and resolve conflicts at home. Schoolchildren who are constantly arguing and fighting are the ones most likely to have problems in school and to have trouble making friends. And these issues can later lead to quitting school, having problems with the law, and abusing alcohol and drugs.

Importantly, helping a child to control angry feelings begins when you respond to the child's anger in a calm, respectful manner:

- Calm an infant by holding and comforting the infant, as well as removing or changing what caused the fussing.
- Encourage a toddler to use words to tell you what he or she feels, even in simple language. "I mad," or "Want doll," is a reasonable response from a little boy or girl.
- Help preschoolers begin to learn and practice a self-calming method taking a few deep breaths, sitting down, counting to 10, or repeating, "Be cool, be calm," for example.
- Encourage kindergarten and elementary school youngsters to explain what happened and how they feel. After a child is calm, ask what is wrong and *LISTEN* to the explanation, without interrupting. Help the child think about and tell ways to change the situation that caused the anger.

If you have trouble, your temper, can help you and your children if you get help through anger management training or by seeing a mental health professional.

1. Social problem solving

Problem solving doesn't just mean doing arithmetic or figuring out how to fix a leaky faucet. Many of the toughest problems, some-times involving strong feelings, occur between people. Adults and children who can manage the strong feelings and resolve conflicts reasonably, without hurting someone, have good skills for social problem solving.

Start early to help young children *stop* and *think* about different ways to solve a problem. Help them choose to act in a way that is nonviolent, safe, and fair. Around age 3, children are usually ready to begin simple steps of thinking and making choices which are part of social problem solving.

As children grow, they get better at solving problems. Around age 4 or 5, children can think of more than one way to solve a problem, and they can predict how people will react to their actions.—"If I hit Ranga when he wants my truck, he will hit me back. If we take turns, he won't grab it any more." They also learn to name their own feelings and those of others. —"I am mad because Santosh won't let me on the swing." "Komal is sad because his balloon popped." Further, they begin to care about other people's feelings and well-being—"Mukesh, I'm sorry you hurt your knee." "Grandma will be happy when she sees the picture I coloured for her."

Children aged 6 to 8 can understand how others might see a problem differently, and they can talk about a situation more clearly. They also develop a conscience and worry about rules and fairness.

Be sure to praise a child who does any of these things:

- Calms down.
- Tells how he or she feels.
- Describes a problem.
- Thinks of solutions to a problem.
- Acts in a way that is safe, fair, and nonviolent.

Make sure that your children understand that it's okay to make mistakes trying to solve problems and that we can learn from our mistakes. Always encourage children to seek help from trusted adults when a problem is too hard for them to handle.

Most of all, remember that children learn by watching you solve problems with respectful words and nonviolent actions.

2. Discipline

No child's behaviour is perfect all of the time, and some kids are harder to deal with than others. When you must act to stop a child's bad behaviour, your goal should always be to do it with self-control and without violence. The goal of discipline is to teach children self-control, not to punish them.

- Discipline is an important job. A young child's constant out-of-control behaviour can:
- Hurt that child or others
- Interfere with the child's learning and making friends
- Damage property
- Lead to school failure
- Create tension and stress at home
- Set the stage for serious problems as the child grows older

Children should be taught self-control by:

- Setting reasonable limits and rules.
- Having consistent, age-appropriate standards for behaviour.
- Showing consistent consequences for misbehaving.
- Letting the child see good behaviour by adult setting an example.

3. When young children "act up":

- Let children know what an adult expects, with simple statements. "Please put away your toys right now."
- Give warnings and reminders, without threats. "When you put away your toys, then you can go outside with your friends."
- Tell a child what to do rather than what not to do. "Please use a soft voice," instead of "Stop yelling!"

- Follow through with praise for following instructions or consequences for disobeying.

Sometimes a youngster's bad behaviour can be so frustrating that a parent or caregiver strikes the child without stopping to think. Yet children become confused, scared, and angry when adults hurt them, especially the adults whom they depend on to love and protect them. And continual, harsh punishment can lead a child to become aggressive and out of control, just the opposite of what you want to accomplish.

Some methods of discipline to try

Ignore some behaviour that is irritating but not dangerous—for example, whining, swearing, or having tantrums. It may be hard to do this, but paying attention to such behaviour may just encourage more of it.

Taking away a privilege can help to stop bad behaviour. Once children are old enough to understand, tell them that something they like (riding a bike, playing at a friend's house, watching a favorite TV show) will be taken away if they continue to misbehave. This sets up a choice: With self-control, they get what they like; if they continue to behave badly, they don't. This kind of approach teaches that actions have consequences.

Natural and logical outcomes can teach lessons.—A child puts her cookie on the floor, you warn her, she persists, the dog eats the cookie, and she has none. Of course, this should never be your approach when safety is at stake, for instance, when a child plays with matches or walks into the street. If a child misbehaves, respond in a way that lets the child see the connection between his or her action and your reaction.—A child colours on the wall, her crayons are taken away, and she helps clean the wall. A youngster screams for candy in the store, the parent takes him home without the treat.

When young children are fighting or arguing, place yourself between them. If possible, kneel to get to the children's eye level. Let them know you as an adult care giver understand that they are upset. If they are fighting over a toy or object, hold the object until the problem is settled. Ask each child to tell you what is wrong and listen to what they say. Ask both children to think of ways they might resolve the problem. Help them think about consequences—"If we do this, then what will happen?". Help them choose a solution that is fair and nonviolent. Watch what happens: If it works, praise them; if not, have them choose another solution and try again.

If one child clearly has been hitting or picking on another, speak to the victim first, allowing him to say what he wants and how he feels. Encourage the victim to face the bully and say how he feels, perhaps something like this: "I don't like it when you push me. It hurts and makes me mad!" Be sure that the bully doesn't get more attention than the victim gets.

4. About spanking

People have a variety of opinions about spanking, but the reality is that hitting or spanking your child sends a confusing message. It says it's okay to hurt someone you love in order to control them or solve a problem. Repeated harshly, over time, it will train children to punish others with force, the same way that they were punished.

5. Media influences

Media includes not only television, but also videos, movies, comic books, music lyrics, and computer games, have a strong influence on children. On the one hand, such media offer powerful tools for learning and entertainment; on the other hand, violence in the media is damaging for young children.

Research shows that violence in the media has the following effects on children:

- It gives children violent heroes to imitate.
- It increases mean-spirited, aggressive behaviour.
- It shows children that violence is all right as a way to handle conflict.
- It makes it easy for children to ignore suffering and the bad effects of violence.
- It causes fear, mistrust, and worry—sometimes including nightmares.
- It whets their appetite for viewing more violence, in more extreme forms.

And, bear in mind that even when the "good guys" win, the effects are the same.

As children get older, those who watch a lot of television also have lower grades, especially in reading. After all, they are substituting TV for homework, study time, reading practice, using their imagination, and interacting with others. Start limiting children's TV viewing while they are young to help prevent later problems in school.

The extent of children's exposure to television violence is stunning. Violence also is a theme in many popular video and computer games for children, and new research suggests that those games may be more harmful than television and movies.

Here are some ways that an adult care-giver can prevent violence in the media from having such a strong influence on young children:

- Watch TV with children and talk about what happens in the shows.
- Monitor what kids watch or play.
- Limit the number of hours children watch TV or play video games.

- Insist that schoolwork and family responsibilities are done before TV is allowed.
- Prevent the children from watching violent shows.
- Help them select shows that promote learning and positive development.
- Tell babysitters, caregivers, and family members about your rules on TV watching.

Talk with children about violence in the media. In those discussions, the care-giver can teach some important lessons:

- Violence in the media is make-believe, not real.
- Real-life violence hurts people.
- Guns, bullets, knives, and other weapons on TV are fake; real weapons hurt or kill people.
- If a show is scary or confusing, talk to an adult about it.

Also, teach children that violent toys may seem exciting in "pretend" games, but that real-life violence is not fun. Encourage children to pretend and play in ways that don't involve violence.

Caution about weapons

A child's curiosity about weapons can be deadly. It is heartbreaking to hear of accidental shootings and serious injuries by children who handle guns or play with them. Teach children to never touch a gun, bullet, or knife. Let them know that if they find one, they should not touch it, but should tell a trusted adult about it.

If you own a gun, never leave it out where a child might get it. Always lock your unloaded guns and bullets separately, in secure places that children cannot reach it.

At home and in your community

The daily experiences you provide for young children are powerful, not only for preventing violence, but also for increasing their chances to have a productive, happy life. If you stay at home with your children, have a schedule and plan activities for them and with them. If your children are in a child-care program while you work outside of home, make sure that it offers chances for constructive play and learning opportunities, with well-qualified staff who promote positive social behaviour. Research shows that high quality child-care programs can reduce behaviour problems in later childhood.

Teach child a sense of community by being part of the community yourself. Participate in activities to keep your neighborhood safe and to prevent violence.

Give children opportunities to play with other children and to interact with people of all ages.

Give children time; play together, eat together, watch their activities, work on projects together, just hang out and share everyday experiences.

As part of a young child's family, you have a critical influence on that young child's development. What you teach children today will make a difference in whom they are tomorrow. You are the best person to show a path to nonviolence for the children, for your family, and for your community.

PREVENTION

Crime brings together honest men and concentrates them." —Giddens, 1972, p. 127; excerpt from *The Division of Labor in Society*.

This quote exemplifies the stance Durkheim took toward crime. He recognised deviance as important to the well-being of society and proposed that challenges to established moral and legal laws—deviance and crime, respectively—acted to unify the law-abiding. Recognition and punishment of crimes is, in effect, the very reaffirmation of the laws and moral boundaries of a society. The existence of laws and the strength thereof are upheld by members of a society when violations are recognised, discussed, and dealt with either by legal punishment—jail, fines, execution—or by social punishment—shame, exile.

Crime actually produces social solidarity, rather than weakens it. Durkheim also proposed that crime and deviance brought people in a society together. When a law is violated, especially within small communities, everyone talks about it. Meetings are sometimes held, articles are written for local news publications, and in general, a social community bristles with activity when a norm is broken. As is most often the case, a violation incites the non-violators—society as a whole—to cling together in opposition to the violation, reaffirming that society's bond and its adherence to certain norms.

A third idea Durkheim held was that deviance and crime also help to promote social change. While most violations of norms are greeted with opposition by the masses, others are sometimes not, and those violations that gain support often are re-examined by that society. Often, those activities that once were considered deviant, are reconsidered and become part of the norms, simply because they gained support by a large portion of the society. In sum, deviance can help a society to rethink its boundaries, and move toward social change, hopefully for the greater benefit of the group.

SOCIAL CONTROL

Many media critics, like George Gerbner and Joanne Cantor, agree that censorship is not the answer. However, they question whose rights are protected when governments give, in Gerbner's words, a "virtual commercial monopoly over the public's airwaves," in effect delivering our "cultural environment to a marketing operation".

As journalist Scott Stossel notes, parents used to tell children scary stories face-to-face, so they could moderate the content and teach life lessons: "Children today, in contrast, grow up in a cultural environment that is designed to the specifications of a marketing strategy.

Shari Graydon, past president of Canada's Media Watch, and Québec activist René Caron remind us that the air waves are a public utility, and those who control their access and distribution must do so in ways that represent the best interests of all Canadians. Caron states, "Violence has been used by the industry to capture the attention of boys, to captivate them and manipulate them." Although this strategy may be profitable, "from a social viewpoint, from a moral viewpoint, this approach has had abominable repercussions".

Many commentators worry that media violence has become embedded in the cultural environment; that, in some sense, its part of the "psychic air" that children and young people constantly breathe. That environment of violence, profanity, crudeness, and meanness may erode civility in society by demeaning and displacing positive social values.

The easiest way to reduce the effects of media violence on children, of course, is to reduce children's exposure to such violence. Prevention programs aimed at reducing exposure could obviously be targeted either at the production sources of the violence or at the child viewing the violence. In a society with strong protections for free speech, it is probably always going to be easier to target prevention efforts at the viewing child than at the producer.

Broadcasters and film and program makers cannot avoid all responsibility for what children are exposed to. The argument that "people watch it so we give it to them" is not valid in a modern socially conscious society, and it is unrealistic to expect parents to control completely what children watch in a society with multiple TVs in each household, VCRs everywhere, and both parents working. Furthermore, it is the exposure of the 2- to 14-year-old child that is of the greatest concern here, as described in this article. The social value of reductions in the exposure of adults and even older teenagers is probably small compared to the social value of reducing younger children's exposure.

With regard to interventions aimed at the viewing child, there are a number of possibilities. Simply reducing children's exposure through parental intervention is an obvious approach. Nathanson—1999—recently found that parental co-viewing of and commenting on the programs seems to reduce the effects of TV violence on the child, probably because it reduces the child's identification with the perpetrator, reduces the child's perception of the violence as real, and reduces the likelihood that the child will rehearse the observed violent script in fantasy or play immediately after observation. Huesmann, Eron, Klein, Brice, and Fischer—1983—showed that the effects of violence on second graders could be reduced by a targeted school-based attitude change intervention that inculcates them with the beliefs that violence on TV does not tell about the world as it is and should not be imitated.

The focus of intervention should address the basic relevant point, such as identification by the child with perpetrators, perception of violent acts as justified, and perception of violent scripts as realistic.

Over the past several years the NYU Center for War, Peace, and the News Media has been developing a program to explore related issues. In the course of doing so, we have begun to inventory media-based initiatives that have already been undertaken to minimise conflict or promote other pro-social ends. We are interested in journalism, but also in soap operas, public affairs programming, sitcoms, advertising, public-interest, public relations, and social marketing. We are also exploring what governments can do through the policy process to promote the utilisation of media resources for preventive purposes; and we are curious about how—through such prosaic means as professional exchanges and international fellowships—journalists and media professionals can enhance their own understanding of the potential of their medium and the obligations—if any—that derive from them.

V-chip

Joanne Cantor criticises the media industry for saying it's up to parents, not the industry, to decide what their children watch: "They make harmful products, which come into our homes automatically through television, they market them to children too young to use them safely, and they try to keep parents in the dark about their effects." Cantor argues parents need tools to help them decide what is healthy and unhealthy for their kids.

One such tool is the V-chip, which enables parents to program their televisions with pre-set industry ratings to screen out certain shows. Keith Spicer, former chair of the Canadian Radio-television and Telecommunications Commission, calls the V-chip a "sexy, telegenic little gizmo that fulfills the fantasy of a magic wand".

The industry has been quick to endorse V-chip technology but critics argue that its real function is to protect the industry from parents, not the other way around. Gerbner states, "It's like major polluters saying, 'We shall continue business as usual, but don't worry, we'll also sell you gas masks to 'protect your children' and have a 'free choice!' ... Programming needs to be diversified, not just 'rated'. A better government regulation is antitrust, which could create a level playing field, admitting new entries and a greater diversity of ownership, employment, and representation. That would reduce violence to its legitimate role and frequency."

Todd Gitlin agrees with Gerbner that the real issue is broadcaster irresponsibility–though he does endorse the V-chip because, "parents deserve all the technology they can get".

Study on V-chip and television ratings usage by the Annenberg Public Policy Center–U.S.

The following findings are from the study "Media in the Home," carried out by the Annenbergy Public Policy Center in the spring of 2000. The results are based on telephone interviews conducted with 1,235 parents of children between the ages of two and 17, and 416 children between the ages of eight and 16. Findings are also sourced from Public Policy, Family Rules and Children's Media Use in the Home, based on 24 focus groups with 87 children and 62 mothers of children in grades three, six and nine.

Family Internet subscriptions are outpacing newspaper subscriptions, and almost half of all families with children ages 2-17 have a television, a VCR, a computer and a video game player in the home.

Parents are more concerned about children's television use than any other medium.

Parents are not using tools available to help them to find educational television for children or to limit the content they deem inappropriate.

Awareness of the Parental Rating Guidelines established through the V-chip legislation has dropped by 20 per cent, from 70 per cent in 1997 to 50 per cent in 2000.

Nine out of ten parents could not accurately identify the age ratings for a sample of programs their children watched.

On average, parents were able to accurately identify the E/I–Educational/Informational–designation for one in three programs their children watched.

Ninety-one per cent of parents report watching TV with their children as a way to mediate what their kids watch.

Forty-three per cent of families could not name one program they encourage their children to watch.

Although parents are concerned about their children's TV viewing, over half of the children surveyed (57 per cent) had a television in their bedroom.

For the first time in the five years that Annenberg has been tracking media in the home, Internet subscriptions have surpassed newspaper subscriptions by 10 per cent.

The number of families with Internet access has more than tripled, going from 15 per cent in 1996 to 52 per cent in 2000.

Across all media, use among children is growing.

Despite the fact that children are likely to spend 4.5 hours per day in front of some form of video screen— television, computer or video game—parents are more concerned about media content than they are about the time children spend using media.

Eighty per cent of parents surveyed reported using the movie ratings to determine the movies their children see — compared to 39 per cent who say they use TV ratings. Mothers in the focus groups knew what the movie ratings are and what they mean, but the same could not be said of their understanding of the TV ratings.

Networks are minimally meeting their responsibility to air three hours' worth of educational programming, offering on average, 3.4 hours of "core educational programming" during a typical week.

Source: News release, June 26 2000, Annenberg Public Policy Center.

Media education

Media education is not going to stop the World Wrestling copycat behaviour of six-year-olds in the playground. It's also unlikely to influence a teen's choice of a video for Saturday-night viewing. But what media education can do is to give young people the tools to respond thoughtfully and critically to media content. It can help kids put media violence into perspective, and perhaps diffuse some of its power.

A critical engagement with the media inspires young people to question how violence is portrayed in films or video games—and even to ask why it's there in the first place. Is violence essential to the plot, or is it factored in for thrills and excitement? Does the violence have realistic consequences, or does it show people smashing through plate glass windows with barely a scratch? And is the psychological trauma of violence and injury shown, or does the story just proceed without skipping a beat? Violence used to be the territory of the "bad guy" but there's been a major shift in the last few decades to violence as the hero's prerogative. Do positive motives justify violent action?

A search for patterns in the portrayal of media violence helps young people to understand media entertainment for what it is—fiction. Crime plays a far greater role in movies than it does in our society. One of the primary lessons of media education is that media productions are not "windows on reality", whatever their producers might like us to believe. They're deliberate constructions, the result of a series of choices. This includes the news. Is *The World Today* really that? Kids need to understand the relationship between how many people watch a TV program (the ratings) and the choices producers make about the news lineup. Most people are familiar with the "If it bleeds it leads" notion, but what about natural disasters and Third World crises where thousands of children can lose families and limbs in Sierra Leone one week, and are never heard of again? And what about the phenomenon of "compassion fatigue": an inability to keep feeling what we would normally feel in the face of human tragedy?

Of course, violence is a time-honored element in stories told through the ages about what it means to live in a society and relate to other people. Media education helps us examine today's media versions of these stories, probe whether the presentation of violence is different than it's been in the past, and ask: Who benefits from this endless menu of violence, and how?

It's an eye opener for young people to realise that the main reason for the proliferation of media violence is money. Films chock-a-block with action and violence are easier to sell abroad because they "translate" with less difficulty and jump over cultural barriers. Comedy and serious drama require intelligent scripting and cultural reference points. People may laugh over different things in *Moose Jaw* and *Dar-es-Salaam* but violence and action are understood by all in a global market.

It's also a revelation to young people when they realise that no one sees the same media production. How we respond to a film, a song, a video game or TV series is coloured by our own personal package of attitudes, values and experiences—including past exposure to media violence. This provides wonderful fodder for self-questioning and healthy discussion.

If kids are growing up in a media-saturated culture—and they are—media education can help them articulate their attitudes and feelings towards violence, in real life as well as on the screen. It can also teach young people that they have a voice and a role to play as active media consumers who can talk to the entertainment industry and present their opinions in public forums. The Internet has opened up important avenues for reaching producers and sharing views.

Talking to Kids about Media Violence

Talking to kids about violence in the media they consume—television, movies, video games, music and the Internet—can help them put media violence into perspective and perhaps diffuse some of its power. The following "discussion starters" are designed to help kids develop the critical thinking skills they need to understand and question the use of violence in media.

Ask kids: What is violence?

Once kids understand what violence is, they can then start to put media violence into context. Ask them to consider both physical and emotional acts of violence in their definition. Can emotional violence be as harmful as physical violence? Yelling, put-downs, name-calling and threats are what kids are most likely to experience in the school-yard. Talk about how these kinds of acts can begin a cycle that leads to physical violence. How do they feel when someone call them names or threatens them?

Discuss how violence is used in different media.

With a definition of violence in mind, kids can start to examine its use in the media they enjoy. Is violence used gratuitously or is it integral to the plot? Is it used in a humorous way and does the humour make it less harmful? Is it there to teach a lesson? Is violence shown to be the only possible solution to a situation which the audience expects?

Discuss the consequences of media violence. Ask kids to think about the realistic consequences of the violence they see in the media:

- How would the people involved in the conflict feel in real life?
- What would be the results of the violence? What injuries might have occurred? What property damages would have resulted?

- How would the perpetrators of violence be punished or made accountable for their actions?

Look for examples in different media—video games, music videos, comic books, TV or movies—where there are no consequences to violence.

Discuss why there is violence in media and why people are attracted to it.

Producers create violent media because it sells both at home and abroad. Many people want their entertainment to be action-packed, but the industry also creates an appetite for violence through marketing—especially to young people. Ask kids if they feel they are being targeted as consumers for violent media.

Consider whether people become increasingly de-sensitised to media violence.

Do kids feel that they need to see graphic violence? Talk about what they expect to see in the next action movie they go to. What does it take to scare them or keep them on the edge of their seat, and why? If people do become desensitised to violence, could that be a problem. Why?

Compare psychological suspense to gratuitous violence.

Can a well-made suspenseful movie be more frightening than a violent action film? Talk about the excitement generated by shootings or explosions in an action movie sequence versus a suspenseful scene that builds tension using music, tempo, camera angles and facial expressions.

Look for creative solutions to conflict in media. Ask kids to look for examples of anger with and without violence in the media. Is there a difference between the two? Does the non-violent approach seem more realistic? Discuss alternative ways to resolve conflict.

Talk about media violence and stereotyping.

Media violence is often used to perpetrate myths and stereotypes about people. Ask kids:

- Who is committing the acts of violence—men, women, white people, minorities?
- Who are the victims of violence—men, women, old people, children, white people, and minorities?

Discuss violence in the news.

War and acts of terrorism need to be put into a historical and cultural context for kids. Random acts of violence and criminal activity need to be discussed and de-sensationalised so children don't become overly fearful of their community or the world in general.

The Rules for Violence on Kids' TV

- Only a small amount of physical or emotional violence is allowed in kids' shows.
- Real-life characters can only use violence when it is needed to develop the story.
- Cartoons can contain *some* non-realistic violence, but not actions that kids might try to imitate.
- Television shows must not make kids feel threatened. They have to be sensitive when they are dealing with issues that kids might be experiencing themselves, like domestic conflict, the death of parents or close relatives, the death of a pet, street crime or the use of drugs.
- Producers of television shows must be careful about how they portray dangerous acts that kids might try to imitate, like using plastic bags as toys, using matches, playing with dangerous household products, or climbing apartment balconies or going on rooftops.
- Violence can't be shown as the only way to handle problems between people.

- Kids' television shows can only contain frightening special effects if they are necessary for the story.
- Adult shows and advertisements that contain scenes of violence, can't be shown before 9 p.m.
- Because older kids might still be watching TV after 9 p.m., broadcasters have to include a warning for parents at the beginning of programs that contain violence.

Source: Canadian Association of Broadcasters—CAB—*Voluntary Code Regarding Violence in Television, 1993.*

Tips on managing your child's media consumption

Family is the most important influence in a child's life, but television is not far behind. Television can inform, entertain, and teach us. However, some of what TV teaches may not be the things you want your child to learn. TV programs and commercials often show violence, alcohol or drug use, and sexual content that may not be suitable for children or teens. Studies show that TV viewing may lead to more aggressive behaviour and less physical activity. By knowing how television affects your children and by setting limits, you can help make your child's TV-watching experience not only enjoyable, but healthy too.

ACTION

At the home level, we can encourage greater awareness of the influence of television on children and enhance understanding of ways that parents and teachers can help children use TV effectively. For example, the U.S. Department of Agriculture Co-operative Extension Service at Kansas State University—Murray & Lonnborg, 1995—has produced a parent guide publication on this topic. This guide is a review of some of the concerns about television and children and provides suggestions for parents in using television in a constructive manner. One of the straightforward techniques for use at home that is very effective is viewing along with your children and talking about what they see on television. With very young children talking about how violence is faked and what would happen if you actually did some of those things that you see on television is a very basic intervention. Such interventions, at the personal or family level, can lead to enhanced understanding of television's influence and more effective use of this medium.

At the school level, interventions such as advocating for the inclusion of media literacy courses in school systems can be very effective. These "critical viewing" programs help children understand how television works and the process of effects. There are many very effective programs, but, in the case of media literacy addressed to the violence issue, one interesting new program has been developed by the Centre for Media Literacy—1995. Called "Beyond Blame—Challenging Violence in the Media, a Multimedia Literacy Program for Community Empowerment"—this program is one that a school system or a community agency might use as a general educational intervention. Another approach to enhancing public awareness is working with parents and communities to address television violence as a public health issue. There has been a long history of public advocacy concern about television violence—Kunkel & Murray, 1991; Montgomery, 1989—and there are several major organisations—Centre for Media Education, Centre for Media Literacy, Mediascope, National Alliance for Non-violent Programming, and the National Telemedia Council —that are producing materials for parents and community organisations. One such videotape, The Kids are Watching, from Mediascope —1993—is very effective in stimulating discussion of the impact of TV violence.

Finally, there are industry and government activities that might be undertaken to change children's television. The Children's Television Act of 1990 did set some limits on the amount of advertising in children's programming and did set some expectations that stations applying for license renewal will have to explain how they have served the educational needs of children in their broadcast area. And, the FCC is now thinking about elaborating that by including quotas—Federal Communications Commission, 1995—such as one hour per day of children's educational television.

Another approach, which is more voluntary than regulatory, involves working with the industry to introduce changes in the role that advertising plays in supporting children's programming. One might encourage advertisers to shift their support of children's programming from advertising to underwriting. Sponsorship of children's TV would then shift from advertising to enhance corporate income to underwriting to enhance corporate image.

Other industry level initiatives might include further development of the parental advisory that the television networks began implementing in 1987. The "viewer discretion" warnings that have been attached to prime time movies since September, 1987 have been shown to have some influence in reducing viewership among the 2- to 11-year-old audiences. Hamilton—1994—conducted an analysis of audience rating data for network movies carrying viewer discretion advisories broadcast during the period September 17, 1987 to September 26, 1993. He found that movies carrying the warnings lost. 59 ratings points among children 2 to 11. This translates into 222,000 fewer children—or a 14% drop in average audience rating for this age group—for movies that contained viewer discretion warnings. There were no changes in viewership for teens or adults. These findings suggest that parents are sensitive to the warnings and will act on the information provided concerning program content.

A related development being considered by the industry is the possible rating of violence levels on television programs and the potential co-ordination with electronic screening devices known as "V-chip" technology. While there is no clear agreement on the implementation of ratings and screening technology, some members of Congress have suggested legislation that would require the FCC to mandate the inclusion of an electronic circuit, or V-chip, in all new television sets. This technology is rather similar to the circuitry required for decoding "closed-caption" program signals. In this instance, the industry would transmit a signal concerning the violent content and parents could program their television set to block programs containing the identified signal. The successful implementation of this type of intervention would require the participation of the industry in rating and coding programs and the involvement of parents in responding to these ratings. Although there are questions about the impact of this V-chip approach, there is evidence from the Hamilton —1994—study that parents may be responsive to viewer warnings in respect of young children.

• • •

INDEX

A

B

C

D

E

S

T

• • •